D0885670

Privacy Law
Fundamentals

Daniel J. Solove
John Marshall Harlan Research Professor of Law
George Washington University Law School
and
President and CEO
TeachPrivacy, LLC

&

Paul M. Schwartz
Jefferson E. Peyser Professor of Law
U.C. Berkeley School of Law
and
Director
Berkeley Center for Law & Technology
and
Special Advisor
Paul Hastings LLC

An IAPP Publication

©2017 by the International Association of Privacy Professionals (IAPP).
All rights reserved. No part of this publication may be reproduced, stored in
a retrieval system or transmitted in any form or by any means, mechanical,
photocopying, recording or otherwise, without the prior, written permission
of the publisher, International Association of Privacy Professionals, Pease
International Tradeport, 75 Rochester Ave., Suite 4, Portsmouth, NH 03801

Cover design by -ing designs, llc.
Book design by Tammy F. Sneddon Design.

ISBN 978-0-9983223-1-5

ABOUT *PRIVACY LAW FUNDAMENTALS*

"Concise, well-organized, and masterfully detailed, *Privacy Law Fundamentals* is the authoritative and most accessible reference for privacy practitioners looking for quick, accurately distilled, and current content from two of the most preeminent scholars in the field."

— *James M. Aquilina, Stroz Friedberg*

"Two giants of privacy scholarship succeed in distilling their legal expertise into an essential guide for a broad range of the legal community. Whether used to learn the basics or for quick reference, *Privacy Law Fundamentals* proves to be concise and authoritative."

— *Jules Polonetsky, Future of Privacy Forum*

"There are no better-qualified authors than Professor Schwartz and Solove to summarize the current state of privacy law and, as a result, there is no better compact privacy law resource than *Privacy Law Fundamentals.*"

— *Christopher Wolf, Hogan Lovells*

"This book is my go-to reference for when I need quick, accurate information on privacy laws across sectors and jurisdictions. Solove and Schwartz masterfully make complex privacy law more accessible and understandable for anyone, from the most experienced practitioner to the first year law student."

— *Nuala O'Connor, Center for Democracy and Technology*

"Professors Solove and Schwartz pack an enormous amount of privacy knowledge into a slim volume in *Privacy Law Fundamentals.* In our fast-paced practice, there's nothing better than a compact and accessible work that is curated by two of the great thinkers of the field. It is a gem."

— *Kurt Wimmer, Covington & Burling*

"The go-to privacy law reference that you will keep going to. Professors Schwartz and Solove manage to distill without distorting and to outline without obscuring. Part reference, part primer and part pathfinder, *Privacy Law Fundamentals* is the ultimate privacy law resource."

— *Tom Counts, Paul Hastings*

"This is the essential primer for all privacy practitioners. Professors Solove and Schwartz have done a remarkable job of keeping this volume current in the fast-changing environment of new technology, case law and legislation."

— *David A. Hoffman, Intel Corporation*

ABOUT THE AUTHORS

Daniel J. Solove is the John Marshall Harlan Research Professor of Law at the George Washington University Law School. He is also the President and CEO of TeachPrivacy, http://teachprivacy.com, a company that provides privacy and data security training to organizations in an array of industries. One of the world's leading experts in privacy law, Solove is the author of numerous books, including *Nothing to Hide: The False Tradeoff Between Privacy and Security* (Yale 2011), *Understanding Privacy* (Harvard 2008), *The Future of Reputation: Gossip and Rumor in the Information Age* (Yale 2007; winner of the 2007 McGannon Award), and *The Digital Person: Technology and Privacy in the Information Age* (NYU 2004). Professor Solove is also the co-author (with Paul Schwartz) of a textbook, *Information Privacy Law*, with Aspen Publishing Co., now in its fifth edition. Additionally, he is the author of several other textbooks, including *Privacy and the Media* (2nd edition, Aspen Publishing Co. 2015), *Privacy, Law Enforcement, and National Security* (1st edition, Aspen Publishing Co. 2015), and *Consumer Privacy and Data Protection* (1st edition, Aspen Publishing Co. 2015), all with Paul Schwartz. He has published more than 50 articles and essays.

Solove has testified before the U.S. Congress and has been involved as an expert and consultant in a number of high-profile privacy cases. His work has been cited by many federal and state courts, including the U.S. Supreme Court. He has been interviewed and featured in several hundred media broadcasts and articles in publications and on networks including *The New York Times, The Wall Street Journal, The Washington Post, Chicago Tribune, USA Today, Time, Newsweek, People, Reader's Digest,* Associated Press, ABC, CBS, NBC, CNN, NPR and C-SPAN's "Book TV."

More information about Professor Solove's work can be found at www. daniel-solove.com. He can also be followed on Twitter at http://twitter.com/ DanielSolove. He blogs at Privacy+Security Blog, www.teachprivacy.com/ privacy-security-training-blog/. As one of a select group of LinkedIn "Influencers," Professor Solove also blogs at LinkedIn, www.linkedin.com/today/post/ articles/2259773. His blog has more than 1 million followers.

Paul M. Schwartz is Jefferson E. Peyser Professor of Law at the University of California–Berkeley Law School and a director of the Berkeley Center for Law & Technology. A leading international expert on informational privacy and information law, he has published widely on these topics. In the U.S., his articles and essays have appeared in periodicals such as the *Harvard Law Review, Yale Law Journal, Stanford Law Review, California Law Review, N.Y.U. Law Review,* and *Chicago Law Review.* With Daniel Solove, he has published the leading casebook *Information Privacy Law* (Aspen, 5th ed., 2015) and other books.

Schwartz has testified as an expert before congressional committees in the United States and provided legal reports to the Commission of the European Community and Department of Justice, Canada. He has assisted numerous corporations in the United States and abroad with information privacy issues. A member of the American Law Institute, Schwartz has received scholarships and grants from the American Academy in Berlin, where he was a Berlin Prize Fellow; the Alexander von Humboldt Foundation; German Marshall Fund; Fulbright Foundation; the German Academic Exchange, and the Harry Frank Guggenheim Foundation. He is a member of the American Law Institute and the organizing committee of the Privacy Law Salon, and is Special Advisor to Paul Hastings LLP.

Schwartz belongs to the editorial boards of *International Data Privacy Law,* the *International Journal of Law and Information Technology,* and the *Zeitschrift für Datenschutz* (Data Protection Journal).

Schwartz received a JD degree from Yale Law School, where he was a senior editor on *The Yale Law Journal,* and a BA degree from Brown University. His homepage is www.paulschwartz.net. His Twitter account is @paulmschwartz.

DEDICATION

To Pamela and Griffin—DJS

To Steffie, Clara and Leo—PMS

PREFACE

This book provides a concise guide to privacy law. Privacy Law Fundamentals is designed to serve as a primer of the essential information that one needs to know about the field. For the student of privacy law or the beginning privacy professional, the book will provide an overview that can be digested readily. For the more seasoned and experienced, the book will serve as a handy reference guide, a way to refresh one's memory of key components of privacy laws and central cases. It will help close gaps in knowledge and inform on areas of the field about which one wants to know more.

In writing this book, we have aimed to avoid the "too much information" problem by singling out the essential provisions of law, regulations, and judicial decisions. A frequent risk in law books is that key definitions, provisions, and concepts will become lost in a litany of long and dense statutes and in a mass of cases. We have endeavored to distill the field down to its fundamentals and present this information in as clear and useful a manner as we could. Wherever possible, we have developed charts and lists to convey the material.

The book is organized in thirteen chapters:

- Chapter One—a review of the key privacy developments since the last edition.

- Chapter Two—an overview of privacy law in all its varied types and forms and a timeline with key points in the development of privacy law.

- Chapter Three—privacy law involving the media, including the privacy torts, defamation, and the First Amendment.

- Chapter Four—the law of domestic law enforcement, focusing on the Fourth Amendment and the statutes regulating electronic surveillance.

- Chapter Five—national security law, including the Foreign Intelligence Surveillance Act.

- Chapter Six—the laws and regulations that pertain to health and genetic data, including HIPAA.

- Chapter Seven—government records and laws, such as the Privacy Act and the Freedom of Information Act.

- Chapter Eight—the laws concerning financial information, including the Fair Credit Reporting Act and the Gramm-Leach-Bliley Act.

- Chapter Nine—legal regulation of the privacy of consumer data and business records, involving statutes, tort protections, and FTC enforcement actions.

- Chapter Ten—data security law, including the varying laws in a majority of the states.

- Chapter Eleven—school privacy, including the Family Educational Rights and Privacy Act.

- Chapter Twelve—the regulation of employment privacy, including the different rules for government and private-sector employees.

- Chapter Thirteen—international privacy law, including the EU Data Protection Directive, the OECD Guidelines, the APEC Privacy Framework, and rules of international data transfers.

For his suggestions on our chapter about school privacy, we wish to thank Steven McDonald. This book also benefitted greatly from the research assistance of Henry Becker, Jordan Bock, Thad Houston, Richard Johnson, Lea Mekhneche, Robert Paris, and Michelle Parker.

For further references, including books, websites, statutes, and other sources of news and legal materials, visit our website (http://informationprivacylaw.com), and for our casebooks, click on the "resources" tab at the top.

We look forward to keeping this book up to date and to finding additional ways to make it as useful as possible. Please feel free to contact us with any suggestions and feedback about the book.

Daniel J. Solove
Washington, DC
dsolove@law.gwu.edu

Paul M. Schwartz
Berkeley, CA
pschwartz@law.berkeley.edu

TABLE OF CONTENTS

CHAPTER 2: AN OVERVIEW OF PRIVACY LAW

CHAPTER 3: PRIVACY AND THE MEDIA

CHAPTER 4: PRIVACY AND LAW ENFORCEMENT

CHAPTER 5: NATIONAL SECURITY AND FOREIGN INTELLIGENCE

CHAPTER 6: HEALTH PRIVACY

CHAPTER 11: EDUCATION PRIVACY

CHAPTER 12: EMPLOYMENT PRIVACY

CHAPTER 1

New Developments

This chapter contains a detailed overview of leading developments in information privacy since the 2015 edition. Only the most important of these developments—those that served as turning points or milestones in the law—are also included in the relevant chapters of this book.

PRIVACY AND THE MEDIA

New Laws of Note

Revenge Porn Statutes

In the past few years, 34 states and the District of Columbia have passed revenge porn laws. In 2013, California led the way when it enacted legislation criminalizing the distribution of images of intimate body parts taken under circumstances where the parties agree or understand that the images would remain private. *See* Cal. Penal Code § 647(j)(4). In December 2014, Noe Iniguez became the first person convicted under the California statute for posting a topless photo of his former girlfriend on her employer's Facebook page. *See People v. Iniguez*, 202 Cal. Rptr. 3d 237 (App. Dep't Super. Ct. 2016) (complaint filed November 3, 2014). Iniguez was sentenced to one year in jail and three years' probation.

First Amendment Restrictions

Elonis v. United States, 135 S. Ct. 2001 (2015)
The U.S. Supreme Court reversed a conviction under 18 U.S.C. § 875(c) that makes it a federal crime to transmit in interstate commerce "any communication containing any threat . . . to injure the person of another." The Court held that a conviction under the statue required a showing that the defendant had either the intent or knowledge that communications would be viewed as threats; negligence was not sufficient.

Music Group Macao Commercial Offshore Ltd. v. Does I-IX, No. 14-mc-80328 LB, **2015 WL 75073 (N.D. Cal. Jan. 6, 2015)**
Music Group sued anonymous Twitter users for tweeting that the company encouraged domestic violence and the CEO visited prostitutes. The court held that the plaintiffs could subpoena Twitter for the identities of the speakers without violating the First Amendment.

Notable Scholarship: Books

Samantha Barbas, *Laws of Image: Privacy and Publicity in America* (2015)
Historical account of how different areas of law—including the right of publicity, defamation, and libel—have regulated the use of one's image in public. Analysis of how "we seek publicity on our own terms" in the United States and the law's reaction to such behavior by individuals.

Lothar Determann, *California Privacy Law* (2d ed. 2017)
Comprehensive analysis of the strict standards of California privacy law.

Jim Dwyer, *More Awesome Than Money: Four Boys and Their Heroic Quest to Save Your Privacy from Facebook* (2014)
Recounting story of four undergraduates who tried, and failed, to build a social media site where people could control their personal data.

Amy Gajda, *The First Amendment Bubble: How Privacy and Paparazzi Threaten a Free Press* (2015)
Discussing how to balance privacy and freedom of the press, including how to define who counts as a "journalist" in the days of blogs and social media.

Jon L. Mills, *Privacy in the New Media Age* (2015)
Describing how to modernize the intrusion tort in a way that emphasizes both human dignity and freedom of the press. Tackles pressing question of how the new media age impacts our approach to privacy.

Jon Ronson, *So You've Been Publicly Shamed* (2015)
Case studies of individuals harmed by Twitter mobs, media attacks and cyber harassment. Ronson warns the public to consider the "level of mercilessness" with which it feels comfortable before joining in public shaming.

PRIVACY AND LAW ENFORCEMENT

Fourth Amendment

United States v. DiTomasso, **56 F. Supp. 3d 584 (S.D.N.Y. 2014)**
Holding users waived their Fourth Amendment rights due to AOL's terms of service, which stated that AOL monitors for criminal activity and reserves the right to reveal

criminal activity to law enforcement. In the court's view, "a reasonable person familiar with AOL's policy would understand that by agreeing to the policy, he was consenting not just to monitoring by AOL as an ISP, but also to monitoring by AOL as a government agent."

Drones

The growth in use of unmanned aerial vehicles has presented a series of privacy issues and public safety concerns.

Registration and Marking Requirements for Small Unmanned Aircraft, 80 Fed. Reg. 78,593 (FAA Dec. 16, 2015) (codified as amended in scattered sections of 14 C.F.R.)
Addresses the registration and marking requirements for small unmanned aircraft, including those operated as model aircraft.

Mail Covers

Office of Inspector Gen., U.S. Postal Serv., HR-AR-14-001, Postal Inspection Service Mail Covers Program (2014)
Recommending better procedures for mail covers program to ensure that the Postal Inspection Service can lead effective investigations and assuage public concerns over privacy of the mail.

Electronic Communications

In re Apple, Inc., **149 F. Supp. 3d 341 (E.D.N.Y. 2016)**
Denying the Government's request for an order requiring Apple, Inc. to bypass the passcode security on an Apple iPhone in order to extract data relevant to an ongoing drug investigation. The court rejected the Government's argument that the All Writs Act provides a court with the authority to grant any relief not outright prohibited by law.

In re the Search of an Apple iPhone, **No. ED 15–0451M, 2016 WL 618401 (C.D. Cal. Feb. 16, 2016)**
After initially requesting that Apple, Inc. assist the Government in unlocking the iPhone used by San Bernardino shooter Syed Farook, the Justice Department announced that it had employed a third party to break into the phone. As a result, the Government requested that the order compelling Apple to assist the government be vacated, resolving a brewing battle between Apple and the Obama administration.

Twitter, *Transparency Report – United States* **(2015)**
Discusses increased demands on Twitter by governments, including an 18% increase in the number of accounts impacted by government information requests.

Google, *Transparency Report* (2015)
Contains data and qualitative explanation of government removal requests. In 2015 Google received 3,467 government requests to remove information from Google products, a slight decrease from the peak of 3,846 requests in 2013.

Microsoft Corp. v. United States, **No. 14-2985, 2016 WL 3770056 (2d Cir. July 14, 2016)**
Finding a lack of extra-territorial reach to a warrant issued pursuant to the Stored Communications Act. The Second Circuit ruled: "Neither explicitly nor implicitly does the statute envision the application of its warrant provisions overseas."

State Electronic Surveillance Law: Recording Police Encounters

Nat'l Inst. Of Justice, Office of Justice Programs, U.S. Dep't of Justice, *A Primer on Body-Worn Cameras for Law Enforcement,* (Sept. 2012)
The National Institute of Justice (NIJ) Sensor, Surveillance, and Biometric Technologies (SSBT) Center of Excellence (CoE) discusses issues that law enforcement organizations should consider both before and during the implementation of body-worn cameras in law enforcement.

Notable Scholarship: Books

After Snowden: Privacy, Secrecy, and Security in the Information Age (Ronald Goldfarb ed., 2015)
Collection of essays by Thomas Blanton, David Cole, John Mills, Hodding Carter, Barry Siegel, and Edward Wasserman. Topics include the Snowden leaks, the state secrets doctrine, journalists and whistleblowers, classification of government documents, and more.

Bernard E. Harcourt, ***Exposed: Desire and Disobedience in the Digital Age*** **(2015)**
Documenting how "[d]igital surveillance capabilities have reached new heights in ordinary digital existence and have begun to converge on carceral monitoring." Calling for "digital disobedience" to "challenge our virtual transparency."

Bruce Schneier, ***Data and Goliath: The Hidden Battles to Collect Your Data and Control Your World*** **(2015)**
Examining NSA surveillance, the Snowden revelations, and other recent issues in privacy and data collection. Developing a core set of principles and solutions for government, corporations, and "the rest of us."

Notable Scholarship: Articles and Other Sources

William Baude & James Y. Stern, *The Positive Law Model of the Fourth Amendment*, 129 Harv. L. Rev. 1821 (2016)
Advocating for a positive law approach to the Fourth Amendment. Fourth Amendment protections should be based on "background positive law," and the key question in search-and-seizure analysis should be "whether government officials have done something forbidden to private parties."

Orin S. Kerr, *Katz Has Only One Step: The Irrelevance of Subjective Expectations*, 82 U. Chi. L. Rev. 113 (2015)
Discusses how the "subjective expectation of privacy" portion of the *Katz* test is a superfluous doctrine and should be excised by the Supreme Court.

Martina Kitzmueller, *Are You Recording This?: Enforcement of Police Videotaping*, 47 Conn. L. Rev. 167 (2014)
Discussing different methods states use for law enforcement to make and preserve videos of their interactions.

Gregory S. McNeal, *Drones and the Future of Aerial Surveillance*, 84 Geo. Wash. L. Rev. 354 (2016)
Arguing that unmanned aerial surveillance could be more protective of privacy than manned surveillance. Proposes looking beyond a warrant-based approach for protecting privacy from aerial surveillance.

Brandon Nagy, *Why They Can Watch You: Assessing the Constitutionality of Warrantless Unmanned Aerial Surveillance by Law Enforcement*, 29 Berkeley Tech. L.J. 135 (2014)
Reviewing current regulatory framework surrounding unmanned aircraft systems and discussing potential constitutional challenges to unmanned aerial surveillance.

NATIONAL SECURITY AND FOREIGN INTELLIGENCE

Foreign Intelligence Gathering

USA Freedom Act of 2015, Pub. L. No. 114-23, 129 Stat. 268 (codified as amended in scattered sections of 50 U.S.C.)
Bans the bulk collection of Americans' Internet metadata and telephonic records under Section 215 of the Patriot Act. The government must now identify a person, account, address, or personal device when requesting records, limiting the scope of tangible things sought "to the greatest extent reasonably possible." However, the bill permits authorities to collect phone records two degrees (or "hops") of separation from targeted individuals.

Leading Cases on Foreign Intelligence Gathering

ACLU v. Clapper, 785 F.3d 787 (2d Cir. 2015)
Holding collection of telephone metadata exceeded authority granted by FISA, as the metadata was not relevant to authorized counterterrorism investigations. The Second Circuit found the Section 215's statutory text did not authorize the telephone metadata program. The opinion did not address the constitutionality of the metadata collection. A follow-up opinion after the enactment of the Freedom Act permitted a 180-day transition period to Congress to wind down the program.

National Security Letters (NSLs)

FBI, *Termination Procedures for National Security Letter Nondisclosure Requirement* (2015)
The FBI revised the NSL disclosure policy, permitting letter recipients to disclose the receipt of the letter at "the earlier of 3 years after the opening of a fully predicated investigation or the investigation's close." Previously, the FBI was permitted to enforce NSL gag orders indefinitely. Gag orders may be enforced beyond the 3-year period if the FBI determines that a statutory exception applies.

Notable Reports

Privacy & Civil Liberties Oversight Board. (PCLOB), *Recommendations Assessment Report* (Feb. 5, 2016)
Report noting full or partial implementation of all 22 recommendations made by PCLOB regarding Section 215 and Section 702 surveillance programs. These recommendations included ending the NSA's bulk collection of metadata, greater transparency by the government and private companies supplying data, expansion of appellate review of FISC decisions, and revised targeting and minimization procedures. PCLOB contends the measures would strengthen civil liberties without hindering counterterrorism efforts.

Nat'l Sec. Agency, *NSA Reports to the President's Intelligence Oversight Board* (2001 – 2013)
Following a FOIA lawsuit filed by the ALCU, the NSA released a series of redacted reports prepared for the Intelligence Oversight Board. The released documents do not make clear the exact number of violations that had occurred during this time period. A declassified Inspector General report noted 12 cases of "intentional misuse" of the organization's monitoring capabilities, including several instances of operators targeting their own significant others.

Notable Scholarship: Books

Laura K. Donohue, *The Future of Foreign Intelligence: Privacy and Surveillance in a Digital Age* (2016)
Examines the expansion of U.S. intelligence gathering and offers solutions for scaling back intrusive national security measures.

Notable Scholarship: Articles and Other Sources

Orin S. Kerr, *The Fourth Amendment and the Global Internet*, 67 Stan. L. Rev 285 (2015)
Examines tensions between the Fourth Amendment and global data transfers, offering proposals on adapting the Amendment to the digital age.

Laura K. Donohue, *Bulk Metadata Collection: Statutory and Constitutional Considerations*, 37 Harv. J.L. & Pub. Pol'y 757 (2014)
Contends that the NSA's bulk telephonic metadata collection runs counter to Congress's original intent in enacting FISA in 1978.

Robert M. Chesney, *Computer Network Operations and U.S. Domestic Law: An Overview*, 89 Int'l L. Stud. 218 (2013)
Examines the use of computer network operations for intelligence gathering purposes with a particular emphasis on Congressional and Executive oversight.

HEALTH PRIVACY

Health Insurance Portability and Accountability Act (HIPAA)

Office for Civil Rights, U.S. Dep't of Health & Human Servs., *HIPAA Privacy in Emergency Situations* (Nov. 2014)
Guidance document from OCR in response to the Ebola crisis. The OCR provides guidance about HIPPA's rules for sharing personal health information in emergency situations.

Office for Civil Rights, U.S. Dep't of Health & Human Servs., *OCR Launches Phase 2 of HIPAA Audit Program* (2015)
HHS Office for Civil Rights began its next phase of audits. After emailing covered entities and business associates to request contact information for the audit, OCR will send a pre-audit questionnaire to gather data about the size, type, and operations of potential auditees. This information will, in turn, be used to create potential audit subject groups.

Notable Cases

Byrne v. Avery Ctr. for Obstetrics & Gynecology, P.C., 314 Conn. 433 (2014)

Holding that HIPAA "does not preempt the plaintiff's state common-law causes of action for negligence or negligent infliction of emotional distress." Even though HIPAA lacks a private right of action, plaintiffs can use HIPAA to inform the standard of care in a negligence case (and other state common law causes of action).

Walgreen Co. v. Hinchy, 21 N.E. 3d 99 (Ind. Ct. App. 2014), *aff'd on reh'g*, 25 N.E.3d 748 (Ind. Ct. App. 2015)

Reviewing a $1.44 million jury verdict, an Indiana appellate court affirmed that the plaintiff had raised a viable claim of negligence based on using HIPAA as the standard of care. Court affirmed original result on rehearing.

United States v. Michel, No. 2:07-cr-00889-JFB, 2013 WL 9903336 (E.D.N.Y. Apr. 10, 2013)

After a three-week jury trial, Helene Michel was convicted of identity theft, Medicare fraud, and wrongful disclosure of private medical information under HIPAA. Michel used her position as owner of a medical equipment company to enter health facilities and steal patient records, which she then used to submit false Medicare billings. Michel was sentenced to twelve years in prison and ordered to forfeit $1.3 million that was seized by the government when she was indicted.

United States v. Hippler, No. 6:14-cr-00018-MHS-JDL (E.D. Tex. Feb. 18, 2015)

Hippler, a former hospital employee, was sentenced to 18 months in prison for HIPAA violations after he pleaded guilty to wrongful disclosure of individually identifiable health information. Hippler had been charged with wrongful disclosure of individual identifiable health information with the intent to sell, transfer, and use the information for personal gain.

New HHS OCR HIPAA Enforcement Cases

Advocate Entities (July 8, 2016)

Three breaches affected the PHI of 4 million individuals. Violations: failed to assess risks to PHI, failed to implement procedures to limit access to files in data support center, failed to ensure that business associate would protect PHI, and failed to secure unencrypted laptop left in unlocked vehicle overnight. $5.55 million penalty.

Univ. of Miss. Med. Ctr. (Jul. 7, 2016)

Breach of PHI affected 10,000 individuals. Violations: failed to implement procedures to correct security lapses, failed to implement physical safeguards for workstations with access to PHI, failed to use a unique user name and/or number to track PHI, and failed to notify individuals whose PHI was likely disclosed. $2.75 million penalty.

Or. Health & Sci. Univ. (Jul. 18, 2016)

Multiple breaches involving unencrypted laptops and a stolen unencrypted thumb drive exposed the PHI of thousands, including 1,361 patients with a significant risk of harm. Violations: did not implement measures to address security risks, did not implement policies to correct security violations, and did not encrypt PHI on workstations. $2.7 million penalty.

Catholic Health Care Servs. of the Archdiocese of Phila. (Jun. 24, 2016)

Theft of mobile device exposed PHI of 412 nursing home residents. Violations: failed to encrypt or physically protect mobile device, failed to implement policies governing mobile devices, and failed to conduct risk analysis. $650,000 penalty.

N.Y. & Presbyterian Hosp. (Apr. 19, 2016)

Hospital released PHI of two patients to film crews and staff during filming of "NY Med" TV series. Violations: allowed individuals receiving urgent medical care to be filmed without their authorization and failed to safeguard PHI during filming. $2.2 million penalty.

Raleigh Orthopaedic Clinic (Apr. 14, 2016)

Clinic gave PHI of 17,300 patients to potential business partner without first implementing a business associate agreement. Violations: disclosed PHI to unauthorized entity and failed to implement business associate agreement. $750,000 penalty.

The Feinstein Inst. for Med. Research (Mar. 16, 2016)

Unencrypted laptop containing PHI of 13,000 patients and research participants stolen from an employee's car. Violations: failed to implement sufficient security procedures, including policies governing devices. $3.9 million penalty.

N. Mem'l Health Care (Mar. 16, 2016)

Unencrypted laptop stolen from locked vehicle belonging to North Memorial's business associate, exposing the PHI of 9,497 individuals. Violations: failed to implement business associate agreement and failed to complete a risk analysis. $1.55 million penalty.

Complete P.T., Pool & Land Physical Therapy, Inc. (Feb. 02, 2016)

Company impermissibly disclosed PHI when it posted patient testimonials to its website without proper authorization. Violations: failed to safeguard PHI, impermissibly disclosed PHI, and failed to implement procedures to comply with HIPAA authorization requirements. $25,000 penalty.

Lincare, Inc. (Mar. 1, 2016)

Employee of in-home medical care provider abandoned documents containing the PHI of 278 individuals after moving residences. Violations: failed to implement procedures to safeguard PHI offsite, despite providing in-home care, and allowed employees to store PHI in personal vehicles for extended periods of time. $239,800 penalty.

Bd. of Regents of the Univ. of Wash. (Dec. 14, 2015)

Employee downloaded an email attachment with malware, infecting the organization's IT system and compromising the data of over 90,000 patients. Violations: failed to implement policies to address security violations and failed to ensure that affiliated entities conducted and responded to risk assessments. $750,000 penalty.

Triple-S Mgmt. Corp. (Nov. 30, 2015)

Series of breaches affected the unsecured PHI of thousands of individuals. Violations: failed to implement administrative, physical, and technical safeguards to protect PHI, impermissibly disclosed PHI to outside vendor without appropriate business associate agreement, failed to conduct and respond to risk assessments, and failed to implement proper security measures. $3.5 million penalty.

Lahey Clinical Hosp., Inc. (Nov. 19, 2015)

Workstation laptop stolen from an unlocked hospital treatment room, exposing the PHI of 599 individuals. Violations: failed to conduct risk analysis, failed to physically safeguard workstations, failed to implement policies regarding PHI maintained on workstations, and failed to use unique user names to track user identity. $850,000 penalty.

Cancer Care Grp., P.C. (Aug. 31, 2015)

Computer and unencrypted backup media stolen from an employee's car, exposing the PHI of 55,000 patients. Violations: widespread non-compliance with the HIPAA Security Rule, including failure to implement policy governing removal of hardware and electronic media and failure to conduct risk analysis. $750,000 penalty.

St. Elizabeth's Med. Ctr. (July 8, 2015)

Employees used an Internet-based document sharing application to store the PHI of at least 498 individuals without assessing the risks associated with the application. Separately, breach of unsecured PHI on former employee's personal laptop and USB flash drive compromised PHI of 595 individuals. Violations: failed to assess risks associated with document practices and failed to identify and respond to known security incident. $218, 400 penalty.

Cornell Prescription Pharmacy (Apr. 22, 2015)

Pharmacy disposed of documents containing PHI of 1,610 patents in an unlocked, open container. Violations: No written policies or procedures and no employee training. $125,000 penalty.

Anchorage Cmty. Mental Health Servs. (Dec. 2, 2014)

Malware infected health facility's technology infrastructure, compromising PHI of 2,743 patients. Violations: did not follow HHS Security Rule policies and procedures and did not address basic technological risks. $150,000 penalty.

New State HIPAA Enforcement Cases

Women & Infants Hosp. of R.I. (Mass. July 22, 2014)
Lawsuit brought under HIPAA and state consumer protection and data security statutes after hospital lost 19 unencrypted backup tapes containing the PHI of 12,127 Massachusetts residents. Violations: failed to implement inventory and tracking system and failed to adequately protect PHI. $110,000 penalty.

Beth Israel Deaconess Med. Ctr. (Mass. Nov. 20, 2014)
Lawsuit brought under HIPAA and state consumer protection and data security statutes after doctor's unencrypted personal laptop was stolen from an unlocked office, exposing the PHI of 4,000 individuals. Violations: failed to encrypt and physically secure laptop. $100,000 penalty.

Bos. Children's Hosp. (Mass. Dec. 19, 2014)
Lawsuit brought under HIPAA and state consumer protection and data security statutes after doctor's unencrypted hospital-issued laptop was stolen at a conference. Breach exposed PHI of 2,159 patients, including 1,700 minors. Violations: failed to encrypt and physically secure laptop. $40,000 penalty.

State Laws

New Jersey, 2014 N.J. Sess. Law Serv. Ch. 88 (West) (effective Aug. 1, 2015)
Provides that health insurance carriers must encrypt patient data; password-protection access is no longer sufficient. Contrast this N.J. law with HIPAA, where encryption is not required. The N.J. statute applies just to health insurance carriers, not to providers. Moreover, a violation of the encryption mandate constitutes a violation of New Jersey's Consumer Fraud Act.

Constitutional Right to Privacy

Stuart v. Camnitz, 774 F.3d 238 (4th Cir. 2014)
On First Amendment grounds, a federal appeals court struck down North Carolina's Woman's Right to Know Act, which compelled doctors to display a sonogram and describe the image of the fetus to a patient before performing an abortion. Statute found to be compelled speech and the restriction to be ideologically motivated.

GOVERNMENT RECORDS

FOIA Amendment

FOIA Improvement Act of 2016, Pub. L. No. 114-185, 130 Stat. 538 (codified at 5 U.S.C. § 552)
The bill, enacted on June 30, 2016, makes key reforms to 1966 FOIA.

Among its key changes:

- Codifies a "foreseeable harm standard" into FOIA; an agency must release information unless it "reasonably foresees that disclosure would harm an interest protected by an exemption" or "disclosure is prohibited by law";

- Requires launch of a "consolidated online request portal" to allow members of the public to use a single website to file FOIA requests;

- Codifies the DOJ guidance that agencies are to make records and documents available to requesters in an electronic format and to post online records that are requested three or more times;

- Creates a Chief FOIA Officers council of Federal Chief Officers; this council to develop recommendations for increasing compliance and efficiency in responding to FOIA requests;

- Excludes the "deliberative process privilege" from records created 25 years or more before the data on which the records were requested; and

- Requires the Office of Government Information Services to offer mediation services to resolve disputes between requesters and agencies "as a non-exclusive alternative to litigation."

Automatic License Plate Readers

***Gannett Co. v Cty. of Monroe*, 4 N.Y.S.3d 847 (Sup. Ct. 2015)**
Holding that New York's FOIA, the Freedom of Information Law, generally permits individuals to find out whether their license plate data has been collected through law enforcement use of License Plate Readers and stored in state databases. Law enforcement agencies also can seek to refuse release on grounds that it would interference with "a current specific ongoing law enforcement investigation."

Government Privacy and Security Management

Office of Mgmt. & Budget, *Circular No. A-130* (2016)
In its Circular A-130, the OMB sets policy and provides guidance on information technology management for federal executive agencies. Before the Obama Administration issued this update in July 2016, Circular A-130 had last been revised in 2000. This update focused on such areas as cyber-security, information governance, privacy, security, and open data. Perhaps most crucially, Circular A-130 calls for strong data governance by the Federal Government to proactively identify risks to privacy and security and to identify and test practical solutions to risk.

Privacy Law Fundamentals

Notable Books

James B. Jacobs, *The Eternal Criminal Record* (2015)
Examines problems with current criminal recordkeeping.

Notable Scholarship: Articles and Other Sources

Erin Murphy, *The Mismatch Between Twenty-First-Century Forensic Evidence and Our Antiquated Criminal Justice System*, 87 S. Cal. L. Rev. 633 (2014)
Argues that the adversarial process is ill suited to twenty-first-century evidence—such as location tracking, biometrics, digital forensics, and other database-driven techniques.

FINANCIAL DATA

Notable FCRA Cases

***Spokeo, Inc. v. Robins*, 136 S. Ct. 1540 (2016)**
Not all FCRA violations qualify for standing, despite congressional intent for the statute to create a private cause of action. To demonstrate the necessary "injury in fact" from the dissemination of false information, plaintiffs must also show a "concrete harm." The concrete harm need not be "tangible," and a sufficient risk of real harm may qualify, but a "bare procedural violation" is insufficient.

***Sweet v. LinkedIn Corp.*, No. 5:14-cv-04531-PSG, 2015 WL 1744254 (N.D. Cal. Apr. 14, 2015)**
LinkedIn's "References Searches" feature, which allowed employers to find people with whom a prospective employee may have worked, did not qualify as a FCRA "consumer report." The report's contents were entirely derived from self-provided information, which is exempted under the statute. Moreover, the district court found that LinkedIn did not qualify under FCRA as a "consumer reporting agency"; the contested feature was only furthering the user's "information-sharing objectives."

CFPB Rulemaking

CFPB, *Rule for Publishing Financial Rules Online* (Oct. 20, 2014)
Financial institutions subject to the GLBA may publish privacy policies online rather than through an annual hard copy. Consumers may be informed about these online privacy policies in a "regular consumer communication," such as a monthly statement.

Notable CFPB Cases

In re Dwolla, Inc., CFPB No. 2016-CFPB-0007 (Mar. 2, 2016)

This consent order stemmed from the first CFPB action related to data security. An online payment platform, Dwolla, allows its members to transfer funds to other members. The company advertised that its data-security practices "exceed[ed]" or "surpass[ed] industry security standards." It also claimed that members' "information is securely encrypted and stored." Among other things, the CFPB found that Dwolla did not reasonably protect consumer data, did not encrypt all sensitive information, and did not exceed industry standards. The CFPB alleged that the company engaged in "deceptive acts or practices." Dwolla agreed to a $100,000 civil penalty, to comply with all statutory requirements in the future, and to implement numerous improvements in its data-security practices.

CONSUMER DATA

New Cases: Standing

Spokeo, Inc. v. Robins, 136 S.Ct. 1540 (2016)

Not all FCRA violations qualify for standing, despite congressional intent for the statute to create a private cause of action. To demonstrate the necessary "injury in fact" from the dissemination of false information, plaintiffs must also show a "concrete harm." The concrete harm need not be "tangible," and a sufficient risk of real harm may qualify, but a "bare procedural violation" is insufficient.

Resnick v. AvMed, Inc., 693 F.3d 1317 (11th Cir. 2012)

Plaintiffs sufficiently pleaded an injury-in-fact by alleging a sufficient nexus between data breach and theft of their identify. Allegation was that the same sensitive information stored on stolen laptops was used by thieves to open bank accounts in plaintiffs' names.

Perkins v. LinkedIn Corp., 53 F. Supp. 3d 1190 (N.D. Cal. 2014)

Class action suit alleging LinkedIn accessed user email accounts and sent correspondence without permission. The court found that the social networking site's users had consented to this usage but had not agreed to follow-up emails LinkedIn sent. The parties entered a settlement wherein LinkedIn agreed to pay $13 million in damages and $3.25 million in legal fees.

Notable FTC Cases

FTC v. Wyndham Worldwide Corp., 799 F.3d 236 (3d Cir. 2015)

Affirmed the FTC's authority to bring actions against companies with inadequate data protection practices. The FTC had pursued a suit against Wyndham, a chain of hospitality suites, alleging a string of data breaches at the company resulted from insufficient security measures. The Third Circuit held that a company's failure to maintain reasonable and appropriate data security could constitute "unfair practices" under Section 5 of the FTC Act. Additionally, the court concluded that prior FTC guidelines and actions provided fair notice that Wyndham's conduct fell within the agency's statutory authority.

Notable FTC Enforcement Actions

In re ASUSTeK Comput., Inc., FTC No. C-4587 (July 18, 2016)
ASUSTeK, a Taiwan-based computer hardware maker, sold routers and cloud services, advertising that these products included multiple security features that would protect customers' computers from viruses and other types of unauthorized access. In fact, ASUSTeK's product possessed security weaknesses that exposed and compromised thousands of consumers' personal information. The FTC's order requires the company to establish and maintain a security program that will be subject to independent audits for the next 20 years.

FTC v. Sitesearch Corp., No. CV-14-02750-PHX-NVW (D. Ariz. Dec. 11, 2015)
The FTC brought an action against data brokers that gathered loan applications that consumers had submitted through payday loan sites. These companies allegedly provided third party scammers with consumers' sensitive personal information, allowing scammers to withdraw money from the consumers' accounts. A settlement now prohibits these companies from providing further sensitive information to third parties and also requires the destruction of previously collected data. The order also includes a $5.7 million suspended judgment against defendants and a $4.1 million default judgment against Sitesearch.

In re Craig Brittain, FTC No. C-4564 (Dec. 28, 2015)
Craig Brittain allegedly operated a "revenge porn" website and deceptively acquired and posted nude images of women. Subsequently, he demanded that the victims pay fees to have the content removed. After the FTC pursued an action against him, Brittain entered into a settlement prohibiting him from publicly sharing any nude content without the express consent of the subjects. The settlement also required the deletion of all previously published content on Brittain's website.

In re PaymentsMD, LLC, FTC No. C-4505 (Jan. 27, 2015)
PaymentsMD provided a billing platform for medical care providers, allowing patients to pay bills online. The FTC alleged that PaymentsMD deceptively collected consumer health information by contacting various health insurance companies, pharmacies, medical offices, and labs without informing consumers. As a result of an FTC order, PaymentsMD must destroy all this collected information; the order also prohibits the company from engaging in similarly deceptive collection and use of consumers' personal information.

In re RadioShack, Corp., 550 B.R. 700 (Bankr. D. Del. 2016)
RadioShack intended to sell their customer database during bankruptcy proceedings. Referring to *In re Toysmart,* the FTC urged the bankruptcy court to protect consumer data through limiting the sale and use of data to ensure RadioShack's privacy promises were honored. RadioShack subsequently entered into an agreement with state attorney generals that limited the company purchaser's access to RadioShack's customer database. The bankruptcy court ultimately approved the sale.

In re Nomi Techs., Inc., FTC No. C-4538 (Aug. 28, 2015)
Nomi Technologies allegedly misled consumers through statements published on the company website falsely indicating that consumers could opt-out of in-store mobile device tracking. The FTC order prohibits Nomi from misleading consumers regarding how their data is collected, processed, used, and shared on any type of electronic device. Furthermore, Nomi may not misrepresent the extent to which consumers will receive notification about the company's privacy practices. Strong dissents in this matter from Commissioners Maureen Ollhausen and Joshua Wright.

FTC v. T-Mobile USA, Inc., No. 2:14-cv-00967-JLR (W.D. Wash. Dec. 19, 2014)
Suit alleging T-Mobile improperly billed customers for unwanted third-party services like horoscopes and celebrity gossip. T-Mobile alleged to have essentially hid these charges from consumers by placing them in extensive phone bills. T-Mobile and the FTC entered a $90 million settlement agreement, including fines in all states and refunds for affected customers.

In re Snapchat, Inc., FTC No. C-4501 (Dec. 23, 2014)
Mobile app Snapchat allows users to share photos and videos that will automatically be deleted after several seconds. In 2014, Snapchat suffered data breaches involving usernames and passwords. The FTC brought a suit against the company, alleging Snapchat users were deceived by a privacy policy that promised less protection than actually provided. In their settlement with the FTC, Snapchat agreed to strengthen privacy and security measures, to provide users with an accurate description of these measures, and to be monitored by an independent privacy professional for 20 years.

In re GMR Transcription Servs., FTC No. C-4482 (Aug. 14, 2014)
Settlement involved allegations that a medical transcription company outsourced services to a third party without adequately checking that it could implement reasonable security measures.

In re Accretive Health, Inc., FTC No. C-4432 (Feb. 5, 2014)
A company providing medical billing and revenue management services to hospitals put consumers' personal information at risk by, among other things, transporting laptops with sensitive data in a way that made them vulnerable to theft. The FTC also said the company gave access to personal information to employees who didn't need it to do their jobs.

Children's Online Privacy Protection Act (COPPA)

FTC COPPA Cases

Video Privacy Protection Act (VPPA)

Video Privacy Protection Act Amendments Act of 2012, Pub. L. No. 112-258, 126 Stat. 2414 (codified as amended at 18 U.S.C. § 2710)
Permitting a videotape service provider to obtain the consumer's informed, written consent through the Internet. Such consent is valid for a period of up to two years or until consent is withdrawn.

VPPA: Leading Cases

Austin-Spearman v. AMC Network Entm't, LLC, 98 F. Supp. 3d 662 (S.D.N.Y. 2015)
AMC Networks allegedly violated the VPPA by sharing user's video-streaming history collected from their website with a social network. The court ruled that these claims were sufficient to constitute an injury-in-fact, required for Article III standing. However, the plaintiff failed to establish that she was a registered user or had any other relationship with the website; the court consequently held she was not a "consumer" protected by the VPPA.

Eichenberger v. ESPN, Inc, No. C14–463 TSZ, 2015 WL 7252985 (W.D. Wash. May 7, 2015)
Class action suit against ESPN alleging that the network's Roku streaming app improperly shared consumer's PII, such as streaming behavior, with third parties. The information given to third parties combined unique Roku serial number with information previously collected about that consumer. The unique serial number of a Roku device was held not to constitute PII under the VPPA.

Locklear v. Dow Jones & Co., 101 F. Supp. 3d 1312 (N.D. Ga. 2015), *abrogated by Ellis v. Cartoon Network, Inc.*, 803 F.3d 1251 (11th Cir. 2015)
Another court reached a similar conclusion to the *Eichenberger* decision, holding that a device's unique serial number was not PII under the VPPA.

Ellis v. Cartoon Network, Inc., 803 F.3d 1251 (11th Cir. 2015)
The Cartoon Network offered free mobile app services that allowed consumers to stream freely available content. A consumer alleged that the company violated the VPPA by disclosing mobile device identification numbers and records about the viewed content with data-analytics companies. The court held that an individual who uses a free mobile app to view freely available content does not qualify as a "subscriber" and consequently is not a "consumer" under the VPPA.

Yershov v. Gannett Satellite Info. Network, Inc., 820 F.3d 482 (1st Cir. 2016)
Newspaper publisher Gannett Satellite offered a mobile app and allegedly disclosed personal information to third-party data-analytics companies, including the unique identifier number of consumers' mobile devices, GPS locations, and content viewed through the app. While the Eleventh Circuit agreed with the district court that this type of information qualifies as PII under the VPPA, it reversed the lower court's dismissal on the grounds that the complaint adequately alleged that the plaintiff was a "consumer" for purposes of the VPPA.

Telephone Consumer Protection Act (TCPA)

Palm Beach Golf Center-Boca, Inc. v. John G. Sarris, D.D.S., P.A., 781 F.3d 1245 (11th Cir. 2015)
Eleventh Circuit ruled transmission of junk faxes conferred Article III standing, even if the faxes in question were unseen by recipients. The court contended that rendering a plaintiff's fax machine unavailable for a period of time constituted an injury-in-fact.

FCC Enforcement

The FCC has increased its enforcement of privacy matters and has handed out large fines. Collaborating with other agencies, the FCC has collected more than $365 million through its settlements, including punitive fines and refunds to consumers.

FCC, *Privacy Guidelines for ISPs* (2016)
Privacy guidelines issued for ISPs, providing three separate categories for using and sharing information. The guidelines also provide ISP customers with increased transparency and power regarding their personal information.

In re Cellco P'ship, FCC No. EB-TCD-14-00017601 (Mar. 7, 2016)
Verizon Wireless had previously added unique identifier headers, or "supercookies," into customer's mobile Internet traffic without notification or consent. According to an FCC suit, these supercookies were employed from 2012 to 2014. A settlement between the parties included a $1.35 million fine and required the adoption a three-year compliance plan. Verizon agreed to notify consumers about tracking and targeting practices, and the company now needs consumer consent in order to share supercookie information with third parties.

In re AT&T Servs., Inc., FCC No. EB-TCD-14-00016243 (Apr. 8, 2015)
AT&T's overseas workers stole personal information from 280,000 customers. In a settlement with the FCC, AT&T agreed to pay a $25 million fine for violating their statutory duty under the Communications Act to reasonably secure and protect their customer data. The FCC noted this failure also constituted "an unjust and unreasonable practice in violation of the Communications Act."

In re TerraCom, Inc., FCC No. EB-TCD-13-00009175 (July 9, 2015)

TerraCom and YourTel exposed consumers' sensitive information to unauthorized individuals when its data storage vendors utilized servers without any encryption or password protection. As a result, the FCC issued an order to the companies that set out a $3.5 million penalty. The companies were also required to implement a comprehensive information security program, a data breach response plan, enhanced employee training, and regular privacy risk assessments. The FCC's order mandated that the two parties designate a certified privacy professional at a senior corporate manager level and to provide compliance reports with the FCC.

In re Cox Commc'ns, Inc., FCC No. EB-IHD-14-00017829 (Nov. 5, 2015)

FCC data security enforcement action against a cable provider following a data breach and subsequent allegations of unreasonable data security practices. The FCC also alleged that Cox failed to notify law enforcement authorities of the security breaches in a timely fashion. Cox entered into a consent decree that included a $595,000 civil penalty and required enhanced security practices including oversight of vendors, privacy risk assessments, a written compliance program, training of employees, and notification issued to affected consumers.

Electronic Communications Privacy Act (ECPA)

Campbell v. Facebook Inc., 77 F. Supp. 3d 836 (N.D. Cal. 2014)

A suit alleging Facebook violated ECPA by scanning users' private messages for targeted advertising purposes. The court held that consumers of Facebook's website neither expressly nor implicitly consented to the alleged interception of their private messages. Facebook's disclosure that it may use information about users for data analysis was not specific enough to constitute valid consent, nor did it provide adequate notice regarding the private communications text-scanning.

Backhaut v. Apple, Inc., 74 F. Supp. 3d 1033 (N.D. Cal. 2014)

Consumers brought a class action alleging that Apple knowingly and intentionally violated ECPA when intercepting and storing text messages sent by current owners of Apple devices to former users, rendering the delivery impossible. The district court held that the plaintiffs' claims failed to allege that Apple accessed messages while in storage and thus did not constitute a proper claim under ECPA. However, Apple's conduct violated the Wiretap Act. Court also noted that the software license agreement failed to adequately notify consumers that Apple's message interception would make the delivery impossible.

In re Carrier IQ, Inc., No. 12-md-02330-EMC, 2016 WL 4474366 (N.D. Cal. Aug. 25, 2016)

Judge granted preliminary approval to a $9 million class action settlement following a federal court's rejection in *In re Carrier IQ, Inc.*, 78 F. Supp.3d 1051 (N.D. Cal. 2015), of smart phone manufacturers' claims that the plaintiffs lacked standing under the Wiretap Act. Plaintiffs had alleged that their phones' performance had been degraded by the error-logging software that collected information about the substance of phone usage, including websites visited and text message contents. The court held plaintiffs had also sufficiently alleged a Wiretap Act claim.

Notable New Books

Kenneth A. Bamberger & Deirdre K. Mulligan, *Privacy on the Ground: Driving Corporate Behavior in the United States and Europe* **(2015)**
Comparing U.S. privacy and data security laws and enforcement strategies with those of Europe, finding certain trends towards convergence as well as a distinctive U.S. model of compliance.

Chris Jay Hoofnagle, *Federal Trade Commission Privacy Law and Policy* **(2016)**
Comprehensive examination of the FTC and its modern role as an inventive regulator in the U.S. privacy marketplace. Valuable analysis of the FTC's history—in the area of privacy and beyond—to explain its current role and predict where it will go in the future.

Notable New Articles

Woodrow Hartzog & Daniel J. Solove, *The Scope and Potential of FTC Data Protection,* **83 Geo. Wash. L. Rev. 2230 (2015)**
Arguing that the FTC's statutory authority permits the agency to reach a broader scope of privacy and data security issues than it currently pursues.

DATA SECURITY

Notable Cases: FTC

FTC v. Wyndham Worldwide Corp., **799 F.3d 236 (3d Cir. 2015)**
Affirming FTC's authority to bring cases against companies with inadequate data protection practices. A company's failure to maintain reasonable and appropriate data security could constitute unfair competition under the FTC's Section 5 authority. FTC Act and prior FTC guidelines and actions were sufficient notice that Wyndham's conduct fell within statutory authority.

Notable FTC Enforcement Actions

In re ASUSTeK Comput. Inc., **FTC No. C-4587 (July 18, 2016)**
Pioneering Internet of Things enforcement action by the FTC. Company alleged to misrepresent its router security features. Among other things, the complaint alleged that ASUSTeK encouraged customers to set up accounts on its private cloud network with weak security presets and authentication bypass vulnerabilities. Company also allegedly failed to provide consumers timely notification of vulnerabilities after receiving customer complaints.

In re Snapchat, Inc., FTC No. C-4501 (Dec. 23, 2014)

Alleging misrepresentations regarding irretrievability of messages sent via mobile app. Complaint alleges that Snapchat privacy promises were deceptive because of behavior of third-party developers using Snapchat's own API. Snapchat also made deceptive promises regarding analytics tracking.

In re Oracle Corp., FTC No. C-4571 (Mar. 28, 2015)

Complaint alleged that Oracle knew of security vulnerabilities in older Java versions, but in update removed only the most recent version of the software. Oracle agreed to refrain from misrepresenting the security of its software. Oracle further agreed to notify consumers of risks associated with older Java versions present on computers and to provide notice of the settlement on its website.

Notable CFPB Enforcement Actions

In re Dwolla, Inc., CFPB No. 2016-CFPB-0007 (Mar. 2, 2016)

CFPB's first data security action. Misrepresentation alleged regarding security of on-line payment system. Dwolla claimed that customer transactions would be "safe" and "secure" in compliance with standards set by the trade group Payment Card Industry Security Standards Counsel, but its practices fell below those standards. Inadequate or unreasonable practices alleged related to adopting and implementing data-security policies, assessing foreseeable security risks, ensuring employee security training, using encryption technology, and practicing secure software development. Pursuant to deceptive acts and practices authority, the CFPB ordered Dwolla to refrain from misrepresenting the security of its online payment system; enact data security measures and policies to correct the above deficiencies; and pay $100,000 civil money penalty.

Notable FCC Enforcement

In re AT&T Servs., Inc., FCC No. EB-TCD-14-00016243 (Apr. 8, 2015)

In its largest data security action, the FTC entered a $25 million settlement with AT&T to resolve investigation into data breaches at AT&T's call centers in Mexico, Colombia, and the Philippines. These breaches resulted from employees' unauthorized use of customers' information, jeopardizing the confidentiality of almost 280,000 customers' personal information. In addition to the financial penalty, FCC ordered AT&T to appoint a compliance officer; develop and implement a compliance plan that included risk assessment, review, and training; and provide notice to affected customers.

In re Cox Commc'ns, Inc., FCC No. EB-IHD-14-00017829 (Nov. 5, 2015)

Cox entered into a consent decree following a 2014 data breach and subsequent FCC allegations of unreasonable data security practices. Unlike enforcement practices typically mandated by the FTC, the FCC consent order required specific security practices rather than general "reasonable" security maintenance. $595,000 civil penalty assessed. FCC's first data security action against a cable provider and first action regarding a hacking incident.

In re TerraCom, Inc., FCC No. EB-TCD-13-00009175 (July 9, 2015)
TerraCom and Yourtel entered into a consent decree following FCC allegations
that they failed to protect the sensitive information of customers applying for their
Lifeline phone services. Specifically, they allegedly stored customer data on online
servers without password protection or encryption, leading to a data breach. The
companies jointly agreed to pay a $3.5 million civil penalty; appoint a compliance
officer and develop a compliance plan; implement an information security program;
and other measures.

Notable Treatises

Cybersecurity: A Practical Guide to the Law of Cyber Risk (Edward R. McNicholas
& Vivek K. Mohan eds., 2016)
Succinct yet thorough treatise on cybersecurity law.

EDUCATION PRIVACY

New Federal Laws

**Every Student Succeeds Act (ESSA), Pub. L. No. 114-95, 129 Stat. 1802 (codi-
fied as amended in scattered sections of 20 U.S.C.) (2015)**

Primary Function: Governs law for K-12 public education policy and replaces No
Child Left Behind Act. The law requires grantees to possess knowledge of FERPA's
responsibilities.

Homeless Students: ESSA mandates that homeless students' living situations not
be listed in directories; instead, this information is considered a part of the student's
educational record and thus protected by FERPA.

Congressional Findings: Congress included a section on the importance of protecting student privacy, calling for recipients of funding to ensure PII is held in strict
confidence.

New Fourth Amendment Cases

G.C. v. Owensboro Public Schs., 711 F.3d 623 (6th Cir. 2013)
School officials lacked reasonable grounds to search a student's cell phone. The student had a history of depression and marijuana-usage, and he violated school policy
regarding cell phone usage in the classroom. These combined factors were deemed
insufficient to justify a cell phone search by school officials.

Notable Scholarship: Articles and Other Sources

Katherine P. McGrath, Note, *Developing a First Amendment Framework for the Regulation of Online Educational Data: Examining California's Student Online Personal Information Protection Act*, 49 U.C. Davis L. Rev. 1149 (2016)
Note examining California's SOPIPA in light of the Supreme Court's *Sorrell v. IMS Health, Inc.* decision about the freedom of commercial speech, hypothesizing that SOPIPA would not survive a First Amendment challenge. The article suggests a number of changes to help SOPIPA better conform to the Supreme Court's views on commercial speech.

Jules Polonetsky & Omer Tene, *The Ethics of Student Privacy: Building Trust for Ed Tech*, 21 Int'l R. Info. Ethics 25 (2014)
Analyzing challenges in the Ed Tech industry, noting the widespread skepticism that apps like InBloom have faced. The authors propose a "solution toolkit" involving transparency and parental access to data. The article also contends that lengthy privacy notices for products may be off-putting and counter-productive for users.

Jules Polonetsky & Omer Tene, *Who is Reading Whom Now: Privacy in Education From Books to MOOCs*, 17 Vand. J. Ent. & Tech. L. 927 (2015)
Focusing on the broad landscape of Ed Tech and arguing for an analytic separation of the privacy issues and education standardization debate surrounding Ed Tech.

EMPLOYMENT PRIVACY

New NLRB Cases

Landry's Inc., 362 N.L.R.B. No. 69 (2015)
NLRB held that a policy was lawful, where it urged employees not to post anything that could result in morale problems, but did not explicitly prohibit employees from posting information related to the job or co-workers.

Boch Imports, Inc., 362 N.L.R.B. No. 83 (2015), *aff'd, Boch Imports, Inc. v. NLRB*, 826 F.3d 558 (1st Cir. 2016)
NLRB found a social media policy violative of Section 8 of the NLRA, which required employees to self-identify when posting comments about the employer, the employer's business, or policy issues.

Chipotle Services LLC, NLRB No. 04-CA-147314 (2016)
In this NLRB action, an administrative law judge concluded that some aspects but not all of Chipotle's social media policy violated Section 8 of the NLRA. A provision prohibiting the disclosure of "confidential information" was violative because the policy did not define "confidential"—a term the NLRB found "vague and subject to interpretation." A provision prohibiting "disparaging" statements was violative because it was overbroad. But the ALJ upheld a provision against "harassing or discriminatory" statements.

Americans with Disabilities Act (ADA)

EEOC, *Living with HIV Infection: Your Legal Rights in the Workplace Under the ADA* (2015)

The EEOC issued this guidance document to address the protections required under the ADA for applicants and employees with HIV infection. Generally, persons with HIV infection are allowed to keep their condition private. If persons disclose their condition, employers have an obligation to keep the medical information confidential, "even from co-workers."

New Employer Access to Employee Social Media Account Laws

Connecticut, An Act Concerning Employee Online Privacy (S.B. 426) (2015)

Prohibits employers from requesting or requiring employees or applicants to provide access to personal online accounts or to invite the employer to join an online network.

Delaware, Employee/Applicant Protection for Social Media Act (H.B. 109) (2015)

Restricts employers from requiring or requesting access to an employee's or applicant's personal social media profile or account.

Maine (H.B. 640) (2015)

Prohibits employers from requiring or coercing employees or applicants to provide passwords to access personal online accounts, provide account information, or add the employer to an account.

Montana (H.B. 343) (2015)

Prohibits employers from requesting employees or applicants to provide passwords or user names to social media accounts.

Nebraska, Workplace Privacy Act (L.B. 821) (2016)

Prohibits employers from accessing personal Internet accounts of applicants or employees. Prohibits employers from taking adverse action against an employee or failing to hire an applicant for not providing personal Internet account information.

Oregon (S.B. 185) (2015)

Prohibits employers from requiring employees or applicants "to establish or maintain a personal social media account," or to allow the employer to use the account for advertising.

Tennessee, Employee Online Privacy Act (S.B. 1808) (2015)

Prohibits employers from requiring employees or applicants to disclose passwords to social media accounts. The Act also prohibits forcing employees or applicants to add the employer as a contact or access the social media account in the employer's presence.

Virginia (H.B. 2081) (2015)

Prohibits employers from "requiring, requesting, or causing" employees or applicants to provide usernames and passwords to social media accounts. The Act also bars employers from requiring employees to change privacy settings or add any other person to the social media account's contacts.

West Virginia, Internet Privacy Protection Act (H.B. 4364) (2016)

Prohibits employers from requiring employees or applicants to disclose user names, passwords, or any other means of access to personal online accounts.

INTERNATIONAL PRIVACY LAW

ECHR Cases

Satakunnan Markkinapörssi Oy and Satamedia Oy v. Finland 931/13 Eur. Ct. H.R. (2015)

Publisher Satakunnan Markkinapörssi Oy printed Finnish individuals' publicly-available tax-related data. The publisher collaborated with service provider Satamedia Oy to send out tax information via text message upon an individual's request. Extensive publication of personal, publicly-available tax information constituted a violation of Article 8, especially in light of Article 10's protection of a free press. The ECJ also found that these text messages had low public interest value.

European Court of Justice (ECJ)

Case C-362/14, Maximillian Schrems v. Data Prot. Comm'r 2015 E.C.R. (Sept. 23, 2015)

In this landmark case, the ECJ ruled, first, that national authorities must be able to independently investigate the Safe Harbor agreement and to decide on the adequacy of mechanisms in place before transfers of personal information to third countries. Second, the Court considered the adequacy of the Safe Harbor agreement itself. It held that it did not provide an adequate level of protection because EU citizens' data were exposed to the mass surveillance programs of U.S. intelligence agencies without limitations and redress.

Case C-230/14, Weltimmo s. r. o. v. Nemzeti Adatvédelmi és Információszabadság Hatóság, Judgment (Oct. 1, 2015)

This case involved Weltimmo, a Slovakian company that ran a Hungarian-language real estate website. The ECJ examined which national data protection law applied to a business operating in more than one EU state. According to the EU Directive, a key factor in determining the applicability of a member state's laws to an entity is whether the company operates a "relevant establishment" in said state. The ECJ held that Weltimmo had an establishment in Hungary for these reasons: (1) website language;

(2) location of advertised property; (3) existence of a representative in Hungary in charge of collecting debts and judicial and administrative proceedings on behalf of Weltimmo; and (4) existence of a business address and bank account in Hungary.

The General Data Protection Regulation (GDPR)

European Commission, Regulation 2016/670 of the European Parliament and of the Council of 27 April 2016 on the protection of individuals with regard to the processing of personal data and on the free movement of such data, and repealing Directive 95/46/EC (General Data Protection Regulation) (May 4, 2016)

After years of discussion and negotiations, the EU adopted the General Data Protection Regulation (GDPR) in April 2016. This new regime will replace the EU Data Protection Directive 95/46 and take effect in May 2018. Unlike the Directive, which required the enactment of harmonizing legislation in Member States, the GDPR will be directly applicable in all Member States. It takes effect in May 2018.

The GDPR includes high penalties for violations, a new and narrower definition of "consent," a requirement for most businesses with more than 250 employees to have a privacy officer, data breach notification requirements, and a "right to erasure." The proposed regulation also contains protections against decisions based exclusively on "automated processing" and safeguards for sensitive data.

Directly Binding in Member States: Unlike the Directive, the GDPR does not require implementation in national law; it will be directly applicable to all member states of the EU. As the Recitals state: "Consistent and homogenous application of the rules for the protection of personal data should be ensured throughout the Union."

National Law-Making and Areas of Exclusion. Although generally directly binding, the GDPR does allow for certain kinds of national law-making. These include national laws that further specify obligations in areas covered under the GDPR, such as "the processing of personal data for compliance with a legal obligation, for the performance of a task carried out in the public interest or in the exercise of official authority vested in a controller." There are also exceptions and national law-making power for freedom of expression and information, national identification numbers, and employee data. Moreover, the GDPR permits "a margin of manoeuvre" for Member States to specify certain kinds of rules, such as those for sensitive data and regarding the conditions under which data processing will be lawful. Finally, the Regulation does not apply to "activities which fall outside the scope of Union law, such as activities concerning national security." It also does not apply to activities by a natural person "in the course of a purely personal or household activity."

Invalidation of the U.S.-EU Safe Harbor Arrangement

Invalidity of Safe Harbor: The **Shrems** *decision*

In 2015, in its *Shrems* decision, the ECJ invalided the 15-year-old, widely-used EU-U.S. Safe Harbor Framework, which provided a mechanism for data transfers between the EU and U.S. Austrian privacy-rights activist Max Schrems sued Facebook Ireland, arguing that his data protection rights were violated when Facebook transferred his personal information to U.S. servers and thus exposing it to the NSA's mass surveillance program. The ECJ held that U.S. surveillance policies did not meet EU privacy rights standards. As a result, the EU invalidated the Safe Harbor for failing to guarantee an adequate level of protection for the personal data of EU citizens.

The EU-U.S. Privacy Shield

The U.S. government and European Commission were already negotiating a new framework for data transfers at the time of ECJ's *Schrems* decision, which invalidated the Safe Harbor agreement. On July 12, 2016 the Commission issued its implementing decision, which found the Privacy Shield to ensure an adequate level of protection for personal data transferred from the EU to self-certified organizations in the U.S. pursuant to it.

Principles of the Privacy Shield

The Privacy Shield seeks to impose strong obligations on U.S. companies to protect the personal data of EU citizens, and to establish robust monitoring and enforcement by the Department of Commerce and the FTC. Furthermore, it provides for stronger individual rights for EU citizens including:

1. *Notice*
   Participating companies must provide individuals with a variety of different information including: (1) type of data collected, (2) purpose of collection, (3) circumstances of onward transfer, (4) third-party identities, (5) rights of the individuals, (6) redress channels for the individuals.

2. *Choice*
   The Privacy Shield gives individuals a right to opt out of their information being disclosed to a third party, or used for a purpose that is materially different than the purpose for which it was originally collected or subsequently authorized by the individual. Opt-out mechanisms must be "clear, conspicuous, and readily available."

3. *Accountability for Onward Transfer*
   Organizations are liable for compliance with the Notice and Choice Principles when transferring information to a third party acting as a controller. To do so, organization must enter into a contract with the third party controller.

---

4. *Security*
Companies must take reasonable and appropriate measures to protect personal information, taking into account the risks involved in the processing and the nature of the personal information.

5. *Data Integrity and Purpose Limitation*
Companies possess a duty to ensure that personal data held and processed by the organization is "reliable for its intended use, accurate, complete, and current."

6. *Access*
Individuals are to have access to personal information about them and be able to correct, amend, or delete that information when it is inaccurate, or has been processed in violation of the Principles. Companies are to reply to individual complaints within 45 days.

7. *Recourse, Enforcement, and Liability*
The Privacy Shield provides the right to file privacy complaints directly with participating companies. The agreement requires independent recourse mechanisms that must be free of charge to individuals.

Other Aspects of the Privacy Shield

Transparency and Safeguards. The U.S. issued written confirmation to the EU Commission that access of public authorities for law enforcement and national security purposes to EU citizens' information will be subject to "clear limitations, safeguards, and oversight." There will be an annual joint review of the Privacy Shield, including the issue of national security access, which will be conducted by the European Commission and U.S. Department of Commerce. The U.S. has also created a new Ombudsperson, separate from U.S. intelligence services, who will handle individual complaints from EU citizens.

Compliance Review by Companies. Participation in the Privacy Shield framework requires an annual compliance review by companies. Companies exiting the Privacy Shield agreement must still comply with its requirements with respect to the data obtained and processed under the Privacy Shield.

Enforcement. The Privacy Shield heightens enforcement mechanisms beyond those of the Safe Harbor agreement. The Department of Commerce and the FTC are given an oversight role under it. Individuals may also bring complaints under it to a national Data Protection Authority.

U.S.-Swiss Safe Harbor Framework (2009)

The U.S.-Swiss Safe Harbor continues to exist after the invalidation of the U.S.-EU Swiss Harbor. The U.S. Department of Commerce continues to maintain its online U.S.-Swiss Safe Harbor List. The Swiss Data Protection Commission has criticized reliance, however, on the U.S.-Swiss Safe Harbor and called for use of contractual safeguards for Swiss-U.S. data transfers. The Swiss Data Protection Commission also advocated adoption of a regulation analogous to the EU-U.S. Privacy Shield between the U.S. and Switzerland.

New Developments: Canada

Digital Privacy Act, S.C. 2015, c. 32 (Can.)
Amending PIPEDA to established breach notification requirements and heightened requirements for valid consent. The amendments also increase penalties for violations of PIPEDA.

New Developments: Japan

In September 2015, an extensive amendment to the Act on Personal Information was enacted. The amendment to APPI will enter into force on a date set by cabinet order and occurs before September 2017. This Amendment places new restrictions on data transfers to foreign countries. It permits transfers to third parties in foreign countries only when there is prior consent; a transfer to a country with protections equivalent to that of Japan; or the transfer is to a third party with an internal protection system that meets standards set by the Japanese Personal Information Protection Commission. The amended APPI contains additional details regarding the law's definition of personal information. Finally, it contains a new definition of sensitive personal information, which will require prior consent before organizations can collect it.

New Developments: Russia

Localization Law, Federal Law No. 242-FZ
A new law requires that the personal data of Russian citizens be stored within Russia. The deadline for compliance was September 1, 2015.

FTC Enforcement of the APEC Cross-Border Privacy Rules System

In re Very Incognito Techs., Inc., FTC No. 162 3034 (May 4, 2016)
On May 4, 2016, the FTC approved its first APEC order, settling a case with Very Incognito Technologies, Inc. ("Vipvape"), a vaporizers manufacturer. Vipvape falsely alleged on its website that it was a certified company under APEC's Cross Border Privacy Rules framework. The settlement prohibits Vipvape from misrepresenting its participation, membership, or certification in any government or self-regulatory privacy or security program.

Notable Scholarship: Treatises and Books

Graham Greenleaf, *Asian Data Privacy Laws: Trade & Human Rights Perspectives* (2014)
Magisterial treatise on the development of and current status of information privacy law in all Asian states

Andrew B. Serwin, *Information Security and Privacy: A Guide to International Law and Compliance* (2016)
Up-to-date treatise examining EU privacy law and that of individual countries worldwide.

Articles and Other Sources

Edward Lee, *Recognizing Rights in Real Time: The Role of Google in the EU*, 49 U.C Davis L. Rev. 1017 (2016)
Discussion of significant role of Google in developing the "right to be forgotten" (RTBF) in the EU. Google plays this role by deciding individual RTBF requests made to it.

CHAPTER 2

An Overview of Privacy Law

ESSENTIAL POINTS

- Information privacy law is a relatively youthful area of law. New developments are still shaping it and changing its form. For example, data breach notification statutes in the United States date only to 2003.

- The development of privacy law in the United States may also be viewed as a dialogue between the courts and the legislature about the scope and application of the legal concept of privacy. In some matters, courts will define new privacy rights. In others, the courts will leave the job to the legislature.

- Privacy problems occur in particular contexts, and different types of problems involve different trade-offs and concerns.

- Technology plays an especially important role in shaping the kinds of privacy concerns that society faces and the role of the law.

- In Europe and most of the rest of the world, this area is called data protection law. International developments have played a highly visible and important part in shaping the role of privacy professionals and the privacy dialogue within the United States.

TYPES OF PRIVACY LAW

Torts

In the United States, tort law is primarily state law. As a result, the particular boundaries of this area of law will differ from state to state—sometimes dramatically. For example, some states recognize all four privacy interests, but Minnesota accepts only three of the four. It does not recognize the false light tort. *Lake v. Wal-Mart Stores, Inc.*, 582 N.W.2d 231 (Minn. 1998).

TORTS MOST COMMONLY INVOLVED IN PRIVACY CASES

- Invasion of Privacy (a collective term for the four privacy torts)
    - Public disclosure of private facts
    - Intrusion upon seclusion
    - False light
    - Appropriation of name or likeness
- Breach of Confidentiality
- Intentional Infliction of Emotional Distress
- Defamation
    - Libel
    - Slander
- Negligence

ORIGINS OF THE PRIVACY TORTS

Samuel D. Warren & Louis D. Brandeis, *The Right to Privacy*, 4 Harv. L. Rev. 193 (1890)
This foundational article, which inspired the development of privacy law in the twentieth century, argued that the common law protected privacy as "the right to be let alone."

William L. Prosser, *Privacy*, 48 Cal. L. Rev. 383 (1960)
The legendary torts scholar William Prosser surveyed all the common law privacy tort cases and identified the central four interests protected. His formulations of the privacy torts remain in widespread use today. The states have widely adopted Prosser's four privacy torts.

Contract/Promissory Estoppel

Confidentiality or other privacy protections can be an express or implied contractual term in a relationship. Promises to protect privacy might be enforced through promissory estoppel.

Criminal Law

Many privacy laws have criminal penalties. Many states have criminalized blackmail, "Peeping Tom" activity, or the surreptitious capture of nude images.

Evidentiary Privileges

In evidence law, many privileges protect the confidentiality of information shared within certain relationships, such as attorney-client and patient-physician.

Federal Constitutional Law

WAYS THE U.S. CONSTITUTION PROTECTS PRIVACY

- The First Amendment right to speak anonymously
- The First Amendment freedom of association, which protects privacy of one's associations
- The Third Amendment's protection of the home from the quartering of troops
- The Fourth Amendment's protection against unreasonable searches and seizures
- The Fifth Amendment's privilege against self-incrimination
- The constitutional right to privacy
- The constitutional right to information privacy

State Constitutional Law

A number of states have directly provided for the protection of privacy in their constitutions. For example, Cal. Const. art. I, § 1 stipulates: "All people are by their nature free and independent and have inalienable rights. Among these are enjoying and defending life and liberty, acquiring, possessing, and protecting property, and pursuing and obtaining safety, happiness and privacy."

STATES WITH EXPRESS CONSTITUTIONAL PRIVACY PROTECTION

AK	Alaska Const. art. I, § 22	IL	Ill. Const. art. I, § 12
AZ	Ariz. Const. art. II, § 8	LA	La. Const. art. I, § 5
CA	Cal. Const. art. I, § 1	MT	Mt. Const. art. II, § 10
FL	Fla. Const. art. I, § 23	SC	S.C. Const. art. I, § 10
HI	Haw. Const. art. I, § 23	WA	Wash. Const. art. I, § 7

Federal Statutory Law

- **Fair Credit Reporting Act of 1970, 15 U.S.C. §§ 1681 *et seq.*—**provides citizens with rights regarding the use and disclosure of their personal information by consumer reporting agencies.

- **Bank Secrecy Act of 1970, Pub. L. No. 91-508**—requires banks to maintain reports of people's financial transactions to assist in government white-collar investigations.

- **Privacy Act of 1974, 5 U.S.C. § 552a**—provides individuals with a number of rights concerning their personal information maintained in government record systems, such as the right to see one's records and to ensure that the information in them is accurate.

- **Family Educational Rights and Privacy Act of 1974, 20 U.S.C. §§ 1221 note, 1232g**—protects the privacy of school records.

- **Right to Financial Privacy Act of 1978, 12 U.S.C. §§ 3401–3422**—requires a subpoena or search warrant for law enforcement officials to obtain financial records.

- **Foreign Intelligence Surveillance Act of 1978, 15 U.S.C. §§ 1801–1811**—regulates foreign intelligence gathering within the U.S.

- **Privacy Protection Act of 1980, 42 U.S.C. § 2000aa**—restricts the government's ability to search and seize the work product of the press and the media.

- **Cable Communications Policy Act of 1984, 47 U.S.C. § 551**—mandates privacy protection for records maintained by cable companies.

- **Electronic Communications Privacy Act of 1986, 18 U.S.C. §§ 2510–2522, 2701–2709**—updates federal electronic surveillance law to respond to the new developments in technology.

- **Computer Matching and Privacy Protection Act of 1988, 5 U.S.C. § 552a**—regulates automated investigations conducted by government agencies comparing computer files.

- **Employee Polygraph Protection Act of 1988, 29 U.S.C. §§ 2001–2009**—governs the use of polygraphs by employers.

- **Video Privacy Protection Act of 1988, 18 U.S.C. §§ 2710–2711**—protects the privacy of videotape rental information.

- **Telephone Consumer Protection Act of 1991, 47 U.S.C. § 227**—provides certain remedies from repeat telephone calls by telemarketers.

- **Driver's Privacy Protection Act of 1994, 18 U.S.C. §§ 2721–2725**—restricts the states from disclosing or selling personal information in their motor vehicle records.

- **Communications Assistance for Law Enforcement Act of 1994, Pub. L. No. 103-414**—requires telecommunication providers to help facilitate government interceptions of communications and surveillance.

- **Personal Responsibility and Work Opportunity Reconciliation Act of 1996, Pub. L. No. 104-193**—requires the collection of personal information (including Social Security numbers, addresses, and wages) of all people who obtain a new job anywhere in the nation. The resulting information is placed into a national database to help government officials track down deadbeat parents.

- **Health Insurance Portability and Accountability Act of 1996, Pub. L. No. 104-191**—gives the Department of Health and Human Services the authority to promulgate regulations governing the privacy of medical records. These regulations, the HIPAA Privacy Rule, were initially finalized in 2000 with modifications then made in 2002. 45 C.F.R. 160, 162, and 164.

- **Identity Theft and Assumption Deterrence Act of 1998, 18 U.S.C. § 1028**—criminalizes the transfer or use of fraudulent identification with the intent to commit unlawful activity.

- **Children's Online Privacy Protection Act of 1998, 15 U.S.C. §§ 6501–6506**—restricts the use by Internet websites of information gathered from children under age 13.

- **Gramm-Leach-Bliley Act of 1999, 15 U.S.C. §§ 6801–6809**—requires privacy notices and provides opt-out rights when financial institutions seek to disclose personal data to other companies.

- **USA Patriot Act of 2001, Pub. L. No. 107-56**—amends a number of electronic surveillance statutes and other statutes to facilitate law enforcement investigations and access to information.

- **CAN-SPAM Act of 2003, Pub. L. No. 180-187**—provides penalties for the transmission of unsolicited e-mail.

- **Video Voyeurism Prevention Act of 2004, 18 U.S.C § 1801**—criminalizes the capturing of nude images of people (when on federal property) under circumstances where they have a reasonable expectation of privacy.

State Statutory Law

Much of privacy law is found in state law. Privacy tort law and data breach notification statutes are predominately state law. In addition, numerous federal statutes permit state laws to exceed their specifications. This issue is regulated under the rubric of "preemption." In Chapter 9 we provide a chart that lists the federal statutes that preempt state laws and those that do not. The U.S. regulation of privacy is best thought of as a dual federal-state system.

Areas of State Legislation on Privacy

Substantial state legislation on privacy exists in the following areas:

Law Enforcement

- Wiretapping and electronic surveillance

Medical and Genetic Information

- Confidentiality of medical information
- Genetic privacy

Government Records

- Public records
- State agency use and disclosure of personal information

Financial Privacy

- Banking privacy
- Consumer reports
- Security freeze

Consumer Data and Business Records

- Spam
- Spyware and phishing
- Telecommunications privacy
- Pretexting
- Use of Social Security numbers
- Data disposal
- Video privacy
- RFID and tracking devices
- Restrictions on ISPs
- Unauthorized access to computers and networks

Data Security

- Identity theft
- Data security breach notification

Employment

- State employee personal information

- Restrictions on employment application questions

For a more detailed analysis of these laws, consult Andrew B. Serwin's *Information Security and Privacy: A Guide to International Law and Compliance* (2016).

International Law

Around the world, numerous countries have endeavored to protect privacy in their laws. There are two general approaches toward protecting privacy:

1. *Omnibus*: A comprehensive approach to protecting privacy that covers personal data across all industries and most contexts. Sometimes a single omnibus law will also regulate the public and private sectors.

2. *Sectoral*: Regulates information on a sector-by-sector basis. Different industries receive different regulation, and some contexts are not regulated at all. Different statutes regulate the public and private sectors.

The world's first comprehensive information privacy statute was a state law; the Hessian Parliament enacted this statute in Wiesbaden, Germany, on September 30, 1970. Like most European data protection laws, this statute is an omnibus law.

In contrast, the United States has generally relied on regulation of information use on a sector-by-sector basis. For example, the Children's Online Privacy Protection Act provides privacy protection for children on the Web, but there is no such law that generally regulates privacy for adults on the Web.

Outside of Europe and the United States, there are many information privacy statutes in the rest of the world. Most countries have adopted the omnibus approach.

There are also important international and transnational accords, guidelines, treaties, directives, and agreements. These include:

- Organisation of Economic Co-operation and Development (OECD) Guidelines (1980), with additional, supplemental OECD Guidelines (2013)

- The Safe Harbor Privacy Principles (2000) established between the United States and the European Commission

- Asia-Pacific Economic Cooperative (APEC) Privacy Framework (2004)

THE CHIEF PRIVACY OFFICER

The chief privacy officer (CPO) is becoming a mainstay at many large organizations. Among other things, a CPO ensures that the organization is complying with the law, that employees are trained about privacy and security practices, and that the organization has an effective privacy policy.

In the public sector, the Homeland Security Act of 2002 established a privacy officer within the Department of Homeland Security. 6 U.S.C. § 142. This statute created the first explicit legal requirement in a federal law for a privacy officer in the United States government. Previously, the Clinton administration had appointed a chief counselor for privacy and located this position in the Office of Management and Budget's Office of Information and Regulatory Affairs (OIRA).

In 2002, Congress also enacted the E-Government Act, which requires administrative agencies to conduct Privacy Impact Assessments (PIAs).

In the private sector, regulations enacted pursuant to the Health Insurance Portability and Accountability Act of 1996 (HIPAA) require "a covered entity" to "designate a privacy official who is responsible for the development and implementation of the policies and procedures of the entity." 45 C.F.R. 164.30(a)(1)(i).

As part of its role implementing the Gramm-Leach-Bliley Act, the Federal Trade Commission issued a Safeguards Rule that requires designation of an employee or employees to coordinate the company's information security program. This requirement can encourage introduction of a chief privacy officer position at organizations that do not yet have one. 16 C.F.R. Part 314.4(a), 67 Federal Register 36484 (2002).

In addition, the Safe Harbor Agreement, negotiated by the U.S. Department of Commerce with the European Commission, called for U.S. companies to engage in either "self-assessment or outside compliance review" of their privacy practices. By mandating these procedures, the Safe Harbor created the obligation for a certain amount of compliance work and an incentive for U.S. organizations that register under it to designate a CPO to take care of these tasks.

Although the European Court of Justice invalidated the Safe Harbor in 2015, the Privacy Shield, a new agreement between the U.S. and European Union, followed in 2016. The Privacy Shield heightens the compliance requirements for U.S. companies, including their obligation to reply promptly to any complaints about their data practices. As a result, the Privacy Shield increased the incentive for companies that enter into it to have a CPO as well as a strong internal compliance program.

In sum, most large companies that handle personal data now have a CPO.

THE DEVELOPMENT OF PRIVACY LAW: A TIMELINE

Antiquity

400 B.C.	Hippocratic Oath provides the first recorded expression of a duty of medical confidentiality.

1000 – 1699

1361	England's Justices of the Peace Act criminalizes eavesdropping and Peeping Toms.
1604	*Semayne's Case* (1604) 77 Eng. Rep. 194, declares that "the house of everyone is to him as his castle and fortress."

THE DEVELOPMENT OF PRIVACY LAW: A TIMELINE

1700 – 1799

1763   *Wilkes v. Wood* (1763) 98 Eng. Rep. 489, repudiates the use of a general warrant to search for documents relating to a pamphlet involving seditious libel. Influential in the creation of the Fourth Amendment.

1765   *Entick v. Carrington* (1765) 95 Eng. Rep. 807, is another repudiation of general warrants in a seditious libel case. Influential in the creation of the Fourth Amendment.

1789   U.S. Constitution—First, Third, Fourth, and Fifth Amendments.

1800 – 1899

1860   U.S. Census becomes more inquisitive. Public outcry for greater census privacy.

1877   *Ex parte Jackson*, 96 U.S. 727 (1877)—U.S. Supreme Court holds that the Fourth Amendment protects sealed letters in the mail.

1886   *Boyd v. United States*, 116 U.S. 616 (1886)—U.S. Supreme Court holds that the government cannot compel people to turn over documents.

1890   Samuel D. Warren & Louis D. Brandeis, *The Right to Privacy*, 4 Harv. L. Rev. 193 (1890). This article inspires the recognition during the twentieth century of privacy torts in the majority of the states.

1900 – 1959

1903   States begin to recognize privacy torts. New York enacts a law creating Warren and Brandeis tort of appropriation. N.Y. Civ. Rights Law §§ 50-51. Georgia Supreme Court recognizes appropriation tort. *Pavesich v. New England Life Ins. Co.*, 50 S.E. 68 (Ga. 1905).

1908   FBI is formed. Originally called the Bureau of Investigation.

1928   *Olmstead v. United States*, 277 U.S. 438 (1928). In a decision later overruled, the U.S. Supreme Court holds that Fourth Amendment protections do not extend to wiretapping. Now on the Supreme Court, Justice Louis Brandeis writes a famous dissent to the majority opinion.

1934   In response to *Olmstead*, Congress enacts § 605 of the Federal Communications Act of 1934 to limit wiretapping.

1936   Social Security system begins. Creation of the Social Security number, which is not intended to be used in other programs or as a form of identification.

1947   Central Intelligence Agency (CIA) is created.

1948   The Universal Declaration of Human Rights is adopted by the UN, protecting a right to privacy in Article 12.

1949   Publication of George Orwell's *1984*. Birth of "Big Brother."

1950   European Convention on Human Rights (ECHR) is adopted, protecting the right to privacy in Article 8.

1952	President Truman creates the National Security Agency (NSA).
1953	Origins of the "right of publicity" tort in *Haelan Laboratories v. Topps Chewing Gum, Inc.*, 202 F.2d 866 (2d Cir. 1953).

1960 – 1979

1960	William L. Prosser, *Privacy*, 48 Cal. L. Rev. 383 (1960).
1961	In *Mapp v. Ohio*, 367 U.S. 643 (1961), the U.S. Supreme Court holds that the exclusionary rule for Fourth Amendment violations applies to the states.
1965	In *Griswold v. Connecticut*, 381 U.S. 479 (1965), the U.S. Supreme Court prevents the government from banning contraceptives. The Griswold Court finds that the Constitution protects a right to privacy through the "penumbras" of many of the 10 amendments of the Bill of Rights.
1966	Congress enacts the Freedom of Information Act (FOIA).
1967	In *Katz v. United States*, 389 U.S. 347 (1967), the U.S. Supreme Court reverses Olmstead. The concurrence in the case by Justice John Marshall Harlan articulates the "reasonable expectation of privacy test," the current approach for determining the Fourth Amendment's applicability.
1967	Alan Westin publishes *Privacy and Freedom*.
1968	Title III of the Omnibus Crime and Control and Safe Streets Act is passed, a major revision of electronic surveillance law. Title III is now known as the Wiretap Act.
1970	In Wiesbaden, Germany, the Hessian Parliament enacts the world's first comprehensive information privacy statute.
1970	The Fair Credit Reporting Act.
1973	According to *Roe v. Wade*, 410 U.S. 113 (1973), the right to privacy "encompass[es] a woman's decision whether or not to terminate her pregnancy."
1973	The U.S. Department of Health, Education and Welfare (HEW) issues a report, *Records, Computers, and the Rights of Citizens*, articulating the FIP.
1974	The Privacy Act.
1974	The Family Educational Rights and Privacy Act.
1975	Congress's Church Committee conducts a thorough investigation of surveillance abuses by the government.
1975	In *Cox Broadcasting Corp. v. Cohn*, 420 U.S. 469 (1975), the U.S. Supreme Court recognizes some First Amendment limitations on the privacy torts.

1976	In *United States v. Miller*, 425 U.S. 435 (1976), the U.S. Supreme Court holds that financial records possessed by third parties are not protected by the Fourth Amendment. The Court articulates the "third party doctrine"—people lack a reasonable expectation of privacy in information conveyed to third parties.
1977	The Supreme Court recognizes the constitutional right to information privacy—the "individual interest in avoiding disclosure of personal matters" in *Whalen v. Roe*, 429 U.S. 589 (1977) and *Nixon v. Administrator of General Services*, 433 U.S. 425 (1977).
1977	German Federal Data Protection Act.
1978	French Data Protection Act.
1979	In *Smith v. Maryland*, 442 U.S. 735 (1979), the U.S. Supreme Court rules that the Fourth Amendment does not apply to a pen register (the telephone numbers a person dials) because of the third party doctrine—people cannot expect privacy in their phone numbers since they expose the information to the phone company.

1980 – 1989

1980	Organisation of Economic Co-operation and Development (OECD) Guidelines.
1981	Israel's Protection of Privacy Law.
1986	Congress passes the Electronic Communications Privacy Act (ECPA), creating the contemporary statutory approach to regulating the electronic surveillance of communications.
1986	Computer Fraud and Abuse Act (CFAA).
1988	Australia passes the Privacy Act, which is based on the OECD Guidelines.
1988	Video Privacy Protection Act (VPPA).

1990 – 1999

1992	The UK begins implementing its CCTV video surveillance system.
1992	Switzerland's Federal Law on Data Protection.
1992	Israel's Basic Law on Human Dignity and Freedom provides for a right to privacy.
1994	Driver's Privacy Protection Act (DPPA).
1995	Communications Decency Act (CDA).
1996	Congress passes the Health Insurance Portability and Accountability Act (HIPAA). Title II of HIPAA requires the establishment of national standards for electronic data exchange and addresses issues concerning the privacy and security of healthcare information.
1996	The European Union promulgates the EU Data Protection Directive.

1996	Hong Kong Personal Data Ordinance.
1998	The FTC begins to bring actions against companies that violate their privacy policies.
1998	Children's Online Privacy Protection Act (COPPA).
1998	The UK Human Rights Act.
1998	The UK Data Protection Act.
1998	Sweden's Personal Data Act.

2000 – 2009

2000	The Safe Harbor Agreement is established between the U.S. and EU for data sharing under the EU Data Protection Directive.
2000	Argentina becomes the first country in South America to adopt a comprehensive data protection statute: the Law for the Protection of Personal Data. The EU Data Protection Directive strongly influences the Argentinean statute.
2001	USA Patriot Act.
2001	Personal Information Protection and Electronic Documents Act (PIPEDA) takes effect in Canada.
2001	In *Kyllo v. United States*, 533 U.S. 27 (2001), the U.S. Supreme Court holds that the Fourth Amendment requires a warrant and probable cause before the government can use thermal sensors to detect activity in people's homes.
2002	Department of Health and Human Services issues final modifications to the HIPAA Privacy Rule.
2003	Japan enacts the Personal Data Protection Act.
2004	Asia-Pacific Economic Cooperation (APEC) Privacy Framework.
2004	The European Court of Human Rights decides *Von Hannover v. Germany*, 2004-VI Eur. Ct. H.R. 41, recognizing privacy rights in certain public settings.
2005	ChoicePoint, one of the largest data brokers, announces that it sold personal data on more than 145,000 people to fraudulent companies established by a ring of identity thieves. Subsequently, numerous companies and organizations began disclosing data security breaches. A vast majority of states enacted data security breach notification legislation in response.
2009	HITECH Act, enacted as part of the American Recovery and Reinvestment Act of 2009, establishes a breach notification requirement for "covered entities" under HIPAA. It also extends HIPAA's requirements for privacy and information security to the business associates of covered entities.

2010 – Present

2010	32nd International Conference of Data Protection and Privacy Commissioners held in Jerusalem. One adopted resolution, proposed by the Information and Privacy Commissioner of Ontario (Canada), calls for adoption of Privacy by Design within organizations in order to make privacy a default mode of operation.
2010	Mexico enacts the Federal Law for the Protection of Personal Data.
2012	In *United States v. Jones*, 132 S. Ct. 945 (2012), the U.S. Supreme Court finds that law enforcement's installation of a GPS device to a car without a warrant is a search under the Fourth Amendment.
2012	Commission proposes EU General Data Protection Regulation.
2013	HHS issues HIPAA Omnibus Final Rule.
2013	Edward Snowden leaks classified documents detailing numerous broad surveillance programs by the NSA.
2013	In *Clapper v. Amnesty International USA*, 133 S. Ct. 1138 (2013), the U.S. Supreme Court denies standing to challengers to NSA surveillance lacked standing to bring their case.
2013	FTC issues Amendments to the COPPA Rule (July 2013).
2013	Supplemental, additional OECD Privacy Guidelines released.
2014	FTC celebrates 100th birthday.
2014	Several prominent large data security breaches are announced by major retailers including Target, Neiman Marcus, Home Depot, Kmart, and others.
2014	In *Riley v. California,* 134 S. Ct. 2473 (2014), the U.S. Supreme Court holds that a warrant is generally required to search digital information on a cell phone seized pursuant to an individual's arrest.
2014	InBloom closed (in part) due to privacy concerns. Numerous states enact new privacy laws for K-12 students.
2014	In Case C-131/12, *Google Spain SL v. Agencia Española de Protección da Datos* (May 13, 2014), the European Court of Justice (ECJ) requires a search engine to remove a link to a search result that violates the "right to be forgotten."
2015	In *FTC v. Wyndham Worldwide Corp.,* 799 F.3d 236 (3d Cir. 2015), the FTC won a case posing the most significant challenge thus far to the FTC's regulatory authority. The U.S. Court of Appeals for the Third Circuit held that the FTC had broad powers to regulate data security under the FTC Act.
2015	In Case C-362/14, *Schrems v. Data Protection Commissioner* (Oct. 6, 2015), the ECJ invalidates the Safe Harbor agreement.

| 2016 | The General Data Protection Regulation is published in the E.U. Office Journal on May 24, 2016. It will become binding throughout the EU on May 25, 2018. |
| 2016 | The Privacy Shield, the successor to the Safe Harbor, entered into force on July 12, 2016. |

FOR FURTHER REFERENCE

Treatises

Kristen J. Mathews, *Proskauer on Privacy: A Guide to Privacy and Data Security Law in the Information Age* (**2016**)
(originally created and edited by Christopher Wolf)

Andrew B. Serwin, *Information Security and Privacy: A Guide to International Law and Compliance* (**2016**)

Lisa J. Sotto, *Privacy and Cybersecurity Law Deskbook* (**2d ed. 2016**)

Lothar Determann, *California Privacy Law* (**2d ed. 2017**)

General Sources

Anita L. Allen, *Uneasy Access: Privacy for Women in a Free Society* (**1988**)
Provides a valuable overview of philosophical accounts of privacy's definition and value.

Colin J. Bennett & Charles D. Raab, *The Governance of Privacy: Policy Instruments in Global Perspective* (**2006**)
A thoughtful study of the political landscape of privacy policymaking around the world.

Michelle Finneran Dennedy, Jonathan Fox, & Thomas R. Finneran, *The Privacy Engineer's Manifesto: Getting from Policy to Code to QA to Value* (**2014**)
A detailed and concrete discussion about Privacy by Design and how to implement privacy in the development of technology.

Viktor Mayer-Schönberger, *Delete: The Virtue of Forgetting in the Digital Age* (**2009**)
A powerful depiction of the legal, social and cultural implications of a world that no longer remembers how to forget. Advocates, among other solutions, an expiration date for information in different settings and contexts.

Helen Nissenbaum, *Privacy in Context: Technology, Policy, and the Integrity of Social Life* (2010)
An illuminating theory for understanding privacy in its social context.

Frank Pasquale, *The Black Box Society: The Secret Algorithms That Control Money and Information* (2015)
Argues that the detailed profiles that companies are creating about people have profound implications for their reputations and opportunities as well as for society. The algorithms used to make automated decisions based on personal data are often hidden, and they should be more transparent. The law should also ensure that important decisions be made fairly and in a non-discriminatory manner.

Richard A. Posner, *The Right of Privacy,* 12 Ga. L. Rev. 393 (1978)
One of the most compelling critiques of privacy.

Robert C. Post, *The Social Foundations of Privacy: Community and Self in the Common Law Tort,* 77 Cal. L. Rev. 957 (1989)
A valuable argument about how privacy is a social value, not just an individual right.

Priscilla M. Regan, *Legislating Privacy: Technology, Social Values, and Public Policy* (1995)
Illuminating study of how and why Congress has passed certain privacy laws.

Neil Richards, *Intellectual Privacy: Rethinking Civil Liberties in the Digital Age* (2015)
Argues that surveillance—by both the government and private-sector entities—threatens freedom of speech, belief, and intellectual exploration.

Jeffrey Rosen, *The Unwanted Gaze: The Destruction of Privacy in America* (2000)
Views privacy as protecting "a space for negotiating legitimately different views of the good life" and examines the loss of private spaces in modern life.

Paul M. Schwartz, *Privacy and Democracy in Cyberspace,* 52 Vand. L. Rev. 1609 (1999)
An account of the importance of protecting the privacy of digital communications.

Daniel J. Solove, *Understanding Privacy* (2008)
A theory of what privacy is and why it is valuable.

Alan Westin, *Privacy and Freedom* (1967)
An early classic work about information privacy, providing an insightful account of the value privacy contributes to individuals and society.

CHAPTER 3

Privacy and the Media

ESSENTIAL POINTS

- Most states recognize the privacy torts.

- The privacy torts and other related torts have wide applicability in a variety of contexts.

- The First Amendment creates significant restrictions on the privacy torts. These reach their apex when public figures or information of public concern are at stake.

THE PRIVACY TORTS

The four privacy torts are:

1. Public disclosure of private facts

2. Intrusion upon seclusion

3. False light

4. Appropriation of name or likeness

Public Disclosure of Private Facts

The public disclosure of private facts tort creates a cause of action for one who publicly discloses a private matter that is "highly offensive to a reasonable person" and "is not of legitimate concern to the public." Restatement (Second) of Torts § 652D (1977). "Publicity" requires widespread disclosure in most jurisdictions. The last element—"not of legitimate concern to the public"—is known as the "newsworthiness test" and is designed to protect free speech interests.

Approaches to the Newsworthiness Test

Courts use at least three newsworthiness tests:

1. *The "Leave It to the Press" Approach*—defer to editorial judgment

2. *The "Community Customs" Approach*—focus on social norms

3. *The "Nexus" Approach*—require a "logical nexus" between the person whose privacy was invaded and a matter of legitimate public interest

Leading Cases

Sipple v. Chronicle Publ'g Co., **201 Cal. Rptr. 665 (Ct. App. 1984)**
A newspaper column that "outed" as gay the hero who thwarted an assassination attempt on President Gerald Ford was newsworthy. Among the reasons for such newsworthiness: The report revealed potential bias by Ford in not publicly thanking the hero.

Sidis v. F-R Publ'g Corp., **113 F.2d 806 (2d Cir. 1940)**
An article about a child prodigy who retreated from the public spotlight for many years was newsworthy because it is of public interest to give a status report on people who were once well known.

Intrusion Upon Seclusion

The intrusion upon seclusion tort provides a remedy when one intrudes "upon the solitude or seclusion of another or his private affairs or concerns" if the intrusion is "highly offensive to a reasonable person." Restatement (Second) of Torts § 652B (1977).

"The intrusion itself makes the defendant subject to liability even though there is no publication or other use of any kind of the photograph or information outlined." *Id.* cmt. b.

Leading Cases

Nader v. Gen. Motors Corp., **255 N.E.2d 765 (N.Y. 1970)**
Although generally people don't have an expectation of privacy in public, "overzealous surveillance" in public can be actionable when the "information sought is of a confidential nature" and the defendant's conduct is "unreasonably intrusive" (beyond the "normal inquiry of observation").

Dietemann v. Time, Inc., **449 F.2d 245 (9th Cir. 1971)**
Entering a person's home under false pretenses and secretly recording his activities is actionable.

In the public disclosure and intrusion upon seclusion torts, a key element involves whether the plaintiff had a privacy interest.

PRIVACY INTEREST

Involuntary exposure in public— certain kinds of involuntary exposure in public, especially involuntary nudity. *Daily Times Democrat v. Graham*, 162 So.2d 474 (Ala. 1964).

Overzealous surveillance in public— surveillance in public that reveals confidential data. *Nader v. Gen. Motors Corp.*, 255 N.E.2d 765 (N.Y. 1970).

Inside the home— activities occurring within people's houses. *Dietemann v. Time, Inc.*, 449 F.2d 245 (9th Cir. 1971).

Known to a certain social group— data known to a discrete social group not likely to circulate it to outsiders. *Y.G. v. Jewish Hosp. of St. Louis*, 795 S.W.2d 488 (Mo. Ct. App. 1990).

Extensive harassment in public— *Linehan v. Linehan*, 285 P.2d 326 (Cal. Dist. Ct. App. 1955).

Photos of corpses of loved ones — *Sellers v. Henry*, 329 S.W.2d 214 (Ky. 1959); *Catsouras v. Dep't of the Cal. Highway Patrol*, 104 Cal. Rptr. 3d 352 (Ct. App. 2010).

NO PRIVACY INTEREST

Public view— anything exposed to public view. *Gill v. Hearst Publ'g Co.*, 253 P.2d 441 (Cal. 1953).

Public domain— any information available in a public record. *Reece v. Grissom*, 267 S.E.2d 839 (Ga. Ct. App. 1980).

Republication— restating facts already publicized. *Heath v. Playboy Enterprises, Inc.*, 732 F. Supp. 1145 (S.D. Fla. 1990).

Known by others— information shared with many people. *Fisher v. Ohio Dep't of Rehab. & Corr.*, 578 N.E.2d 901 (Ohio Ct. Cl. 1988).

PRIVACY AND THE MEDIA

3

In the public disclosure, intrusion upon seclusion and false light torts, a key element involves whether the violation is highly offensive to a reasonable person. Courts are not always consistent in their holdings, but generally, the following things have been found either highly offensive or not highly offensive.

HIGHLY OFFENSIVE	NOT HIGHLY OFFENSIVE
Peeping into home windows. *Pritchett v. Board of Comm'rs*, 85 N.E. 32 (Ind. App. 1908).	**Disclosure of reputation-enhancing information.** *Wood v. Nat'l Comput. Sys., Inc.*, 643 F. Supp. 1093 (W.D. Ark. 1986).
Harassing telephone calls. *Rogers v. Loews L'Enfant Plaza Hotel*, 526 F. Supp. 523 (D.D.C. 1981).	**Disclosure of union membership.** *Int'l Union v. Garner*, 601 F. Supp. 187 (M.D. Tenn. 1985).
Snooping into mail. *Doe v. Kohn Nast & Graf, P.C.*, 866 F. Supp. 190 (E.D. Pa. 1994).	**Disclosure of non-embarrassing information.** *Bisbee v. John C. Conover Agency, Inc.*, 452 A.2d 689 (N.J. Super. Ct. App. Div. 1982).
Secretly recording conversations. *Fischer v. Hooper*, 732 A.2d 396 (N.H. 1999).	**Disclosure of employment duties.** *Budik v. Howard Univ. Hosp.*, 986 F. Supp. 2d 1 (D.D.C. 2013)
Illegally accessing credit card records. *Pulla v. Amoco Oil Co.*, 882 F. Supp. 836 (S.D. Iowa 1994).	**Disclosure of family photographs.** *Hart v. World Wrestling Entm't, Inc.*, No. 3:10cv0975(SRU), 2012 WL 1233022 (D. Conn. 2012)
Distribution of nude photos. *Taylor v. K.T.V.B., Inc.*, 525 P.2d 984 (Idaho 1974).	**Disclosure of minor injury.** Restatement (Second) of Torts § 652D cmt. c (1977).
Disclosure of autopsy photos. *Reid v. Pierce Cty.*, 961 P.2d 333 (Wash. 1998).	**Disclosures causing "minor and moderate annoyance."** Restatement (Second) of Torts § 652D cmt. c (1977).
Disclosure of confidential medical data. *Crippen v. Charter Southland Hosp., Inc.*, 534 So.2d 286 (Ala. 1988).	
Public disclosure of mental health records. *Susan S. v. Israels,* 67 Cal. Rptr. 2d 42 (Ct. App. 1997).	
Disclosure of a teacher's medical and personnel information. *Munoz v. Chi. Sch. Reform Bd.*, No. 99 C 4723, 2000 WL 152138 (N.D. Ill. Feb. 4, 2000)	
Identifying a rape victim. *Nappier v. Jefferson Standard Life Ins. Co.*, 322 F.2d 502 (4th Cir. 1963).	
Disclosure of debts. *Brents v. Morgan,* 299 S.W. 967 (Ky. 1927).	

False Light

The false light tort creates a cause of action when one publicly discloses a matter that places a person "in a false light" that is "highly offensive to a reasonable person." Restatement (Second) of Torts § 652E (1977).

Leading Case

Time, Inc. v. Hill, **385 U.S. 374 (1967)**
The U.S. Constitution's First Amendment permits liability in false light cases only if the plaintiff publicly discloses the matter with a reckless disregard for the truth or with actual knowledge of falsity.

Appropriation of Name or Likeness

A plaintiff has a remedy against one "who appropriates to his own use or benefit the name or likeness" of the plaintiff. Restatement (Second) of Torts § 652C (1977). From the right against appropriation, courts have also developed a "right of publicity" that provides famous people an exclusive right to exploit the value of their identity as celebrities.

Leading Cases

Carson v. Here's Johnny Portable Toilets, Inc., **698 F.2d 831 (6th Cir. 1983)**
A right of publicity protects against an unauthorized commercial exploitation of celebrity identity. An unauthorized use of a famous phrase, "Here's Johnny," that is associated with a celebrity appropriates his identity as celebrity and violates his right of publicity.

Finger v. Omni Publ'ns Int'l, Ltd., **566 N.E.2d 141 (N.Y. 1990)**
A photograph of plaintiffs, used to illustrate a magazine article without their permission, does not violate their privacy interests so long as there is a "real relationship" between their photograph and the topic of the article.

OTHER TORTS

Intentional Infliction of Emotional Distress

The tort of intentional infliction of emotional distress can also serve as a remedy for certain privacy invasions. This tort provides a remedy when one "by extreme and outrageous conduct intentionally or recklessly causes severe emotional distress to another." Restatement (Second) of Torts § 46 (1977). Since privacy invasions can often result in severe emotional distress, this tort may provide a remedy. However, it is limited by the requirement of "extreme and outrageous conduct."

Breach of Confidentiality

The tort of breach of confidentiality provides a remedy when a professional (i.e., doctor, lawyer, banker) divulges a patient's or client's confidential information. A plaintiff must prove that the defendant owed the plaintiff a duty of confidentiality and that the defendant breached that duty. Unlike the tort of public disclosure, the breach of confidentiality tort does not require the tests of "highly offensive," publicity or newsworthiness.

PUBLIC DISCLOSURE TORT VS. BREACH OF CONFIDENTIALITY TORT	
PUBLIC DISCLOSURE	**BREACH OF CONFIDENTIALITY**
Publicity—widespread disclosure	Breach of a duty of confidentiality—need not be widespread disclosure
Private matter	Confidential information
Highly offensive to a reasonable person	N/A
Not of legitimate concern to the public	N/A

OTHER PRIVACY LAWS OF NOTE

Video Voyeurism Prevention Act (VVPA), 18 U.S.C. § 1801 (2004)
Prohibits capturing images or videos of people's private parts. Provides protection when a reasonable person expects to be able to disrobe without being photographed or recorded as well as when a person expects his or her private parts not to be publicly visible "regardless of whether that person is in a public or private area." The statutory jurisdiction of this federal law is limited to the special maritime and territorial jurisdiction of the U.S.

State Video Voyeurism Statutes
Many states have laws prohibiting the capturing of photos or videos of people's private parts. Some of these include criminal penalties. *See, e.g.,* Cal. Penal Code § 647(k); Fla. Stat. Ann. § 810.145; La. Stat. Ann. § 14:283; N.J. Stat. Ann. § 2C:18-3; N.Y. Penal Law § 250.45; Wash. Rev. Code § 9A.44.115.

"Peeping Tom" Laws
A number of states criminalize peeping into people's homes or other places where they expect privacy. Many state statutes require that the perpetrator trespass onto private property in order to peep or that the perpetrator see the victim wholly or partially nude. Other states lack such restrictions. For example, Hawaii makes it a crime when one "[p]eers or peeps into a window or other opening of a dwelling or other structure adapted for sojourn or overnight accommodations for the purpose of spying on the occupant thereof or invading the privacy of another person with a lewd or unlawful purpose, under circumstances in which a reasonable person in the dwelling or other structure would not expect to be observed." Haw. Rev. Stat. § 711-1111.

Blackmail Laws

Blackmail laws address threats to expose discreditable secrets unless a person pays money. Example: "A person extorts if he purposely threatens to: … (c) expose or publicize any secret or any asserted fact, whether true or false, tending to subject any person to hatred, contempt or ridicule, or impair his credit or business repute." N.J. Stat. Ann. § 2C:20-5.

California Anti-Paparazzi Act, Cal Civ. Code § 1708.8

The first anti-paparazzi law in the United States. Among other things, it prohibits capturing images, video, or audio with enhancing devices. Although it is similar to the tort of intrusion upon seclusion, the statute only requires that the violation be offensive rather than highly offensive, and the statute provides for treble damages.

Revenge Porn Statutes

Non-consensual pornography, known as "revenge porn," occurs when people post nude or sexual images or videos of another person without their consent (often motivated by vengeance). In 2004, New Jersey adopted the first criminal invasion of privacy statute prohibiting the disclosure of someone's sexually explicit images without that person's consent. See N.J. Stat. Ann. § 2C: 14-9.

In the past few years, many states have passed similar laws. Currently, there are revenge porn laws in 34 states and the District of Columbia. In 2013, California led the way when it enacted legislation criminalizing the distribution of images of intimate body parts taken under circumstances where the parties agree or understand that the images would remain private. *See* Cal. Penal Code § 647(j)(4). In December 2014, Noe Iniguez became the first person convicted under the California statute for posting a topless photo of his former girlfriend on her employer's Facebook page. *See People v. Iniguez*, 202 Cal. Rptr. 3d 237 (App. Dep't Super. Ct. 2016) (complaint filed, November 3, 2014). Iniguez was sentenced to one year in jail and three years' probation.

DEFAMATION LAW

Libel and Slander

Defamation: A person is liable for defamation if he makes "a false and defamatory statement concerning another" to a third party with the applicable fault standard. Restatement (Second) of Torts § 558 (1977). A "defamatory" statement "tends so to harm the reputation of another as to lower him in the estimation of the community or to deter third persons from associating or dealing with him." Restatement (Second) of Torts § 559 (1977).

Libel vs. Slander: Defamation law consists of two torts—libel and slander. Libel is defamation in tangible form—written or broadcast via TV or radio. Slander is defamation spoken directly to other people.

Republication: "[O]ne who repeats or otherwise republishes defamatory matter is subject to liability as if he had originally published it." Restatement (Second) of Torts § 578 (1977).

Distribution: One who distributes, transmits, or broadcasts on television or radio defamatory material is also liable if she knows or would have reason to know of its defamatory character. Restatement (Second) of Torts § 581 (1977).

First Amendment Restrictions

New York Times Co. v. Sullivan, **376 U.S. 254 (1964)**
Libel law must be constrained by the First Amendment to ensure speech is "uninhibited, robust and wide-open." A public official must prove "actual malice" to prevail.

> ## Actual Malice
>
> "Actual malice" involves making a statement "with knowledge that it was false or with reckless disregard of whether it was false or not." *New York Times Co. v. Sullivan,* 376 U.S. 254 (1964).

Curtis Publ'g Co. v. Butts, **388 U.S. 130 (1967)**
Public figures, in addition to public officials, must prove actual malice to prevail in a defamation case.

Gertz v. Robert Welch, Inc., **418 U.S. 323 (1974)**
Private figures do not need to establish actual malice in order to prevail in a defamation lawsuit.

> ## Public vs. Private Figures
>
> 1. **All-Purpose Public Figures**—people who have "general fame or notoriety." Deemed a public figure for all issues.
>
> 2. **Limited Public Figures**—people who are involved in a particular controversy. They are deemed public figures with regard to stories about the context or controversy that makes them public figures, but for everything else, they remain private.

Dun & Bradstreet, Inc. v. Greenmoss Builders, Inc., **472 U.S. 749 (1985)**
For matters of purely private concern, such as providing a report on one's financial condition for use by another person or company, actual malice is not required by the First Amendment, nor any other limitations on the defamation torts.

Privacy Law Fundamentals

DEFAMATION: FAULT STANDARDS

	PUBLIC FIGURE (includes public officials)	PRIVATE FIGURE
Speech of Public Concern	*Curtis Publ'g Co. v. Butts* Compensatory Damages = Malice Punitive Damages = Malice Presume Damages = Malice	*Gertz v. Robert Welch, Inc.* Compensatory Damages = Negligence Punitive Damages = Malice Presumed Damages = Malice
Speech of Private Concern	Unclear. Probably same as above, but might be Gertz rule. Communications Decency Act (CDA) § 230(c), 47 U.S.C. § 230(c) (1996)	*Dun & Bradstreet v. Greenmoss Builders* Compensatory Damages = Negligence Punitive Damages = Negligence Presumed Damages = Negligence (or possibly strict liability for all forms of damages)

Communications Decency Act (CDA)
§ 230(c), 47 U.S.C. § 230(c) (1996)

"No provider or user of an interactive computer service shall be treated as the publisher or speaker of any information provided by another information content provider." Immunizes ISPs, blogs, social network sites and others from liability for the content posted by users.

Leading Cases

Zeran v. Am. Online, Inc., 129 F.3d 327 (4th Cir. 1997)
The CDA § 230 immunizes an ISP that fails to remove a defamatory posting by a user even after the ISP knows it is defamatory.

Carafano v. Metrosplash.com, Inc., 339 F.3d 1119 (9th Cir. 2003)
Dating website immune under CDA § 230 for false profile of plaintiff posted by a third party.

Batzel v. Smith, 333 F.3d 1018 (9th Cir. 2003)
Listserv operator who forwarded defamatory e-mail was immune under CDA § 230 because a third party authored the e-mail.

Fair Hous. Council v. Roommates.com, LLC, 521 F.3d 1157 (9th Cir. 2008)
Roommates.com not immune under CDA § 230 when it created questions and answer choices for users to select. By providing "pre-populated answers, Roommates becomes much more than a passive transmitter of information provided by others; it becomes the developer, at least in part, of the information."

FIRST AMENDMENT

The First Amendment provides restrictions to tort liability for the disclosure of true and false information:

- For content-based restrictions on the disclosure of true information, the First Amendment requires strict scrutiny when the data pertains to a matter of public significance. When the data involves a private matter, the Supreme Court has not indicated what, if any, First Amendment restrictions would be involved.

- For false information, the First Amendment follows the rules set forth in its line of cases involving defamation, generally requiring actual malice for public figures.

- For the enforcement of contract or promissory estoppel that involves restrictions on the disclosure of information, the First Amendment does not provide restrictions.

Leading Cases

Cox Broad. Corp. v. Cohn, 420 U.S. 469 (1975)
If the information is released in court records by the government, the tort of public disclosure cannot apply (even if the information is private and not newsworthy).

The Fla. Star v. B.J.F., 491 U.S. 524 (1989)
"[I]f a newspaper lawfully obtains truthful information about a matter of public significance then state officials may not constitutionally punish publication of the information, absent a need to further a state interest of the highest order."

Bartnicki v. Vopper, 532 U.S. 514 (2001)
A provision in the federal Wiretap Act prohibits one from intentionally disclosing the contents of a communication "knowing or having reason to know that the communication was obtained" in violation of the wiretap law. The Supreme Court held that the First Amendment prevents the application of the statute when the illegally obtained communication involves a matter of public concern.

Time, Inc. v. Hill, 385 U.S. 374 (1967)
Actual malice rule applies to the false light tort. After *Gertz,* it appears the actual malice rule would apply to cases brought only by public figures.

Hustler Magazine, Inc. v. Falwell, 485 U.S. 46 (1988)
Public figures must prove actual malice to recover for intentional infliction of emotional distress.

Snyder v. Phelps, 562 U.S. 443 (2011)
For speech of public concern, plaintiffs must prove actual malice in order to prevail under the intentional infliction of emotional distress tort. The First Amendment also restricts intrusion upon seclusion liability for picketing near a funeral.

Zacchini v. Scripps-Howard Broad. Co., 433 U.S. 562 (1977)
Actual malice rule does not apply to the appropriation tort.

Cohen v. Cowles Media Co., 501 U.S. 663 (1991)
The First Amendment does not limit contracts and promissory estoppel when they involve restrictions on speaking.

Elonis v. United States, 135 S. Ct. 2001 (2015)
The U.S. Supreme Court reversed a conviction under 18 U.S.C. § 875(c), which makes it a federal crime to transmit in interstate commerce "any communication containing any threat . . . to injure the person of another." The Court held that a conviction under the statue required a showing that the defendant had either the intent or knowledge that communications would be viewed as threats; negligence was not sufficient.

THE FIRST AMENDMENT AND TORTS

Public Disclosure of Private Facts
The First Amendment requires strict scrutiny if the information is truthful and involves a matter of public concern. *The Fla. Star v. B.J.F.*, 491 U.S. 524 (1989); *Bartnicki v. Vopper*, 532 U.S. 514 (2001).

Intrusion Upon Seclusion
Intrusion upon seclusion tort action used improperly to impose liability on protesting near a funeral violates the First Amendment. *Snyder v. Phelps*, 562 U.S. 443 (2011). When the tort does not involve direct restrictions on speech, it will likely have no First Amendment problems.

False Light
Actual malice required. *Time, Inc. v. Hill*, 385 U.S. 374 (1967). It is likely that the same standards apply as in defamation law.

Appropriation of Name or Likeness
No actual malice required. *Zacchini v. Scripps-Howard Broad. Co.*, 433 U.S. 562 (1977).

Intentional Infliction of Emotional Distress
Actual malice required for public figures. *Hustler Magazine, Inc. v. Falwell*, 485 U.S. 46 (1988).

Breach of Confidentiality
No U.S. Supreme Court First Amendment case yet. If seen as akin to tort, then might be treated akin to the public disclosure tort. But if seen as akin to contract or promissory estoppel, then no First Amendment limitation. *Cohen v. Cowles Media Co.*, 501 U.S. 663 (1991).

Defamation Torts

See the Defamation: Fault Standards chart on page 55.

> ## Anti-SLAPP
>
> When lawsuits implicate a defendant's speech, 30 states and the District of Columbia provide special anti-SLAPP protections.
>
> A SLAPP lawsuit—or a "strategic lawsuit against public participation"—is a lawsuit designed to censor or retaliate against a person for their speech. Fearing significant legal defense costs, defendants might retract their speech or stop engaging in new speech about a matter. SLAPP suits can successfully silence people engaging in protected speech even when the suit is without merit because the costs of getting the suit dismissed can still be significant.
>
> Anti-SLAPP legislation typically has the following elements: (1) requirements that the plaintiff demonstrate early that the case has merit; (2) provisions that allow the defendant to seek an expedited hearing; (3) limits on long costly discovery; (4) the right of a prevailing defendant to recover attorney fees and costs.

ANONYMOUS SPEECH

The First Amendment protects anonymous speech. Unless narrowly tailored to a compelling government interest, a law or regulation cannot:

- Require people to include their true identities on handbills and pamphlets. *Talley v. California*, 362 U.S. 60 (1960); *McIntyre v. Ohio Elections Comm'n*, 514 U.S. 334 (1995).

- Require individuals handing out petitions to wear name tags. *Buckley v. Am. Constitutional Law Found.*, 525 U.S. 182 (1999).

- Force solicitors of private residences to obtain a permit requiring they supply their identities. *Watchtower Bible & Tract Soc'y v. Vill. of Stratton*, 536 U.S. 150 (2002).

> ### Standards for Unmasking Anonymous Speakers
>
> Courts have articulated several different standards for a plaintiff to find out the identity of an anonymous speaker:
>
> 1. ***The Motion to Dismiss Standard.*** The plaintiff must show the case can survive a motion to dismiss in order to ascertain the identity of the anonymous speaker. *Columbia Ins. Co. v. seescandy.com*, 185 F.R.D. 573 (N.D. Cal. 1999).

2. **The Prima Facie Case Standard.** The plaintiff must produce evidence showing a prima facie case on all elements and must demonstrate that revealing the identity of the anonymous speaker will not severely harm the speaker's free speech or privacy rights and will be "necessary to enable plaintiff to protect against or remedy serious wrongs." *Highfields Capital Mgmt., L.P. v. Doe*, 385 F. Supp. 2d 969 (N.D. Cal. 2005); *Dendrite Int'l, Inc. v. Doe*, No. 3, 775 A.2d 756 (N.J. Super. Ct. App. Div. 2001).

3. **The Summary Judgment Standard.** The plaintiff must prove the case could survive a motion for summary judgment. *Doe v. Cahill*, 884 A.2d 451 (Del. 2005); *Sinclair v. TubeSockTedD*, 596 F. Supp. 2d 128 (D.D.C. 2009).

4. **The Variable Standard.** The standard varies depending on the nature of the speech, with commercial speech afforded less protection than political, religious, or literary speech. *In re Anonymous Online Speakers*, 661 F.3d 1168 (9th Cir. 2011), *withdrawing* 611 F.3d 653 (9th Cir. 2010) (known as the "*Quixtar*" case).

PRIVACY OF READING AND INTELLECTUAL EXPLORATION

Stanley v. Georgia, 394 U.S. 557 (1969)
The First and Fourteenth Amendments prohibit making mere private possession of obscene material a crime.

Osborne v. Ohio, 495 U.S. 103 (1990)
The rule in *Stanley* does not apply to the possession of child pornography in the home.

Reporter's Privilege

In *Branzburg v. Hayes*, 408 U.S. 665 (1972), the Supreme Court held that there is no First Amendment reporter's privilege against grand jury requests for evidence. Following *Branzburg*, many federal circuit courts have recognized a qualified reporter's privilege. The reporter's privilege has fared much better in civil cases than in criminal ones.

In the states, the reporter's privilege has been recognized, with sources in state constitutions, state statutes, and common law. Forty-nine states and the District of Columbia have recognized it. In most states, there is a qualified reporter's privilege, which can be overridden if the government establishes that it has no alternative way to obtain the information and that there is a compelling interest to do so. About 13 states have an absolute privilege, which cannot be overridden.

Currently, the Federal Rules of Evidence do not recognize a reporter's privilege.

FOR FURTHER REFERENCE

Treatises

J. Thomas McCarthy, *The Rights of Publicity and Privacy* (2015)

Books

Samantha Barbas, *Laws of Image: Privacy and Publicity in America* (2015)
Historical account of how different areas of law, including the right of publicity, defamation, and libel, have regulated the use of one's image in public. Analysis of how "we seek publicity on our own terms" in the United States and the law's reaction to such behavior by individuals.

Danielle Keats Citron, *Hate Crimes in Cyberspace* (2014)
A discussion of how the Internet provides a platform for systematized targeting of individuals (most frequently women and minorities) for repeated cyber-attacks. These attacks are vicious and threatening, and they create severe emotional distress and other harm in victims. Currently, legislators and policymakers frequently underestimate the need for adequate legal proscriptions and punishments of this behavior. Recommends the use of civil rights law to combat the problem.

Lawrence M. Friedman, *Guarding Life's Dark Secrets: Legal and Social Controls Over Reputation, Propriety, and Privacy* (2007)
An illuminating history of gossip and reputation, with a focus on the Victorian Age.

Amy Gajda, *The First Amendment Bubble: How Privacy and Paparazzi Threaten a Free Press* (2015)
Discussing how to balance privacy and freedom of the press, including how to define who counts as a "journalist" in the days of blogs and social media.

The Offensive Internet: Speech, Privacy, and Reputation (Saul Levmore & Martha C. Nussbaum eds., 2010)
A compilation of pieces from distinguished scholars connecting the absence of legal oversight of the Internet with harassment and discrimination.

Jon L. Mills, *Privacy in the New Media Age* (2015)
Describing how to modernize the intrusion tort in a way that emphasizes both human dignity and freedom of the press. Tackles pressing question of how the new media age impacts our approach to privacy.

Don R. Pember, *Privacy and the Press: The Law, the Mass Media, and the First Amendment* (1972)
A good historical account of the development of the privacy torts, with an extensive discussion of how the torts evolved in each decade following Warren and Brandeis' seminal 1890 article on privacy.

Daniel J. Solove, *The Future of Reputation: Gossip, Rumor, and Privacy on the Internet* (2007)
A discussion of how new forms of social media are transforming the nature of gossip and rumor in troubling ways.

Articles and Other Sources

Danielle Keats Citron, *Cyber Civil Rights*, 89 B.U. L. Rev. 61 (2009)
An insightful account of how civil rights laws can regulate offensive online speech directed toward attacking women and minorities.

Amy Gajda, *Judging Journalism: The Turn Toward Privacy and Judicial Regulation of the Press*, 97 Cal. L. Rev. 1039 (2009)
Describes and explains the weakening judicial deference to the media in privacy cases.

Woodrow Hartzog & Frederic Stutzman, *The Case for Online Obscurity*, 101 Cal. L. Rev. 1 (2013)
Arguing that obscurity is a key component of privacy but often lacking in legal protection. Proposes four indicia that define obscurity for the purposes of protecting it.

William L. Prosser, *Privacy*, 48 Cal. L. Rev. 383 (1960)
An influential article organizing the privacy tort into four categories.

Daniel J. Solove & Neil M. Richards, *Rethinking Free Speech and Civil Liability,* **109 Colum. L. Rev. 1650 (2009)**
Examines why the First Amendment generally restricts civil liability for tort but not for contract or property law.

Lior Jacob Strahilevitz, *A Social Networks Theory of Privacy,* **72 U. Chi. L. Rev. 919 (2005)**
Examines how social network theory can resolve the question of when privacy expectations are eliminated by disclosure of secrets to other people.

Eugene Volokh, Freedom of Speech and Information Privacy: The Troubling Implications of a Right to Stop People from Speaking About You, 52 Stan. L. Rev. 1049 (2000)
A strong critique of civil liability for the disclosure of true personal information.

Eugene Volokh, *Tort Law vs. Privacy,* **114 Colum. L. Rev 879 (2014)**
A discussion of which legal institutions—juries, judges, or legislatures—should resolve the privacy vs. safety questions that routinely arise within tort law.

Samuel D. Warren & Louis D. Brandeis, *The Right to Privacy,* **4 Harv. L. Rev. 193 (1890)**
The article that inspired the privacy torts and that has been called the most influential law review publication ever.

Diane L. Zimmerman, *Requiem for a Heavyweight: A Farewell to Warren and Brandeis's Privacy Tort,* **68 Cornell L. Rev. 291 (1983)**
A powerful attack on the Warren and Brandeis privacy torts.

CHAPTER 4

Privacy and Law Enforcement

ESSENTIAL POINTS

- There are fundamental distinctions between how the law regulates access by law enforcement to personal information and how it treats that of intelligence agencies. This chapter examines the former; the next chapter, the latter.

- The Fourth Amendment provides protection whenever a person has a reasonable expectation of privacy. Generally, though subject to numerous exceptions, the Fourth Amendment requires a warrant supported by probable cause in order for law enforcement officers to conduct a search.

- Even if the Fourth Amendment does not apply, federal statutory law may require safeguards and impose process requirements on the governmental party seeking the information. The following federal statutes may apply:

  1. Electronic Communications Privacy Act (ECPA), consisting of the
     - Wiretap Act
     - Stored Communications Act
     - Pen Register Act
  2. Privacy Protection Act (PPA)
  3. Right to Financial Privacy Act (RFPA)

- States also have statutes that regulate electronic surveillance and access to computers. In some states, these laws provide stricter privacy protections than their federal counterparts.

- Highly intricate electronic surveillance law regulates the government's access to personal data. This area of law draws complex and sometimes confusing distinctions based on different types of communications ("wire communications," "oral communications" and "electronic communications").

- Many electronic surveillance laws apply to the private sector and not just to the government.

- Under certain federal statutes, companies can be liable for disclosing data to law enforcement officials if the companies do not comply with legal standards.

- The government has a number of tools to access private-sector records. These include:
    - Statutes with reporting requirements (e.g., Bank Secrecy Act)
    - National Security Letters (NSLs)
    - Subpoenas

- The Fourth Amendment does not apply to much government information gathering because of the third-party doctrine. Even if a company promises privacy, a customer lacks an expectation of privacy under the Fourth Amendment.

- Many federal privacy statutes provide for government access to records through a court order or subpoena, which have loose standards for access, much lower than probable cause.

FOURTH AMENDMENT

The Fourth Amendment to the U.S. Constitution

"The right of the people to be secure in their persons, houses, papers, and effects, against unreasonable searches and seizures, shall not be violated, and no Warrants shall issue, but upon probable cause, supported by Oath or affirmation, and particularly describing the place to be searched, and the persons or things to be seized."

How the Fourth Amendment Works

In Fourth Amendment cases, a court must answer two important questions:

1. **Is the Fourth Amendment applicable?**
   The government must engage in a "search" or "seizure" in order to trigger Fourth Amendment protection. A search occurs whenever the government activity invades a person's reasonable expectation of privacy. A seizure occurs when government officials exercise control over a person or thing.

2. **If the Fourth Amendment applies, is the search reasonable?**
   A search with a warrant supported by probable cause is generally reasonable, with only a few rare exceptions.

Privacy Law Fundamentals

How the Fourth Amendment Works

Probable cause exists when a reasonable person would believe that the place to be searched will turn up evidence of a crime or that the person arrested committed a crime.

A search without a warrant and probable cause is often deemed unreasonable, but there are many exceptions to the warrant and probable cause requirements, such as exigent circumstances, plain view, automobile searches, searches incident to arrest, stop and frisk and the special needs doctrine.

Evidence obtained in violation of the Fourth Amendment is generally to be excluded from trial. But there are a number of exceptions to this rule.

Leading Cases

Katz v. United States, 389 U.S. 347 (1967)
Overrules *Olmstead v. United States*, 277 U.S. 438 (1928). The Katz Court agreed with Justice Louis Brandeis' dissent in *Olmstead* and found that the Fourth Amendment applies to wiretapping. Justice Harlan's concurrence in *Katz* established the "reasonable expectation of privacy test," which the majority of the Supreme Court later adopted as its governing standard to determine whether a search falls under the scope of the Fourth Amendment. Under this test: (1) a person must exhibit an "actual (subjective) expectation of privacy" and (2) "the expectation [must] be one that society is prepared to recognize as 'reasonable.'"

Terry v. Ohio, 392 U.S. 1 (1968)
A police officer can "stop" an individual if the officer has "reasonable suspicion" that criminal activity is afoot. During the stop, the officer may "frisk" an individual for weapons if the officer has reasonable suspicion that the person is armed and dangerous.

Smith v. Maryland, 442 U.S. 735 (1979)
The Supreme Court held that no reasonable expectation of privacy exists in the numbers that a person dials when the police record them with a pen register. The court reached this conclusion because (1) the numbers do not involve the "content" of the communications and (2) when a person conveys information to another (the phone company), that person must assume the risk that the company will reveal the information to others.

Florida v. Riley, 488 U.S. 445 (1989)
The Fourth Amendment is not triggered by the police flying a helicopter over a greenhouse and peering from above through the greenhouse's missing roof panels. There is no reasonable expectation of privacy if something is visible from a vantage point accessible to the public.

Kyllo v. United States, 533 U.S. 27 (2001)

Use of a thermal imaging device to monitor activities in a home triggers Fourth Amendment protection because of the importance of protecting privacy at home and the fact that the thermal imaging device "is not in general public use."

United States v. Jones, 132 S. Ct. 945 (2012)

Law enforcement's installation of a GPS device in a car without a warrant is a search under the Fourth Amendment because it represents a trespass on a person's property. Concurring opinions also argue that the use of extensive long-term surveillance violates a reasonable expectation of privacy.

Riley v. California, 134 S. Ct. 2473 (2014)

A warrant is required to search digital information on a cell phone seized pursuant to an individual's arrest because cell phones are qualitatively different from other physical "papers and effects" found on the arrestee's person. Law enforcement must either obtain a warrant or fall within the exigent circumstances exception.

Key Fourth Amendment Doctrines

1. **Third Party Doctrine:** If a person exposes information to a third party, she can no longer expect privacy in that information. *United States v. Miller*, 425 U.S. 435 (1976) (bank records); *Smith v. Maryland*, 442 U.S. 735 (1979) (phone numbers).

2. **Misplaced Trust Doctrine:** A person has no Fourth Amendment protection against being betrayed by an informant or undercover agent because the person assumes the risk of betrayal. *Hoffa v. United States*, 385 U.S. 293 (1966).

3. **Plain View Doctrine:** If something is seen in plain view, it is not a search and does not trigger any Fourth Amendment protection. *Harris v. United States*, 390 U.S. 234 (1968).

4. **Special Needs Doctrine:** Under certain circumstances, typically when searches are by non-law-enforcement government officials (school officials, government employers), a search need only be "reasonable." *O'Connor v. Ortega*, 480 U.S. 709 (1987).

FOURTH AMENDMENT REASONABLE EXPECTATION OF PRIVACY

YES

- Wiretapping private conversation. *Katz v. United States, 389 U.S. 347 (1967).*

- Searching a home. *Minnesota v. Olson*, 495 U.S. 91 (1990).

- Using sense enhancement not in general use to reveal activities in the home. *Kyllo v. United States, 533 U.S. 27 (2001).*

- Tracking device that monitors a person's movements at home. *United States v. Karo*, 468 U.S. 705 (1984).

- Searching a bag or container. *Arkansas v. Sanders*, 442 U.S. 753 (1979), *abrogated by California v. Acevedo*, 500 U.S. 565 (1991).

- Searching a personal computer. *Trulock v. Freeh*, 275 F.3d 391 (4th Cir. 2001).

- Opening a sealed letter. *Ex parte Jackson*, 96 U.S. 727 (1877).

- Searching an office desk. *O'Connor v. Ortega*, 480 U.S. 709 (1987).

NO

- Obtaining phone numbers dialed from a phone company. *Smith v. Maryland*, 442 U.S. 735 (1979).

- Obtaining financial records from a bank. *United States v. Miller*, 425 U.S. 435 (1976).

- Dog sniff for drugs. *Illinois v. Caballes*, 543 U.S. 405 (2005).

- Search of trash left on the curb for collection. *California v. Greenwood*, 486 U.S. 35 (1988).

- Viewing a person's property overhead from a helicopter. *Florida v. Riley*, 488 U.S. 445 (1989).

- Using sense enhancement technology in general public use. *Dow Chem. Co. v. United States*, 476 U.S. 227 (1986).

- Tracking device that monitors a person's movements in public. *United States v. Knotts*, 460 U.S. 276 (1983).

- Requiring a person to provide a voice sample. *United States v. Dionisio*, 410 U.S. 1 (1973).

- Requiring a person to provide a handwriting sample. *United States v. Mara*, 410 U.S. 19 (1973).

- Searching a workplace computer where the user was notified that the device is subject to monitoring. *United States v. Angevine*, 281 F.3d 1130 (10th Cir. 2002).

EXCEPTIONS TO THE WARRANT
AND PROBABLE CAUSE REQUIREMENTS

NO WARRANT REQUIRED (BUT MUST HAVE PROBABLE CAUSE)

- Exigent Circumstances

  No warrant is required if delay of obtaining it would endanger the public, permit escape, or allow destruction of evidence.

- Plain View

  Objects may be seized if there is probable cause to believe they are contraband or evidence of a crime.

- Vehicle Searches

  Mobile vehicles can be searched if there is probable cause to believe they contain evidence of criminal activity.

- Arrests

  A person can be arrested without a warrant outside of her home.

- Searches Incident to Arrest

  If there is probable cause to arrest, a search for weapons or evidence on the arrestee and in the immediate area is permissible.

NO WARRANT OR PROBABLE CAUSE REQUIRED

- Consent

  If permission is given for the search, no warrant or probable cause is needed.

- Stop and Frisk

  A brief stop can be made with reasonable suspicion crime is afoot and a frisk can be done for weapons.

- Special Needs

  Searches in schools or government workplaces must be reasonable under the circumstances.

- Administrative Searches

  Searches of homes for code violations and of closely regulated businesses can be made without specific suspicion.

- Checkpoints

  Certain kinds of checkpoints do not require a warrant or probable cause if reasonable.

- Border Searches

  The special need to collect duties and intercept contraband coming into the U.S. often does not require probable suspicion.

ELECTRONIC COMMUNICATIONS

Electronic Communications Privacy Act of 1986 (ECPA)
18 U.S.C. §§ 2510-2522, 2701-2711, 3121-3127

The ECPA amended Title III (the Wiretap Act) and also included two new acts in response to developments in computer technology and communication networks. As a result, federal electronic surveillance law for domestic law enforcement agencies contains three parts:

1. Wiretap Act (updated version of Title III), 18 U.S.C. §§ 2510–2522

2. Stored Communications Act (SCA), 18 U.S.C. §§ 2701–2711

3. Pen Register Act, 18 U.S.C. §§ 3121–3127

Note: The next chapter discusses the legal regulations in place for intelligence agencies that seek to carry out electronic surveillance for the purpose of foreign intelligence gathering (as opposed to domestic law enforcement).

Types of Communications in ECPA

1. **Wire Communications:** A "wire communication" involves "aural transfer[s]" (communications containing the human voice) that travel in part or whole through wire (i.e., telephone wires or cable wires) or a similar medium. 18 U.S.C. § 2510(1).

2. **Oral Communications:** An "oral communication" is a communication "uttered by a person exhibiting an expectation that such communication is not subject to interception under circumstances justifying such expectation." Such communications are typically intercepted through bugs or other recording or transmitting devices. 18 U.S.C. § 2510(2).

3. **Electronic Communications:** An "electronic communication" consists of all non-wire and non-oral communications (i.e., signals, images, data) that can be transmitted through a wide range of transmission mediums (wire as well as radio, electromagnetic, photoelectronic, etc.). E-mail is an example of electronic communication.18 U.S.C. § 2510(12).

Wiretap Act
18 U.S.C. §§ 2510–2522

THE WIRETAP ACT	
Applies to	Interception of communications in flight.
Key Provisions	*Interception:* Provides strict controls on the interception of communications. "Interception" is the acquiring of the contents of a communication through an electronic, mechanical, or other device while the communication is being transmitted.
Court Order	Application for court order to intercept must contain details justifying the interception and information about how the interception will occur and its duration. 18 U.S.C. § 2518.
	These statutory standards are stricter than those that the Supreme Court has identified in the Fourth Amendment. Hence, the Wiretap Act is said to require a "super warrant."
	The judge must find:
	1. Probable cause
	2. That alternatives to interception have failed, are unlikely to succeed or will be too dangerous
	Orders must require that interception be conducted to "minimize the interception of the communications not otherwise subject to interception."
	Only high-level government prosecutors can apply for orders.
	Orders are limited to certain felonies ("predicate offenses").
Exceptions	*Consent:* Title I does not apply if one party to the communication consents. 18 U.S.C. § 2511(2)(c).
	Service Provider: Title I does not apply to the interception of communications by a communications service provider. 18 U.S.C. § 2511(2)(a)(i).
Exclusionary Rule	Yes, for wire and oral communications.
	No, for electronic communications.
Penalties	Damages (minimum $10,000 per violation). Up to five years imprisonment.

Stored Communications Act (SCA)
18 U.S.C. §§ 2701–2711

THE STORED COMMUNICATIONS ACT	
Applies to	1. Accessing communications in "electronic storage" 2. Records of ISPs
Key Provisions	*Stored Communications:* Requires the government to obtain via court order, subpoena, or warrant. 18 U.S.C. § 2703. *ISP Records:* Requires the government to obtain a warrant or court order to access specified customer data held by ISPs, including name, address, length of service, means of payment, etc. 18 U.S.C. § 2703(c).
Court Order	*Communications Stored 180 Days or Less:* Government must obtain warrant supported by probable cause. 18 U.S.C. § 2703(a). *Communications Stored Over 180 Days (Prior Notice):* Government must provide prior notice to subscriber and obtain a subpoena or court order. Court order requires "specific and articulable facts showing that there are reasonable grounds" to believe communications are relevant to the criminal investigation. 18 U.S.C. § 2703(d). *Communications Stored Over 180 Days (No Prior Notice):* If government does not provide prior notice to subscriber, it must obtain a warrant. 18 U.S.C. § 2703(a). *ISP Records:* Government must obtain court order; same standard as that for communications stored over 180 days.
Exceptions	*Consent:* SCA does not apply if the subscriber consents. 18 U.S.C.§ 2702(b)(3). *Service Provider:* SCA does not apply to the accessing of stored communications by communications service providers. 18 U.S.C. § 2701(c)(1).
Exclusionary Rule	No
Penalties	Damages (minimum $1,000 per violation). Up to one year imprisonment (if done for commercial gain). 18 U.S.C. § 2701(b).

THE PEN REGISTER ACT	
Applies to	Pen registers or trap and trace devices.
Key Provisions	Requires court order before installation of pen registers.
	A "pen register" is a "device or process" that records outgoing "dialing, routing, addressing or signaling information," but "such information shall not include the contents of any communication." 18 U.S.C. § 3127(3).
	A "trap and trace device" is a "device or process" that captures incoming "dialing, routing, addressing and signaling information" but "such information shall not include the contents of any communication." 18 U.S.C. § 3127(4).
Court Order	The government must obtain a court order to install pen register and trap and trace devices.
	The court shall grant the order if the government has demonstrated that "the information likely to be obtained by such installation and use is relevant to an ongoing criminal investigation." 18 U.S.C. § 3123(a)(1).
Exceptions	*Service Provider:* The Pen Register Act does not apply to the use of a pen register or trap and trace device by a communications service provider relating to the provision of the service. 18 U.S.C. § 3121(b)(1).
	Abuse Protection: The act does not apply when a communications service provider records the existence of the communication to protect against unlawful or abusive use of the service. 18 U.S.C. § 3121(b)(2).
	Consent: The act does not apply if the user consents. 18 U.S.C. § 3121(b)(3).
Exclusionary Rule	No
Penalties	Fines.
	Up to one-year imprisonment. 18 U.S.C. § 3121(d).

Leading Cases

Microsoft Corp. v. United States, No. 14-2985, 2016 WL 3770056 (2d Cir. July 14, 2016)

Finding a lack of extra-territorial reach to a warrant issued pursuant to the Stored Communications Act. The Second Circuit ruled: "Neither explicitly nor implicitly does the statute envision the application of its warrant provisions overseas."

United States v. Forrester, 512 F.3d 500 (9th Cir. 2007)

E-mail headers and IP addresses are akin to pen registers and have no Fourth Amendment protection. The Ninth Circuit notes in dicta that URLs "might be more constitutionally problematic" because a URL "identifies the particular document within a website that a person views and thus reveals much more information about the person's Internet activity."

United States v. Councilman, 418 F.3d 67 (1st Cir. 2005) (en banc)

An Internet bookseller provided e-mail service for its customers, and it intercepted all incoming communications from Amazon.com. The First Circuit concluded that "the term 'electronic communication' includes transient electronic storage that is intrinsic to the communication process, and, hence, interception of an e-mail message in such storage is an offense under the Wiretap Act."

Theofel v. Farey-Jones, 359 F.3d 1066 (9th Cir. 2003)

E-mail messages delivered to a recipient are still covered by the Stored Communications Act because they are stored as a "backup" for the user.

Fraser v. Nationwide Mut. Ins. Co., 352 F.3d 108 (3d Cir. 2003) (same result as Theofel)

United States v. Warshak, 631 F.3d 266 (6th Cir. 2010)

Compelling an ISP to turn over the contents of a subscriber's e-mails violates a reasonable expectation of privacy—and hence violates the Fourth Amendment—even though the ISP itself may have access to the e-mails.

Key Facts About ECPA

1. The Wiretap Act provides the strongest level of protection, followed by the Stored Communications Act. The Pen Register Act provides the weakest level of protection.

2. ECPA applies not only to government officials, but also to everyone. Private-sector employers and regular citizens are regulated.

3. ECPA provides for an exclusionary rule only for Wiretap Act violations involving wire or oral communications.

4. ECPA does not regulate silent video surveillance or location-tracking devices.

5. ECPA is a one-party consent statute—surveillance is permissible when only one party to a communication consents. Most state electronic surveillance statutes are one-party consent, but several states have two-party consent statutes. In these states, all parties to the communication must consent to the surveillance.

THE FOURTH AMENDMENT VS. ELECTRONIC SURVEILLANCE LAW

	THE FOURTH AMENDMENT	FEDERAL ELECTRONIC SURVEILLANCE LAW
Applicability	The Fourth Amendment applies to electronic surveillance when there is a reasonable expectation of privacy. The Fourth Amendment applies only to government officials (subject to limited exceptions).	Federal electronic surveillance law applies to all interceptions of communications and to accessing stored communications (even if there is no reasonable expectation of privacy). Federal electronic surveillance law applies to pen registers and trap and trace devices (Pen Register Act). The Fourth Amendment does not apply to these devices. See Smith v. Maryland, 442 U.S. 735 (1979). Federal electronic surveillance law applies to government officials and to private parties.
Judicial Authority to Obtain Access	Subject to a number of exceptions, the Fourth Amendment requires a warrant supported by probable cause.	Federal electronic surveillance law contains a wide variety of forms of judicial authority, including subpoenas, court orders with varying levels of notice to the subject of the investigation, warrants, and the super warrant required by the Wiretap Act.
Duration of Authority to Obtain Access	Fourth Amendment warrants authorize a single entry and prompt search. Warrants must be narrowly circumscribed.	Federal wiretap orders can have a broad duration. A judge can authorize 24-hour surveillance for a 30-day period.
Enforcement	The Fourth Amendment is enforced by the exclusionary rule. The Fourth Amendment can serve as the basis for a § 1983 or Bivens action.	Federal electronic surveillance law is enforced through the exclusionary rule only sometimes—for interceptions of wire or oral communications under the Wiretap Act. Federal electronic surveillance law also has civil and criminal penalties.

Communications Assistance for Law Enforcement Act of 1994 (CALEA) 47 U.S.C. §§ 1001-1010, 1021

Primary Function: Requires "telecommunications carriers" to design their networks to make them compliant with authorized governmental requests for surveillance.

Facilitate Law Enforcement Access: Requires all telecommunications providers to be able to isolate and intercept electronic communications and be able to deliver them to law enforcement personnel.

Privacy and Security: Carriers must "facilitat[e] authorized communications interceptions and access to call-identifying information … in a manner that protects … the privacy and security of communications and call-identifying information not authorized to be intercepted." 47 U.S.C. § 1002(a)(4)(A).

Limitations: CALEA does not apply to "information services," an important and long-standing term of art in telecommunications law. It does apply to "telecommunication carriers." Drawing the distinction between the two categories can be quite complex, but it is an absolutely critical issue; information service providers fall outside of CALEA, which means that they need not design their networks to be accessible to law enforcement agencies. 47 U.S.C. § 1002(b)(2).

Leading Case

Am. Council on Educ. v. FCC, 451 F.3d 266 (D.C. Cir. 2006)
The DC Circuit upheld the FCC's classification of broadband Internet access and voice over Internet protocol (VoIP) as "telecommunications carriers" under CALEA. As a consequence, broadband and VoIP providers must ensure that law enforcement officials can intercept communications that are transmitted over their networks.

Drones

Registration and Marking Requirements for Small Unmanned Aircraft, 80 Fed. Reg. 78,593 (FAA Dec. 16, 2015) (codified as amended in scattered sections of 14 C.F.R.)
Addresses the registration and marking requirements for small unmanned aircraft, including those operated as model aircraft.

STATE ELECTRONIC SURVEILLANCE LAW
The vast majority of states have electronic surveillance statutes. Many are quite similar to ECPA. The majority, like ECPA, permit surveillance if one party to a communication consents. But several states have all-party consent laws, requiring all parties to a communication to consent.

Many people unwittingly violate all-party consent statutes. If they secretly record a conversation between themselves and another person, they violate this kind of statute.

If a person records a call made from a one-party consent state to an all-party consent state, the law of the all-party consent state governs. *Kearney v. Salomon Smith Barney, Inc.*, 137 P.3d 914 (Cal. 2006).

Recording Police Encounters

In some instances, people recording their encounters with police officers have been prosecuted under state electronic surveillance laws because the police officer did not consent. *Commonwealth v. Hyde*, 750 N.E.2d 963 (Mass. 2001) (upholding felony conviction under Massachusetts electronic surveillance law for recording a traffic stop with a police officer).

Some courts have held that the First Amendment prohibits the criminalization of secretly recording encounters with police when performing official duties. *ACLU v. Alvarez*, 679 F.3d 583 (7th Cir. 2012) (striking down application of Illinois electronic surveillance law when recording police officers).

STATE ELECTRONIC SURVEILLANCE LAW

ONE-PARTY CONSENT STATES		ALL-PARTY CONSENT STATES	
AL	Ala. Code §§ 13A-11-30 to -31	CA	Cal. Penal Code § 630 *et seq.*
AK	Alaska Stat. § 42.20.310	CT	Conn. Gen. Stat. § 52-570d
AZ	Ariz. Rev. Stat. Ann. § 13-3005	FL	Fla. Stat. §§ 934.01-.03
AK	Ark. Code Ann. § 5-60-120	IL	720 Ill. Comp. Stat. 5/14-1 to -2
CO	Colo. Rev. Stat. §§ 18-9-301, 18-9-303	MD	Md. Code Ann., Cts. & Jud. Proc. § 10-402
DE	Del. Code Ann. tit. 11, § 2402	MA	Mass. Gen. Laws ch. 272, § 99
DC	D.C. Code §§ 23-541, 23-542	MT	Mont. Code Ann. § 45-8-213
GA	Ga. Code Ann. §§ 16-11-62, 16-11-66	NV	Nev. Rev. Stat. §§ 200.610-.620
HI	Haw. Rev. Stat. § 803-42	NH	N.H. Rev. Stat. Ann. §§ 570-A:1 to -A:2
ID	Idaho Code Ann. § 18-6702	PA	18 Pa. Cons. Stat. § 5701 *et seq.*
IN	Ind. Code § 35-33.5-1 *et seq.*	WA	Wash. Rev. Code § 9.73.030
IA	Iowa Code § 727.8	*No Electronic Surveillance Statute*	
		VT	
KS	Kan. Stat. Ann. §§ 21-4001, 21-4002		

KY	Ky. Rev. Stat. Ann. §§ 526.010-.020
LA	La. Stat. Ann. § 15:1303
ME	Me. Rev. Stat. Ann. tit. 15, §§ 709-10
MI	Mich. Comp. Laws § 750.539c
MN	Minn. Stat. §§ 626A.01-.02
MS	Miss. Code Ann. § 41-29-501 *et seq.*
MO	Mo. Rev. Stat. § 542.402
NE	Neb. Rev. Stat. § 86-290
NJ	N.J. Stat. Ann. § 2A:156A-1 *et seq.*
NM	N.M. Stat. Ann. § 30-12-1
NY	N.Y. Penal Law §§ 250.00-.05
NC	N.C. Gen. Stat. § 15A-287
ND	N.D. Cent. Code § 12.1-15-02
OH	Ohio Rev. Code Ann. § 2933.51 *et seq.*
OK	Okla. Stat. tit. 13, § 176.1 *et seq.*
OR	Or. Rev. Stat. §§ 165.540-.543
RI	R.I. Gen. Laws § 11-35-21
SC	S.C. Code Ann. §§ 17-30-20 to -30
SD	S.D. Codified Laws §§ 23A-35A-1
TN	Tenn. Code Ann. § 39-13-601
TX	Tex. Penal Code Ann. § 16.02
UT	Utah Code Ann. § 77-23a-1 *et seq.*
VA	Va. Code Ann. §§ 19.2-61 to -62
WV	W. Va. Code § 62-1D-1 *et seq.*
WI	Wis. Stat. §§ 968.27-.31
WY	Wyo. Stat. Ann. §§ 7-3-701 to -702

Source: Scott P. Cooper et al., Proskauer on Privacy § 5:10.1 (2010)

GOVERNMENT ACCESS TO PERSONAL DATA

Fourth Amendment: Third-Party Doctrine
In several cases, the U.S. Supreme Court concluded that whenever a third party possesses a person's information, that person can no longer have a reasonable expectation of privacy in the data.

Couch v. United States, 409 U.S. 322 (1973)
The government could obtain documents that a person provided to his accountant without violating the Fourth Amendment.

United States v. Miller, 425 U.S. 435 (1976)
Financial records possessed by third parties are not protected by the Fourth Amendment because people lack a reasonable expectation of privacy in their bank records. This information is "voluntarily conveyed to the banks and exposed to their employees in the ordinary course of business."

Smith v. Maryland, 442 U.S. 735 (1979)
The court held that there is no reasonable expectation of privacy in the numbers a person dials that the police record with a pen register. The numbers do not involve the "content" of the communications, and when a person conveys information to another (the phone company), that person must assume the risk that the company will reveal the information to others.

Lower courts have applied the third-party doctrine widely, including to records about a person's Internet use held by ISPs. *United States v. Forrester*, 512 F.3d 500 (9th Cir. 2007); *Guest v. Leis*, 255 F.3d 325 (6th Cir. 2001).

Bank Secrecy Act of 1970

Recordkeeping: Requires the retention of bank records and creation of reports that would be useful in criminal, tax, or regulatory investigations or proceedings. Requires that federally insured banks record the identities of account holders as well as copies of each check, draft, or other financial instrument. Not all records and financial instruments must be maintained, only those that the secretary of the treasury designates as having a "high degree of usefulness." 12 U.S.C. § 1829(b)(1).

Reporting: The act authorizes the secretary of the treasury to promulgate regulations for the reporting of domestic financial transactions. 31 C.F.R. § 103.25 (citing 5 U.S.C. § 553(b)). The regulations require that a report be made for every deposit, withdrawal or other transfer of currency exceeding $10,000. 31 C.F.R. § 103.22(b)(1). For transactions exceeding $10,000 into or out of the United States, the amount, the date of receipt, the form of financial instrument and the person who received it must be reported. 31 C.F.R. §§ 103.23, 103.25.

Cal. Bankers Ass'n v. Shultz, **416 U.S. 21 (1974)**

Upholds the Bank Secrecy Act against a Fourth Amendment challenge.

Right to Financial Privacy Act of 1978 (RFPA)
29 U.S.C. §§ 3401–3422

Primary Function: The RFPA prevents banks and other financial institutions from disclosing a person's financial information to the government unless the records are disclosed pursuant to a subpoena or search warrant.

Subpoenas

A subpoena is an order to obtain testimony or documents. Numerous statutes authorize federal agencies to issue subpoenas. "A subpoena may order the witness to produce any books, papers, documents, data, or other objects the subpoena designates. The court may direct the witness to produce the designated items in court before trial or before they are to be offered in evidence. When the items arrive, the court may permit the parties and their attorneys to inspect all or part of them." Fed. R. Crim. P. 17(c)(1).

If the party served with the subpoena has an objection, she may bring a motion to quash or modify the subpoena. "[T]he court may quash or modify the subpoena if compliance would be unreasonable or oppressive." Fed. R. Crim. P. 17(c)(2).

Leading Case

United States v. Dionisio, **410 U.S. 1 (1973)**

Concludes that a grand jury subpoena does not trigger any Fourth Amendment protection.

Gonzales v. Google, Inc., **234 F.R.D. 674 (N.D. Cal. 2006)**

The government subpoenaed search records from Google to assist in examining the effectiveness of content filtering software. The court did not permit the government to obtain the search query information because "there is a potential burden as to Google's loss of goodwill if Google is forced to disclose search queries to the Government."

Federal Statutory Provisions for Government Access to Records

(see Chapter 5 for National Security Letter provisions)

Cable Communications Policy Act of 1984 (CCPA), 47 U.S.C. § 551(h)

The government can obtain cable subscriber data pursuant to a court order justified by "clear and convincing evidence" that the subscriber is "reasonably suspected of engaging in criminal activity and that the information sought would be material evidence in the case." The subscriber must be notified and allowed to challenge the order.

Fair Credit Report Act of 1970 (FCRA), 15 U.S.C. § 1681f

"[A] consumer reporting agency may furnish identifying information respecting any customer, limited to his name, address, former addresses, places of employment or former places of employment, to a governmental agency."

Health Insurance Portability and Accountability Act of 1996 (HIPAA), 45 C.F.R. § 164.512(f)(1).

Law enforcement officials may access medical records with a warrant, court order or subpoena. Health information may also be disclosed "in response to a law enforcement official's request for such information for the purpose of identifying or locating a suspect, fugitive, material witness or missing person."

Pen Register Act, 18 U.S.C. § 3123(a)(1)

To obtain pen register information, the government must obtain a court order by certifying that "the information likely to be obtained by such installation and use is relevant to an ongoing criminal investigation."

Right to Financial Privacy Act of 1978 (RFPA), 12 U.S.C. § 3407(1)

The government must first obtain a warrant or subpoena in order to access financial information. The subpoena requires a "reason to believe that the records sought are relevant to a legitimate law enforcement inquiry."

Stored Communications Act (SCA), 18 U.S.C. § 2703(d)

Requires the government to obtain a court order or warrant in order to access stored e-mail messages. The government must obtain a warrant or court order to obtain a customer's ISP records. The court order requires "specific and articulable facts showing that there are reasonable grounds to believe" communications are relevant to the criminal investigation.

Video Privacy Protection Act of 1988 (VPPA), 18 U.S.C. § 2710(b)(2)(C)

Permits disclosure to a law enforcement agency pursuant to a warrant, court order or subpoena.

SEARCHES AND SEIZURES OF MEDIA DOCUMENTS

Privacy Protection Act of 1980 (PPA)
42 U.S.C. § 2000aa

Primary Function: Protects media documents and work product from government searches and seizures.

Key Provisions: During a criminal investigation, government officials cannot search or seize work product or documents that are "reasonably believed" to be intended to be disseminated to the public. These include a newspaper, book, broadcast or other similar form of public communication. 42 U.S.C. § 2000aa(a).

How the PPA Works: The effect of the PPA is to require law enforcement officials to obtain a subpoena in order to obtain such information. Unlike search warrants, subpoenas permit the party subject to them to challenge them in court before having to comply. Further, instead of law enforcement officials searching through offices or records, the persons served with the subpoena must produce the documents themselves.

Exceptions: The government can search or seize the work product or documents if they relate to a crime the possessor has committed, if necessary to prevent death or serious injury, or if the documents might be destroyed or concealed. 42 U.S.C. § 2000aa(a)(2), (b)(3).

Leading Case

Zurcher v. Stanford Daily, **436 U.S. 547 (1978)**
The Supreme Court held that the First and Fourth Amendments permit law enforcement to search media offices with a warrant supported by probable cause rather than a heightened standard. This holding led Congress to enact the PPA.

FOR FURTHER REFERENCE

Treatises

Thomas K. Clancy, *The Fourth Amendment: Its History and Interpretation* (2008)
A great resource on current Fourth Amendment law.

William J. Cuddihy, *The Fourth Amendment: Origins and Original Meaning, 602–1791* (2009)
The most comprehensive intellectual history of the origins of the Fourth Amendment.

Wayne R. LaFave, Jerold H. Israel, Nancy J. King & Orin S. Kerr, *Criminal Procedure* (4th ed. 2015)
Leading multivolume treatise contains a detailed look at scope of the exclusionary rule and search and seizure issues, including electronic surveillance. Also available abridged in a hornbook format.

Books

Samuel Dash, *The Intruders: Unreasonable Searches and Seizures from King John to John Ashcroft* (2004)
A short, accessible history of the Fourth Amendment, filled with interesting stories about the key cases.

Jeffrey Rosen, *The Naked Crowd: Reclaiming Security and Freedom in an Anxious Age* (2004)
A sociological account of fear, liberty, and security following the September 11 attacks.

Bruce Schneier, *Data and Goliath: The Hidden Battles to Collect Your Data and Control Your World* (2015)
Examining NSA surveillance, the Snowden revelations, and other recent issues in privacy and data collection. Developing a core set of principles and solutions for government, corporations, and "the rest of us."

Christopher Slobogin, *Privacy at Risk: The New Government Surveillance and the Fourth Amendment* (2007)
The government engages in both physical surveillance, through means such as CCTV, and transaction surveillance when it examines records of our daily activities. This book advocates that legislatures and courts create stronger constraints on such governmental activities.

Daniel J. Solove, *Nothing to Hide: The False Tradeoff Between Privacy and Security* (2011)
Argues that the current debate between privacy and security is skewed toward the security side based on faulty arguments.

Articles and Other Sources

Anthony G. Amsterdam, *Perspectives on the Fourth Amendment*, 58 Minn. L. Rev. 349 (1974)
A classic article about the Fourth Amendment and one of the most influential on this topic.

William Baude & James Y. Stern, *The Positive Law Model of the Fourth Amendment*, 129 Harv. L. Rev. 1821 (2016)
Advocating for a positive law approach to the Fourth Amendment. Fourth Amendment protections should be based on "background positive law," and the key question in search-and-seizure analysis should be "whether government officials have done something forbidden to private parties."

Orin S. Kerr, *Fourth Amendment Seizures of Computer Data*, 119 Yale L.J. 700 (2010)
Analysis of what it means to "seize" computer data for Fourth Amendment purposes and the kinds of police action that govern digital evidence investigations.

Orin S. Kerr, *The Case for the Third-Party Doctrine*, 107 Mich. L. Rev. 561 (2009)
The most extensive defense of the third-party doctrine in an academic article.

Orin S. Kerr, *The Fourth Amendment and New Technologies: Constitutional Myths and the Case for Caution*, 102 Mich. L. Rev. 801 (2004)
Makes the provocative argument that courts should defer to legislatures in Fourth Amendment cases involving new technologies.

Winston Maxwell & Christopher Wolf, *A Global Reality: Governmental Access to Data in the Cloud* (July 18, 2012)
White Paper compares protections against government access to data in the cloud in ten industrialized nations and concludes that the protections in other countries often do not exceed those in the U.S.

Neil M. Richards, *The Dangers of Surveillance*, 126 Harv. L. Rev. 1934 (2013)
Apart from vague Orwellian threats, we lack a clear sense of the dangers of government surveillance. Richards explores the boundaries of legitimate surveillance activities, proposing principles to guide the future of surveillance law.

Paul M. Schwartz, *Reviving Telecommunications Surveillance Law*, 75 U. Chi. L. Rev. 287 (2008)
Description of each of the main parts of statutory telecommunications law and analysis of the extent to which numerical data is collected to track the extent of governmental activity in these areas.

Christopher Slobogin, *Subpoenas and Privacy,* **54 DePaul L. Rev. 805 (2005)**
A thorough examination of subpoenas and their implications for accessing data.

Daniel J. Solove, *Digital Dossiers and the Dissipation of Fourth Amendment Privacy,* **75 S. Cal. L. Rev. 1083 (2002)**
A discussion of how the third-party doctrine eviscerates Fourth Amendment protection in the Information Age.

William J. Stuntz, *Privacy's Problem and the Law of Criminal Procedure,* **93 Mich. L. Rev. 1016 (1995)**
Contends that the Fourth Amendment should focus on police coercion and violence rather than privacy.

CHAPTER 5

National Security and Foreign Intelligence

ESSENTIAL POINTS

- Although the Fourth Amendment regulates domestic criminal investigations and national security investigations, how the Fourth Amendment regulates foreign intelligence gathering within the United States remains an open question.

- The Foreign Intelligence Surveillance Act (FISA) is the main statute that regulates the government's electronic surveillance. It applies when foreign intelligence gathering is "a significant purpose" of the investigation.

- There are other legal authorities that permit the gathering of information for national security purposes, including National Security Letters.

THE FOURTH AMENDMENT

There is not much U.S. Supreme Court guidance about how the Fourth Amendment addresses national security issues and foreign intelligence gathering. The Court has distinguished between three categories of searches and surveillance:

- *Criminal Investigations*—ordinary Fourth Amendment protections apply.

- *Domestic National Security Investigations*—protected by the Fourth Amendment but may require standards other than warrants and probable cause.

- *Foreign Intelligence Gathering*—no determination by the court as to whether the Fourth Amendment applies and, if so, what the standards are.

United States v. U.S. Dist. Court, 407 U.S. 297 (1972) (the "Keith" Case)

Rejects Nixon administration argument that the Fourth Amendment does not apply when the president conducts electronic surveillance for domestic national security investigations. Notes that domestic security surveillance "may involve different policy and practical considerations from the surveillance of 'ordinary crime,'" and concludes that "[d]ifferent standards may be compatible with the Fourth Amendment if they are reasonable both in relation to the legitimate need of Government for intelligence information and the protected rights of our citizens."

United States v. Butenko, 494 F.2d 593 (3d Cir. 1974)

Concludes that the Fourth Amendment does not require a warrant for foreign intelligence gathering because "foreign intelligence gathering is a clandestine and highly unstructured activity, and the need for electronic surveillance often cannot be anticipated in advance."

United States v. Truong Dinh Hung, 629 F.2d 908 (4th Cir. 1980)

Concludes that the Fourth Amendment does not require a warrant for foreign intelligence gathering.

FOREIGN INTELLIGENCE GATHERING

Foreign Intelligence Surveillance Act of 1978 (FISA)
50 U.S.C. §§ 1801–1811

Primary Function: FISA establishes standards and procedures for the government's use of electronic surveillance to collect "foreign intelligence" within the United States. FISA requires the government, if seeking evidence of domestic security violations, to follow the authorities granted by the usual criminal law.

Applies to: Foreign intelligence gathering as "a significant purpose" of the investigation. 50 U.S.C. § 1804(a)(6)(B) and § 1823(a)(6)(B).

The Foreign Intelligence Surveillance Court (FISC): Requests for FISA orders are reviewed by a special court of 11 federal district court judges. The proceedings are ex parte, and the court meets in secret.

The Foreign Intelligence Surveillance Court of Review (FISCR): The government may appeal decisions of the FISC to a three-judge appellate court. This judicial entity is called the Foreign Intelligence Surveillance Court of Review.

Court Orders: FISA orders are granted when the FISC finds probable cause that the party to be monitored is a "foreign power" or "an agent of a foreign power." 50 U.S.C. § 1801. Therefore, unlike ECPA or the Fourth Amendment, FISA surveillance is not tied to any required showing of a connection to criminal activity. However, if the

Privacy Law Fundamentals

monitored party is a "United States person" (a citizen or permanent resident alien), the government must establish probable cause that the party's activities "may" or "are about to" involve a criminal violation. 50 U.S.C. § 1801(b)(2)(A)-(B). Under special limited circumstances, FISA authorizes surveillance without having to first obtain a court order.

The FISA Amendments Act (FAA) of 2008: The FAA explicitly permits collection of information from U.S. telecommunications facilities where it is not possible in advance to know whether a communication is purely international (that is, all parties to it are located outside of the United States) or whether the communication involves a foreign power or its agents. The collection of this information must be carried out in accordance with certain "targeting procedures" to ensure that the collection is directed at persons located outside the United States. The FISC is to review certifications and the targeting and minimization procedures adopted.

USA Freedom Act of 2015
Pub. L. No. 114-23, 129 Stat. 268 (codified as amended in scattered sections of 50 U.S.C.)

Bans the bulk collection of Americans' Internet metadata and telephonic records under Section 215 of the Patriot Act. The government must now identify a person, account, address, or personal device when requesting records, limiting the scope of tangible things sought "to the greatest extent reasonably possible." However, the bill permits authorities to collect phone records two degrees (or "hops") of separation from targeted individuals.

Leading Cases

ACLU v. Clapper, 785 F.3d 787 (2d Cir. 2015)
Holding collection of telephone metadata exceeded authority granted by FISA, as the metadata was not relevant to authorized counterterrorism investigations. The Second Circuit found that Section 215's statutory text did not authorize the telephone metadata program. The opinion did not address the constitutionality of the metadata collection. A follow-up opinion after enactment of the Freedom Act's passing permitted Congress a 180-day transition period to wind down the program.

Clapper v. Amnesty Int'l USA, 133 S. Ct. 1138 (2013)
Lawyers, journalists, human rights advocates, and others challenged Section 702 of the Foreign Intelligence Surveillance Act. In a 5–4 opinion, the Supreme Court held that the challengers lacked standing because they could not demonstrate a threatened injury that was "certainly impeding." Plaintiffs could point only to a "speculative chain of possibilities."

In re Sealed Case, 310 F.3d 717 (FISA Ct. Rev. 2002)
This case, the first published decision of the FISCR, concerns "Intelligence Sharing Procedures" implemented by Attorney General John Ashcroft. The court up-

held the new Department of Justice procedures and concluded that the new regulations correctly interpreted applicable statutory requirements for information sharing between criminal enforcement officials and intelligence officials working on shared investigations. "FISA, as amended, does not oblige the government to demonstrate to the FISA court that its primary purpose in conducting electronic surveillance is *not* criminal prosecution . . . ." The FISCR also concluded that the Patriot Act's amendment to FISA does not violate the Fourth Amendment by making FISA applicable when foreign intelligence gathering is a "significant purpose" of the investigation.

In re Directives Pursuant to Section 105B, 551 F.3d 1004 (FISA Ct. Rev. 2008)
In its second published opinion, released only in redacted form, the FISCR identified a foreign intelligence exception to the Fourth Amendment warrant requirement. The exception applies to surveillance undertaken for national security purposes and directed at a foreign power or an agent of a foreign power reasonably believed to be located outside the United States. The court declared "that there is a high degree of probability that requiring a warrant would hinder the government's ability to collect time-sensitive information and, thus, would impede the vital national security interests that are at stake."

United States v. Duggan, 743 F.2d 59 (2d Cir. 1984)
Concludes that FISA (in its version prior to the Patriot Act changes) does not violate the Fourth Amendment because the Supreme Court in the Keith case had indicated that "the governmental interests presented in national security investigations differ substantially from those presented in traditional criminal investigations."

GOVERNMENT ACCESS TO PERSONAL DATA FOR NATIONAL SECURITY PURPOSES

National Security Letters (NSLs)

Several provisions of law provide for national security letters (NSLs), which allow the FBI to demand the production of information when relevant to foreign intelligence gathering or a terrorism investigation:

- Stored Communications Act, 18 U.S.C. § 2709—customer records of communications companies

- Right to Financial Privacy Act of 1978, 12 U.S.C. § 3414(a)(5)(A)—financial records

- Fair Credit Reporting Act of 1970, 15 U.S.C. § 1681u—credit records and consumer reports

The FBI revised the NSL disclosure policy, permitting letter recipients to disclose the receipt of the letter at "the earlier of 3 years after the opening of a fully predicated investigation or the investigation's close." Previously, the FBI was permitted to enforce NSL gag orders indefinitely. Gag orders may be enforced beyond the 3-year period if the FBI determines that a statutory exception applies.

USA Patriot Act of 2001, § 215

Section 215 of the USA Patriot Act added a new section to FISA that gives the director of the FBI or her designee the authority to make "an application for an order requiring the production of any tangible things (including books, records, papers, documents and other items) for an investigation . . . to protect against international terrorism or clandestine activities." 50 U.S.C. § 1861(a)(1).

Section 215 has expired, and the USA Freedom Act has altered the way in which investigators may request data, now requiring a specific target with leeway to make two "hops" of separation.

STATE SECRETS

The state secrets doctrine is an evidentiary privilege that protects information from discovery when its disclosure would harm national security. The doctrine first occurred in *United States v. Reynolds*, 345 U.S. 1 (1953). In this Cold War era case, the Supreme Court drew on English precedents regarding crown privilege to permit the Air Force to decline to share an accident investigation report with civilians who were suing the government under the Federal Tort Claims Act.

The state secrets doctrine has been used in numerous cases after 9/11. Private industry has also asserted state secrets in many cases, a strategy to provoke the federal government to join the litigation to prevent certain documents from being discovered or even to block the underlying lawsuit.

THE INTELLIGENCE COMMUNITY

Intelligence Agencies

Federal Bureau of Investigation (FBI)
Originally created in 1908 as the Bureau of Investigation, the FBI received its current name in 1935. Beyond its focus on domestic criminal investigations involving federal crimes, the FBI also has intelligence, counterintelligence, and counterterrorism functions. It has a National Security Branch, established in 2005, which is run by an executive assistant director of the FBI.

Central Intelligence Agency (CIA)
Originally, the CIA's functions were handled by the Office of Strategic Services (OSS), created in 1942 by President Franklin D. Roosevelt. The OSS was eliminated at the end of World War II. President Harry Truman created the CIA with the National Security Act of 1947.

National Security Agency (NSA)
Located within the Department of Defense, the NSA was created by President Truman in 1952 to engage in cryptology—deciphering encryption codes used in foreign communications.

Additionally, there are intelligence agencies within the Department of Defense, the Department of Homeland Security, the Department of State, and the Department of the Treasury, among others. Some of these entities include the Defense Intelligence Agency (DIA), the State Department's Bureau of Intelligence and Research (INR), and the Treasury Department's Office of Terrorism and Financial Intelligence.

Intelligence Reform and Terrorism Prevention Act of 2004 (IRTPA)
Pub. L. No. 108-458, 118 Stat. 3638 (codified as amended in scattered sections of the U.S.C.)

Primary Function: The IRTPA reorganized the intelligence community and implemented several recommendations of the 9/11 Commission. It created the position of the director of national intelligence and established the National Counterterrorism Center.

New Information Sharing: The act authorizes the creation of a new "Information Sharing Environment" to link federal and state entities as well as the private sector. 6 U.S.C. § 485(a)(2). It states that the president is to "create an information sharing environment for the sharing of terrorism information in a manner consistent with national security and with applicable legal standards relating to privacy and civil liberties." 6 U.S.C. § 485(b)(1)(A).

"Secure Flight," Biometrics, and Identification: IRTPA contains provisions for "Secure Flight," which is a TSA passenger-screening system. 49 U.S.C. § 44903. It authorizes the creation of a biometric entry and exit data system to the United States, seeks improved pre-inspection of travelers to the United States at foreign airports, sets minimum standards for domestic birth certificates and driver's licenses, and prohibits the display of Social Security numbers on driver's licenses or motor vehicle registrations. IRTPA also requires the Secretary of Homeland Security to establish minimum standards for the identification documents required of domestic air travelers.

Privacy and Civil Liberties Oversight Board: IRTPA establishes a Privacy and Civil Liberties Oversight Board within the executive branch. Through subsequent amendments, the board is an independent agency and has subpoena power.

FOR FURTHER REFERENCE

Treatises

David S. Kris & J. Douglas Wilson, *National Security Investigations & Prosecutions* (2d ed. 2012)
A detailed description of how FISA works, the process for obtaining National Security Letters, and other issues, such as the process for searches and seizures abroad.

Books

Laura K. Donohue, *The Future of Foreign Intelligence: Privacy and Surveillance in a Digital Age* (2016)
Examines the expansion of U.S. intelligence gathering and offers solutions for scaling back intrusive national security measures.

Government Reports

President's Review Grp. on Intelligence & Commc'ns Techs., *Liberty and Security in a Changing World: Report and Recommendations* (Dec. 12, 2013)
In the wake of the Snowden revelations, President Obama convened a group of experts to review the government's surveillance activities. This report contains 46 recommendations. The recommendations include limiting collection of bulk telephony metadata; increasing transparency regarding telephone, Internet, and other providers; and enhancing privacy protections of non-U.S. persons.

Privacy & Civil Liberties Oversight Bd. (PCLOB), *Report on the Telephone Records Program Conducted under Section 215 of the USA PATRIOT Act* (Jan. 23, 2014)
PCLOB reached negative conclusions about the NSA's bulk collection of telephone metadata conducted under Section 215 of the USA PATRIOT Act. It called for an end to the program because it did not meet the "strong showing of efficacy" required of a government program with such "serious implications for privacy and civil liberties." Short of this recommendation, the PCLB also called for immediate changes to the program, including reducing the retention period for bulk telephone records from five years to three and restricting the number of "hops" used in contact chaining from three to two.

Privacy & Civil Liberties Oversight Bd. (PCLOB), *Report on the Surveillance Program Operated Pursuant to Section 702 of the Foreign Intelligence Surveillance Act* (July 2, 2014)
PCLOB's Report on NSA bulk data collection program that drew on Internet Service Providers and the Internet's basic infrastructure and was justified under Section 702, FISA. PCLOB found the program to be legal under Section 702. While the report

noted that components of the program "push the program close to the line of constitutional reasonableness," it concluded that the program was useful for gathering intelligence, reasonable under the Fourth Amendment, and authorized by Congress.

Privacy & Civil Liberties Oversight Bd. (PCLOB), *Recommendations Assessment Report* (Feb. 5, 2016)
Report noting full or partial implementation of all 22 recommendations made by PCLOB regarding Section 215 and Section 702 surveillance programs. These recommendations included ending the NSA's bulk collection of metadata, greater transparency by the government and private companies supplying data, expansion of appellate review of FISC decisions, and revised targeting and minimization procedures. PCLOB contends the measures would strengthen civil liberties without hindering counterterrorism efforts.

Articles and Other Sources

William C. Banks, *The Death of FISA*, 91 Minn. L. Rev. 1209 (2007)
Argues that FISA is no longer effective and that there has been a decline in effective oversight of national security surveillance by Congress and the judiciary.

Robert M. Chesney, *State Secrets and the Limits of National Security Litigation*, 75 Geo. Wash. L. Rev. 1249 (2007)
Examines the state secrets doctrine and proposes alternatives.

Robert M. Chesney, *Computer Network Operations and U.S. Domestic Law: An Overview*, 89 Int'l L. Stud. 218 (2013)
Examines the use of computer network operations for intelligence gathering purposes with a particular emphasis on Congressional and Executive oversight.

Laura K. Donohue, *The Shadow of State Secrets*, 159 U. Pa. L. Rev. 77 (2010)
Major empirical study of the use of the state secrets evidentiary privilege, including how private-sector companies are now relying on it.

Laura K. Donohue, *Bulk Metadata Collection: Statutory and Constitutional Considerations*, 37 Harv. J.L. & Pub. Pol'y 757 (2014)
Contends that the NSA's bulk telephonic metadata collection runs counter to Congress's original intent in enacting FISA in 1978.

Orin S. Kerr, *Updating the Foreign Intelligence Surveillance Act*, 75 U. Chi. L. Rev. 225 (2008)
Calls for a rewriting of FISA to account for changes in communications technology and Fourth Amendment doctrine that have occurred since the 1970s.

Orin S. Kerr, *The Fourth Amendment and the Global Internet*, 67 **Stan. L. Rev 285 (2015)**
Examines tensions between the Fourth Amendment and global data transfers, offering proposals on adapting the Amendment to the digital age.

Susan Landau, *Making Sense from Snowden: What's Significant in the NSA Surveillance Revelations*, **IEEE Sec. & Privacy (2013); and** *Making Sense of Snowden, Part II: What's Significant in the NSA Revelations*, **IEEE Sec. & Privacy (2014)**
In these two articles, security researcher Susan Landau summarizes key points of NSA surveillance activities revealed by Edward Snowden's disclosures regarding the NSA. The first article discusses the leaked materials, the scope of the government's powers, and the NSA's international spying activities. The second article discusses wiretap law, the NSA's collection of communications metadata and content, and the government's ability to undermine widely used security technologies.

Mark M. Lowenthal, *Intelligence: From Secrets to Policy* (**6th ed. 2015**)
Classic reference work explaining the organization and workings of the U.S. intelligence community.

Jon D. Michaels, *Deputizing Homeland Security*, **88 Tex. L. Rev. 1435 (2010)**
Identification of a dramatic rise of corporate participation in efforts to identify and counter threats of terrorism as well as the legal uncertainties and ambiguities about some of these "deputization programs."

Paul M. Schwartz, *Warrantless Wiretapping, FISA Reform, and the Lessons of Public Liberty*, **97 Cal. L. Rev. 407 (2009)**
Detailed analysis of FISA Amendments Act of 2008, current status of FISA and institutional lessons from this amendment process.

Peter P. Swire, *The System of Foreign Intelligence Surveillance Law*, **72 Geo. Wash. L. Rev. 1306 (2004)**
Thoughtful analysis of FISA and practical suggestions for reform.

Stephen I. Vladeck, *The Case Against National Security Courts*, **45 Willamette L. Rev. 505 (2009)**
Discusses the pros and cons of national security courts and ultimately finds that the negative aspects predominate.

CHAPTER 6

Health Privacy

ESSENTIAL POINTS

- HIPAA lacks a private right of action.

- The HIPAA regulations permit the enactment of stronger state law provisions. Some states, such as Texas, have health privacy laws that have a broader scope than HIPAA as well as certain more stringent protections.

- The HITECH Act requires notification of a data security breach of HIPAA-covered entities when protected health information is involved.

- Many HIPAA rules apply directly to business associates of covered entities.

- State institutions must be aware of constitutional protections, including the constitutional right to information privacy.

- In certain cases, medical providers have legal duties to disclose personal data about dangerous patients or to protect public safety.

- Physicians and psychotherapists need to walk a fine line when dealing with the confidentiality of a patient who potentially poses a danger to others. If they disclose improperly, they can be liable for breach of confidentiality. If they fail to disclose or warn, they can be liable to victims if a patient attacks a reasonably identifiable future victim.

PATIENT-PHYSICIAN CONFIDENTIALITY

Ethical Rules
Current Opinions of the Judicial Council of the American Medical Association, Canon 5.05

"The physician should not reveal confidential communications or information without the express consent of the patient, unless required to do so by law."

Evidentiary Privileges

Physician-Patient Privilege: A majority of the states (more than 40) have a physician-patient privilege. The privilege protects communications and information relating to the patient's medical treatment. With the privilege, a patient can prohibit a doctor from disclosing the confidential information. States have restricted the use of the privilege in many types of criminal cases, as well as in worker compensation cases and child custody cases. Physicians are also required by statute to disclose certain data to state authorities, such as child abuse and communicable disease.

In federal proceedings, where privileges are left to the courts to recognize under Federal Rule of Evidence 501, most courts have not recognized a physician-patient privilege.

Psychotherapist-Patient Privilege: Every state has adopted a psychotherapist-patient privilege. Exceptions to the psychotherapist-patient privilege are similar to those for the physician-patient privilege.

The psychotherapist-patient privilege is also recognized under the Federal Rules of Civil Procedure. *Jaffee v. Redmond,* 518 U.S. 1 (1996).

The Breach of Confidentiality Tort

Applies to: When a physician reveals a patient's confidential information, in a majority of states the patient can bring a tort action for breach of confidentiality. A cause of action exists whenever a person (1) is under a duty of confidentiality and (2) breaches that duty.

The Source of the Duty of Confidentiality: The source of the duty of confidentiality can be found in: "(1) state physician licensing statutes, (2) evidentiary rules and privileged communication statutes which prohibit a physician from testifying in judicial proceedings, (3) common law principles of trust, and (4) the Hippocratic Oath and principles of medical ethics which proscribe the revelation of patient confidences." *McCormick v. England,* 494 S.E.2d 431 (S.C. Ct. App. 1997).

Liability for Inducing a Breach of Confidentiality: Inducing a breach of physician-patient confidentiality can also make one liable under the breach of confidentiality tort: "The law is settled in Ohio and elsewhere that a third party who induces a breach of a trustee's duty of loyalty, or participates in such a breach, or knowingly accepts any benefit from such a breach, becomes directly liable to the aggrieved party." *Hammonds v. Aetna Cas. & Sur. Co.*, 243 F. Supp. 793 (N.D. Ohio 1965).

Exception: Physicians will not be liable for disclosing confidential medical information when it is necessary to protect others from danger or when it is required by law. *Simonsen v. Swenson,* 177 N.W. 831 (Neb. 1920).

Public Disclosure of Private Facts

Many courts have found that the disclosure of medical information can give rise to a claim for public disclosure of private facts, which is one of the four privacy torts. In *Urbaniak v. Newton,* 277 Cal. Rptr. 354 (Ct. App. 1991), the court held that the disclosure of a patient's HIV status was "clearly a 'private fact' of which the disclosure may 'be offensive and objectionable to a reasonable [person] of ordinary sensibilities.'" *See also Susan S. v. Israels,* 67 Cal. Rptr. 2d 42 (Ct. App. 1997) (public disclosure action for disclosure of mental health records).

> ## Key Points:
> ## Common Law Torts and Medical Information
>
> 1. Healthcare providers must not only heed HIPAA but also be aware of the common law torts of breach of confidentiality and public disclosure of private facts.
>
> 2. Breach of confidentiality has significantly fewer requirements than the pubic disclosure tort:
>   - No requirement of "high offensiveness" or widespread disclosure
>   - No requirement that the disclosure not be of "legitimate public concern"
>   - No First Amendment case limiting liability under the tort

Tort Liability for Failing to Disclose Personal Data

Duty to Warn: In the famous case *Tarasoff v. Regents of University of California,* 551 P.2d 334 (Cal. 1976), the California Supreme Court declared: "We conclude that the public policy favoring protection of the confidential character of patient-psychotherapist communications must yield to the extent to which disclosure is essential to avert dangers to others. The protective privilege ends where the public peril begins."

A psychotherapist can be liable for failing to warn a victim if:

1. The doctor has a "special relationship" with the harm-causer;
2. The victim is a person who is reasonably identifiable; and
3. The harm to the victim is foreseeable and serious.

Thus, a psychotherapist's treatment of a dangerous patient can create an affirmative duty to a third party, namely, a reasonably identifiable future victim of the patient.

Through subsequent codification in California, the *Tarasoff* duty requires a psychotherapist to make "reasonable efforts to communicate the threat to the victim or victims and to a law enforcement agency." Cal. Civil Code § 43.92(b).

A majority of states have a duty to warn similar to that in *Tarasoff.*

Mandatory Reporting Laws: Many states require that medical personnel or institutions report certain health information to state agencies or to others.

Research Disclosure Laws: A number of states regulate the use of medical data for research purposes.

MEDICAL INFORMATION

State Regulation

Medical Confidentiality Laws: Many states have specific statutes providing civil and criminal protection against the disclosure of medical information. Some laws restrict disclosure of medical data by particular entities: government agencies, HMOs, insurance companies, employers, pharmacists, and health data clearinghouses. Other laws prohibit the disclosure by any entity of particular types of medical data, such as AIDS/HIV, alcohol or drug abuse, mental health, and genetic information. *See, e.g.,* Cal. Civil Code § 199.21 (prohibiting disclosure of HIV test results); N.Y. Pub. Health Law § 17 (prohibiting the nonconsensual disclosure of medical records of minors relating to sexually transmitted diseases and abortion; even the disclosure to parents is prohibited without consent); 71 Pa. Cons. Stat. § 1690.108 (prohibiting the disclosure of all records prepared during alcohol or drug abuse treatment).

Patient Access Laws: The vast majority of states have statutes providing patients with a right to access certain medical records. A few states grant wide access to medical records held by all types of entities. On the other end of the spectrum, some states have no right of access, and others have only a limited right to access mental health records. The remaining states fall somewhere in between, permitting access to records from certain healthcare providers but not others (e.g., from some but not all of the following entities: hospitals, HMOs, insurers, and pharmacists).

Comprehensive Health Privacy Laws: Most states do not have a comprehensive law governing medical privacy, but some states do.

Texas Medical Privacy Act, Tex. Health & Safety Code Ann §§ 181.001 *et seq.*

After new amendments (H.B. 300) effective in 2012, Texas now has one of the broadest and strictest medical privacy laws in the country. The law mandates broader coverage and requires stricter rules in many areas than HIPAA. The law covers any organization that (1) assembles, collects, stores, or transmits protected health information (PHI); (2) comes into possession of, obtains, or stores PHI; or (3) is an employee, agent or contractor of an entity that fits within the preceding two categories. Thus, many law firms and accounting firms may be covered entities.

All employees of covered entities must be trained in the applicable obligations of federal and state law at least every two years, with initial training of all employees occurring within 60 days of hiring. The statute also mandates that people have access to their electronic health data in 15 days (a shorter period than HIPAA's 30-day requirement). Notification of a health data breach must be made "as quickly as possible" to "any individual whose sensitive personal information" was affected. Thus, the law covers all affected parties and not just Texas residents. The law's fines mirror HIPAA's.

Health Insurance Portability and Accountability Act of 1996 (HIPAA) Regulations 45 C.F.R. §§ 160-164

Primary Function: Pursuant to the Health Insurance Portability and Accountability Act of 1996, the Department of Health and Human Services (HHS) promulgated regulations to regulate the privacy and security of medical information—the "Privacy Rule" and the "Security Rule."

In 2009, Congress passed the HITECH Act as part of the American Recovery and Reinvestment Act. The act extends HIPAA rules to business associates (previously regulated by contractual arrangements with covered entities) and provides for direct HHS enforcement over business associates. Among other things, the act increases the fines for HIPAA violations and requires data security breach notification. In 2013, HHS issued a regulation (the Omnibus Rule) to implement the HITECH Act changes.

Applies to: Covered entities include health plans, healthcare clearinghouses, and healthcare providers. 45 C.F.R. § 160.102(a). The regulations apply only to those who transmit health information electronically in HIPAA's standard format. Most healthcare providers who deal with insurance—physicians, hospitals, insurance companies, and pharmacists—are covered. Business associates that receive PHI from covered entities (and subcontractors that receive PHI from business associates) are also directly subject to the HIPAA Security Rule and parts of the Privacy Rule.

Hybrid Entities: When an organization provides a variety of products and services, only some of which pertain to healthcare, they are known as "hybrid entities." Only the component that performs the healthcare functions must comply with HIPAA.

Protected Health Information: The data protected by HIPAA is called PHI, which consists of "individually identifiable health information." 45 C.F.R. § 160.103.

The Right to Request Restrictions: An individual retains the right to request restrictions on the use or disclosure of health information by all covered entities. 45 C.F.R. § 164.502(c).

Notice: Covered entities must produce a notice of privacy practices.

Right of Access: Individuals have a right to access any protected health information that is used in whole or in part to make decisions about the individual.

Authorization: For all uses and disclosures beyond those for treatment, payment, or healthcare operations, a patient's authorization is required. 45 C.F.R. § 164.508(a). Treatment cannot be made conditional on authorization unless the covered entity's purpose is research, determining health plan eligibility, or underwriting.

Marketing: Authorization is required for data use in marketing. But, a covered entity can use PHI to market its own healthcare products, and the individual cannot opt out. 45 C.F.R. § 164.501.

Business Associates: Entities that contract with a covered entity are "business associates" and are permitted to receive PHI "if the covered entity obtains satisfactory assurance that the business associate will appropriately safeguard the information." 45 C.F.R. § 164.502. Business associates that violate HIPAA are subject to the same punishments as covered entities. The HITECH Act provides for direct HHS enforcement power over business associates. Subcontractors of business associates that receive PHI are deemed to be business associates.

Psychotherapy Notes: Authorization is required "for any use or disclosure of psychotherapy notes" even if that use or disclosure is for treatment, payment, and healthcare operations. 45 C.F.R. § 164.508(a)(2). According to the regulation commentary, psychotherapy notes require authorization because they "do not include information that covered entities typically need for treatment, payment or other types of healthcare operations."

Disclosure and Use Without Authorization: The regulation provides for a number of situations where health information can be used or disclosed without authorization: (1) required by law; (2) for public health activities; (3) regarding victims of abuse, neglect, or domestic violence (under certain circumstances); (4) for health oversight activities; (5) for judicial and administrative proceedings; (6) for law enforcement purposes; (7) to avert a serious threat to health or safety; (8) for specialized government functions; and (9) for workers' compensation. 45 C.F.R. § 164.512.

De-Identified Health Information: HIPAA does not place restrictions on the use or disclosure of de-identified data.

De-Identifying Data Under HIPAA

There are two methods to de-identify data:

Statistician Method

Have an expert certify that the data is not individually identifiable. This expert must have the appropriate statistical and scientific knowledge for data de-identification. The expert must determine that the risk of re-identifying individuals is "very small" and must document the methods and results of the analysis that justifies this determination.

Safe Harbor Method

Remove 18 identifying data elements that HIPAA specifies and have no actual knowledge that the remaining data could be used to identify the individual. If all these identifying data elements are removed, then the data is de-identified. No expert is required. The 18 identifiers are:

1. Names
2. All geographic subdivisions smaller than a state
   - Includes street address, city, county, precinct, or zip code
   - May use the first three digits of the zip code if the geographic unit formed by combining all zip codes with the same three initial digits contains more than 20,000 people and the initial three digits of the zip codes for geographic units containing 20,000 or fewer people are changed to 000)
3. All elements of dates related to an individual except the year
   - Includes birth date, admission date, discharge date, date of death, and all ages over 80
4. Telephone numbers
5. Fax numbers
6. E-mail addresses
7. Social Security numbers
8. Medical record numbers
9. Health plan beneficiary numbers
10. Account numbers
11. Certificate/license numbers

	De-Identifying Data Under HIPAA
12.	Vehicle identifiers, such as serial numbers and license plate numbers
13.	Device identifiers and serial numbers
14.	URLs
15.	IP addresses
16.	Biometric identifiers (fingerprint, voice print)
17.	Full-face photographs
18.	Any other unique identifying number, characteristic, or code

Disclosure to Law Enforcement Officials: PHI may be disclosed to law enforcement officials without consent or authorization if required by a court order, warrant, or subpoena. Moreover, certain health information may also be disclosed "in response to a law enforcement official's request for such information for the purpose of identifying or locating a suspect, fugitive, material witness or missing person." 45 C.F.R. § 164.512(f)(2).

Privacy Officials: Covered entities must have a designated privacy official.

Enforcement: Under the HIPAA statute, 42 U.S.C. § 1320d-6(a), a person who knowingly obtains or discloses individually identifiable health information in violation of the Privacy Rule can be fined up to $50,000 and imprisoned for up to one year. If the violation occurred via false pretenses, the fine is up to $100,000 and five years imprisonment. If the violation was done for commercial advantage, personal gain, or malicious harm, then the penalties are up to a $250,000 fine and 10 years imprisonment. The maximum penalties under HIPAA are $50,000 per violation, with an annual maximum of $1.5 million. The HIPAA regulations do not grant a private cause of action. Criminal enforcement is via the Department of Justice. Civil enforcement is via the Department of Health and Human Services, Office for Civil Rights (OCR).

Preemption: HIPAA does not preempt more stringent state law. 45 C.F.R. § 160.203(b).

The Security Rule: Unlike the Privacy Rule, which applies to all PHI, the Security Rule applies only to "electronic protected health information" (e-PHI). The Security Rule requires covered entities to "protect against any reasonably anticipated threats or hazards to the security or integrity of [e-PHI]." 45 C.F.R. § 164.306(a)(2). Requires a security officer, security training, and other procedures.

Data Breach Notification: The HITECH Act of 2009 establishes a data breach notification requirement. A breach consists of an unauthorized disclosure of "unsecured PHI," which is unencrypted PHI. Affected individuals must be notified "without reasonable delay" and no later than 60 days after discovery of the breach. Breaches of 500 people or more require notice to the media and to HHS.

Court Cases

United States v. Zhou, 678 F.3d 1110 (9th Cir. 2012)
The court concluded that for the purpose of a misdemeanor violation of HIPAA under 42 U.S.C. § 1320d-6(a), a violator need only knowingly obtain "individually identifiable health information relating to an individual." The court held there was no requirement of knowledge of violating HIPAA.

Byrne v. Avery Ctr. for Obstetrics & Gynecology, P.C., 314 Conn. 433 (2014)
Holding that HIPAA "does not preempt the plaintiff's state common-law causes of action for negligence or negligent information of emotional distress." Even though HIPAA lacks a private right of action, plaintiffs can use HIPAA to inform the standard of care in a negligence case (and other state common law causes of action).

Walgreen Co. v. Hinchy, 21 N.E. 3d 99 (Ind. Ct. App. 2014), *aff'd on reh'g,* 25 N.E. 3d 748 (Ind. Ct. App. 2015)
Reviewing a $1.44 million jury verdict, an Indiana appellate court affirmed that the plaintiff had raised a viable claim of negligence based on using HIPAA as the standard of care. Court affirmed original result on rehearing.

HIPAA Myths and Facts

MYTH: HIPAA regulates all medical information.

FACT: HIPAA regulates only medical information maintained by "covered entities" that use the standard HIPAA format.

MYTH: Complying with HIPAA will ensure a healthcare provider is properly protecting privacy under the law.

FACT: HIPAA is often weaker than state law protections. Since it does not preempt more stringent state laws, healthcare providers must be familiar with state statutory and common law privacy protections. Public hospitals must also comply with the U.S. Constitution and state constitutions.

MYTH: HIPAA prevents physicians from disclosing information about a person's care to relatives or from having office sign-in sheets.

FACT: HIPAA does not make such restrictions.

HIPAA Problems to Avoid

- **Removing unencrypted data:** Providence Health & Services stored unencrypted PHI in electronic storage devices and laptops that were taken outside the institution and then lost. Penalty: Providence agreed to pay the Department of Health & Human Services (HHS) a $100,000 fine plus establish a three-year corrective action plan.

- **Improperly disposing of prescription data:** CVS inadequately discarded labels from prescription bottles. Penalty: $2.25 million fine plus a corrective action plan.

- **Failure to provide adequate training:** HHS settlements with Phoenix Cardiac Surgery for $100,000 and with the Alaska Department of Health and Social Services (DHSS) for $1.7 million involved, in part, inadequate training.

- **Inadequate policies and safeguards:** HHS's settlement with the Alaska DHSS was due, in part, to these deficiencies.

- **Failure to conduct risk analysis:** HHS's settlement with Phoenix Cardiac Surgery was due, in part, to the failure to conduct risk analysis.

- **Failure to cooperate with HHS's investigation:** HHS fined Cignet Health $4.3 million for denying 41 patients access to their records and for not cooperating in the investigation. Most of the fine was for the failure to cooperate.

OCR HIPAA Enforcement Actions

Advocate Entities (July 8, 2016)
Three breaches affected the PHI of 4 million individuals. Violations: failed to assess risks to PHI, failed to implement procedures to limit access to files in data support center, failed to ensure that business associate would protect PHI, and failed to secure unencrypted laptop left in unlocked vehicle overnight. $5.55 million penalty.

Or. Health & Sci. Univ. (Jul. 18, 2016)
Multiple breaches involving unencrypted laptops and a stolen unencrypted thumb drive exposed the PHI of thousands, including 1,361 patients with a significant risk of harm. Violations: did not implement measures to address security risks, did not implement policies to correct security violations, and did not encrypt PHI on workstations. $2.7 million penalty.

Catholic Health Care Servs. of the Archdiocese of Phila. (Jun. 24, 2016)
Theft of mobile device exposed PHI of 412 nursing home residents. Violations: failed to encrypt or physically protect mobile device, failed to implement policies governing mobile devices, and failed to conduct risk analysis. $650,000 penalty.

N.Y. Presbyterian Hosp. (Apr. 19, 2016)

Hospital released PHI of two patients to film crews and staff during filming of "NY Med" TV series. Violations: allowed individuals receiving urgent medical care to be filmed without their authorization and failed to safeguard PHI during filming. $2.2 million penalty.

Raleigh Orthopaedic Clinic (Apr. 14, 2016)

Clinic gave PHI of 17,3000 patients to potential business partner without first implementing a business associate agreement. Violations: disclosed PHI to unauthorized entity and failed to implement business associate agreement. $750,000 penalty.

The Feinstein Inst. for Med. Research (Mar. 16, 2016)

Unencrypted laptop containing PHI of 13,000 patients and research participants stolen from an employee's car. Violations: failed to implement sufficient security procedures, including policies governing devices. $3.9 million penalty.

N. Mem'l Health Care (Mar. 16, 2016)

Unencrypted laptop stolen from locked vehicle belonging to North Memorial's business associate, exposing the PHI of 9,497 individuals. Violations: failed to implement business associate agreement and failed to complete a risk analysis. $1.55 million penalty.

Bd. of Regents of the Univ. of Wash. (Dec. 14, 2015)

Employee downloaded an email attachment with malware, infecting the organization's IT system and compromising the data of over 90,000 patients. Violations: failed to implement policies to address security violations and failed to ensure that affiliated entities conducted and responded to risk assessments. $750,000 penalty.

Lahey Clinical Hosp., Inc. (Nov. 19, 2015)

Workstation laptop stolen from an unlocked hospital treatment room, exposing the PHI of 599 individuals. Violations: failed to conduct risk analysis, failed to physically safeguard workstations, failed to implement policies regarding PHI maintained on workstations, and failed to use unique user names to track user identity. $850,000 penalty.

Parkview Health Sys., Inc. (June 23, 2014)

Boxes of medical records were left unattended in physician's driveway, compromising the PHI of 8,000 patients. Violations: failed to implement safeguards to physically protect PHI. $800,000 penalty.

N.Y. Presbyterian Hosp. (May 7, 2014)

Improperly reconfigured computer server made PHI of 6,800 patients available to Internet search engines. Violations: failed to implement processes for monitoring IT equipment, failed to implement security measures to reduce risks to PHI, and failed to implement procedures for authorizing access to patient databases. $3.3 million penalty.

Trustees of Columbia Univ. (May 7, 2014)

Physician attempted to deactivate personal computer server on network containing PHI, resulting in release of PHI to Internet search engines. Violations: failed to implement processes for monitoring IT equipment and failed to implement security measures to reduce risk of disclosure. $1.5 million penalty.

QCA Health Plan, Inc. (Apr. 11, 2014)

Unencrypted laptop containing PHI of 148 individuals was stolen from an employee's car. Violations: failed to implement procedures governing PHI and failed to implement security measures to assess and reduce potential risks and vulnerabilities. $250,000 penalty.

Skagit Cty. (Mar. 6, 2014)

Facility inadvertently moved records to a publically accessible server, compromising PHI of 1,581 individuals. Violations: failed to notify individuals whose PHI had been compromised, failed to implement sufficient security procedures, and failed to implement written policies to ensure compliance with HIPAA Security Rule. $215,000 penalty.

Adult & Pediatric Dermatology, P.C. (Dec. 24, 2013)

Unencrypted thumb drive stolen from employee's car, compromising PHI of 2,200 individuals. Violations: did not properly train employees, did not implement written security procedures, and did not conduct risk assessment. $150,000 penalty.

Affinity Health Plan, Inc. (Aug. 7, 2013)

Company returned leased photocopiers without erasing hard drive, disclosing the PHI of 344,579 individuals. Violations: failed to incorporate photocopier in its risk analysis and failed to implement relevant procedures when returning equipment. $1.2 million penalty.

WellPoint, Inc. (July 8, 2013)

Online application database left PHI of 612,402 individuals accessible to unauthorized individuals over the internet. Violations: did not implement appropriate technical safeguards, did not perform adequate technical evaluations, and did not implement technology to verify identity of persons seeking access to PHI.

Shasta Reg'l Med. Ctr. (June 3, 2013)

Senior executives discussed medical services provided to a patient without valid written authorization. Violation: failed to safeguard PHI from intentional or unintentional disclosure and failed to sanction employees pursuant to internal policies. $275,000 penalty.

Alaska Dep't of Health & Soc. Servs. (June 25, 2012)

USB hard drive stolen from employee vehicle. Violations: failed to complete risk analysis, failed to properly train employees, and failed to encrypt devices. $1.7 million penalty.

Phx. Cardiac Surgery, P.C. (Apr. 11, 2012)
Facility posted clinical and surgical appointments on publically accessible Internet-based calendar. Violations: did not properly train employees, did not implement appropriate administrative and technical safeguards, and did not obtain sufficient business associate agreements. $100,000 penalty.

BlueCross BlueShield of Tenn. (Mar. 9, 2012)
Fifty-seven unencrypted computer hard drives containing the PHI of over 1 million individuals were stolen from a leased facility. Violation of HHS Privacy and Security Rules. $1.5 million penalty.

Regents of the Univ. of Cal. (July 6, 2011)
Unauthorized employees repeatedly viewed patient PHI. Violations: did not provide appropriate employee training, did not sanction employees who impermissibly accessed PHI, and did not implement proper security measures. $865,000 penalty.

Cignet Health (Feb. 4, 2011)
Denied 41 patients access to their medical records. Violations: failed to cooperate with HHS investigation and failed to provide patients with a copy of their medical records within 30 days of the patients' request. $4.3 million penalty.

Mgmt. Servs. Org. Wash., Inc. (Dec. 13, 2010)
Disclosed PHI to subsidiary for marketing purposes. Violations: did not implement appropriate administrative, technical, or physical safeguards. $35,000 penalty.

Rite Aid Corp. (June 7, 2010)
Disposed of prescriptions and pill bolls in open dumpsters. Violations: did not establish physical and administrative safeguards, did not properly train employees on disposal of PHI, and did not sanction employees who failed to comply with procedures. $1 million penalty.

CVS Pharmacy, Inc. (Jan. 16, 2009)
Disposed of PHI in open dumpsters. Violations: did not establish physical and administrative safeguards, did not sanction employees who failed to comply with procedures, and did not properly train employees on disposal of PHI. $1 million penalty.

State Enforcement Actions

Women & Infants Hosp. of R.I. (Mass. July 22, 2014)
Lawsuit brought under HIPAA and state consumer protection and data security statutes after hospital lost 19 unencrypted backup tapes containing the PHI of 12,127 Massachusetts residents. Violations: failed to implement inventory and tracking system and failed to adequately protect PHI. $110,000 penalty.

Beth Israel Deaconess Med. Ctr. (Mass. Nov. 20, 2014)

Lawsuit brought under HIPAA and state consumer protection and data security statutes after doctor's unencrypted personal laptop was stolen from an unlocked office, exposing the PHI of 4,000 individuals. Violations: failed to encrypt and physically secure laptop. $100,000 penalty.

Bos. Children's Hosp. (Mass. Dec. 19, 2014)

Lawsuit brought under HIPAA and state consumer protection and data security statutes after doctor's unencrypted hospital-issued laptop was stolen at a conference. Breach exposed PHI of 2,159 patients, including 1,700 minors. Violations: failed to encrypt and physically secure laptop. $40,000 penalty.

Accretive Health (Minn. July 31, 2012)

Lawsuit brought under HIPAA and Minnesota debt collection and consumer protection statutes after an employee left an unencrypted laptop in a rental car, exposing the PHI of 23,000 individuals. Violations: failed to encrypt and physically secure laptop. $2.5 million penalty.

WellPoint, Inc. (Ind. June 23, 2011)

Lawsuit brought under Indiana's Security Breach Act after health insurance application records accessible through the company's website exposed the PHI of 32,000 individuals. Violations: failed to adequately safeguard PHI and failed to promptly notify individuals affected by the breach. $100,000 penalty.

Health Net (Vt. Jan. 19, 2011)

Lawsuit brought under HIPAA and state consumer protection and data security statutes after loss of unencrypted computer hard drive exposed PHI of 525 Vermont residents. Violations: failed to adequately safeguard PHI and failed to promptly notify individuals affected by the breach. $55,000 penalty.

Health Net (Conn. July 6, 2010)

Lawsuit brought under HIPAA and state privacy statutes after hard drive with the unencrypted PHI of 446,000 individuals went missing. Connecticut was the first state to pursue actions under HITECH. Violations: failed to adequately safeguard PHI and failed to promptly notify individuals affected by the breach. $250,000 fine.

The Common Rule
45 C.F.R. § 46.101

Primary Function: To ensure that the rights of a human subject are protected throughout a research project.

Applies to: Most federally funded research conducted on humans. 45 C.F.R. § 46.101.

Key Protections: The key protections of the Common Rule concern individual autonomy and consent, the need for independent review of research by an institutional review board (IRB), and the minimization of physical and mental harm to research subjects. Privacy and confidentiality are considered important components of the risk of harm from any research project.

Exceptions: The Common Rule also exempts from its requirements research that involves publicly available information or information "recorded by the investigator in such a manner that subjects cannot be identified, directly or through identifiers linked to the subjects." 45 C.F.R. § 46.101(b)(4).

Preemption: The Common Rule's requirements for informed consent do not preempt any applicable federal, state, or local laws that set stricter standards for legally effective informed consent.

Federal Drug and Alcohol Confidentiality Statute
42 U.S.C. § 290dd-2

Primary Purpose: To protect the confidentiality of records of drug and alcohol abuse treatment.

Applies to: Regulates "any program or activity relating to substance abuse education, prevention, training, treatment, rehabilitation or research which is conducted, regulated, or directly or indirectly assisted by any department or agency of the United States." 42 U.S.C. § 290dd-2(a).

Regulations: The regulations relating to this statute are at 42 C.F.R. §§ 2.1-2.67.

Relationship to HIPAA: A drug and alcohol treatment program can be covered under both HIPAA and the federal drug and alcohol confidentiality rules. The confidentiality rules are more privacy-protective than HIPAA.

Confidentiality Protections: The confidentiality rules generally restrict disclosure of personal information. There are only a few exceptions: (1) written consent from the patient, (2) scientific research and evaluation of the program, provided the records are de-identified, (3) emergencies, (4) court orders, (5) data relating to a crime on the program premises or against program employees and (6) suspicion of child abuse or neglect.

Restriction from Use in Criminal Cases: With limited exceptions (e.g., crime on program premises), records of drug and alcohol abuse treatment cannot be used "to initiate or substantiate any criminal charges against a patient or to conduct any investigation of a patient." 42 U.S.C. § 290dd-2(c).

Subpoenas for Medical Information

Although the law governing subpoenas is generally permissive in allowing demands for information, courts tend to be more exacting when they face challenges to subpoenas for medical information.

Nw. Mem'l Hosp. v. Ashcroft, 362 F.3d 923 (7th Cir. 2004)
Quashing a subpoena to doctors for partial birth abortion records even though they would be de-identified. The court noted a risk of re-identification and noted that even if they could not be re-identified, the patients might still feel their privacy was invaded by the revelation of details about their abortions.

In re Grand Jury Investigation, 779 N.E.2d 173 (N.Y. 2002)
Quashing a subpoena to obtain emergency room data from hospitals to locate a bleeding suspect who fled a crime scene. Divulging medical records pertaining to all people treated for stab wounds would violate the physician-patient privilege.

CONSTITUTIONAL PROTECTIONS

Constitutional Right to Privacy

Although the U.S. Constitution does not explicitly mention privacy, in a line of cases commonly referred to as concerning "substantive due process," the Supreme Court has held that there exists a "right to privacy" in the U.S. Constitution.

Griswold v. Connecticut, 381 U.S. 479 (1965)
Recognizes a "right to privacy" in the Constitution based on the "penumbras" of the Bill of Rights. The right to privacy protects against a state law prohibiting the use of contraceptives in the "sacred precincts of marital bedrooms."

Eisenstadt v. Baird, 405 U.S. 438 (1972)
Strikes down a statute permitting contraceptives only to married couples. The right of privacy "is the right of the individual, married or single, to be free from unwarranted government intrusion into matters so fundamentally affecting a person as the decision whether to bear or beget a child."

Roe v. Wade, 410 U.S. 113 (1973)
The right to privacy "is broad enough to encompass a woman's decision whether or not to terminate her pregnancy."

Planned Parenthood of Se. Penn. v. Casey, 505 U.S. 833 (1992)
Reaffirms Roe v. Wade, though it suggests a different standard—that no law place an "undue burden" on the right to have an abortion.

Washington v. Glucksberg, 521 U.S. 702 (1997)
Concludes that a ban on physician-assisted suicide did not run afoul of the right to privacy.

Lawrence v. Texas, 539 U.S. 558 (2003)
Overrules *Bowers v. Hardwick*, 478 U.S. 186 (1986), and concludes that the right to privacy prohibits the criminalization of homosexual sex.

Constitutional Right to Information Privacy

Whalen v. Roe, 429 U.S. 589 (1977)
The court recognizes that the constitutional right to privacy also encompasses "the individual interest in avoiding disclosure of personal matters"—which is now called the "constitutional right to information privacy."

Nixon v. Adm'r of Gen. Servs., 433 U.S. 425 (1977)
Concludes that President Richard Nixon had a constitutional privacy interest in records of his private communications with his family, but not in records involving his official duties.

United States v. Westinghouse Elec. Corp., 638 F.2d 570 (3d Cir. 1980)
The court set forth the predominant test for determining whether there is a violation of the constitutional right to information privacy by listing seven factors that "should be considered in deciding whether an intrusion into an individual's privacy is justified": (1) "the type of record requested," (2) "the information it does or might contain," (3) "the potential for harm in any subsequent nonconsensual disclosure," (4) "the injury from disclosure to the relationship in which the record was generated," (5) "the adequacy of safeguards to prevent unauthorized disclosure," (6) "the degree of need for access" and (7) "whether there is an express statutory mandate, articulated public policy, or other recognizable public interest militating toward access."

Fourth Amendment

The Fourth Amendment protects the privacy of medical information when government officials are seeking to obtain it.

GENETIC INFORMATION

Genetic Testing and Discrimination

State Genetic Privacy Statutes: Many states have passed statutes protecting the privacy of genetic information.

Genetic Information Nondiscrimination Act of 2008 (GINA), Pub. L. No. 110-223: This federal statute prevents insurance companies and employers from using genetic tests to deny individuals health coverage or employment. GINA does not preempt stricter state laws.

Exec. Order No. 13145, 2 C.F.R. § 13,145 (2000): Requires all executive branch departments and agencies to refrain from genetic discrimination. Also states that the "employing department or agency shall not request, require, collect or purchase protected genetic information with respect to an employee, or information about a request for or the receipt of genetic services by such employee."

FOR FURTHER REFERENCE

Treatises

Lisa M. Boyle, *HIPAA: A Guide to Health Care Privacy and Security Law* (2015)
A 1,400-page volume on HIPAA.

Patricia I. Carter, *HIPAA Compliance Handbook* (2015)
In-depth examination of the privacy and security regulations in HIPAA and enforcement mechanisms.

Khaled El Emam, *Guide to the De-Identification of Personal Health Information* (2013)
Detailed discussion about why and how to de-identify PHI.

Khaled El Emam & Luk Arbuckle, *Anonymizing Health Data: Case Studies and Methods to Get You Started* (2013)
Practical and concrete discussion of how to de-identify PHI.

Rebecca Herold & Kevin Beaver, *The Practical Guide to HIPAA Privacy and Security Compliance* (2d ed. 2015)
A detailed guide to HIPAA and how to develop an effective compliance program.

A Guide to HIPAA Security and the Law **(Stephen S. Wu ed., 2007)**
Focuses on liability issues and the scope of applicability of the HIPAA Security Rule.

Books

Genetic Secrets: Protecting Privacy and Confidentiality in the Genetic Era **(Mark A. Rothstein ed., 1997)**
A sterling collection of interdisciplinary essays by leading scholars regarding privacy and genetic information.

Articles and Other Sources

Fred H. Cate, *Protecting Privacy in Health Research: The Limits of Individual Choice*, 98 Cal. L. Rev. 1765 (2010)
Argues that the policy and legal reliance on individual choice concerning the use of personal information health research is a flawed approach.

Lawrence O. Gostin, *Health Information Privacy*, 80 Cornell L. Rev. 451 (1995)
A classic article that identifies the key issues in the health privacy debate.

Institute of Medicine, *Beyond the HIPPA Privacy Rule: Enhancing Privacy, Improving Health Through Research* (2009)
Report of Blue Ribbon panel proposed changes to HIPPA Privacy Rule and other privacy regulations with goal of improving healthcare research while also protecting personal privacy.

Peter H. Schuck & Daniel J. Givelber, Tarasoff v. Regents of the University of California*: The Therapist's Dilemma, in* Torts Stories 99 (Robert L. Rabin & Stephen D. Sugarman eds., 2003)
Fascinating background and valuable information on the leading case about a health-care professional's duty to warn a victim about a threat from a potential harm-causer whom the professional is treating.

Paul M. Schwartz, *Privacy and Participation: Personal Information and Public Sector Regulation in the United States*, 80 Iowa L. Rev. 553 (1995)
Examination of the constitutional right to informational privacy, including discussion of lower court opinions.

Peter A. Winn, *Criminal Prosecutions Under HIPAA*, 53 U.S. Att'ys Bull. 21 (2005)
Advances an influential theory about prosecutions of employees and business associates of covered entities under HIPAA pursuant to 18 U.S.C. § 2(b).

CHAPTER 7

Government Records

ESSENTIAL POINTS

- Federal agencies have statutory and constitutional duties both to make information available to the public and to protect the privacy of people's personal data in record systems.

- The privacy of court records is primarily governed by judicial discretion, and there is a presumption of public access.

- The privacy of other government records is primarily governed by the Freedom of Information Act and state analogues. Many of these laws have exemptions from disclosure to protect privacy.

- Under the First Amendment, once the government releases information to the public, nobody can be sanctioned for further disclosing it. But the government can make information available on the condition of agreeing to curtail how one disseminates it.

- The federal Privacy Act regulates the way that federal agencies collect, use, and disclose personal data. In general, it does not apply to private-sector entities or state or local governments. The one exception to this rule concerns its limitations on the use of Social Security numbers.

- The constitutional right to information privacy requires that the government avoid making unwarranted disclosures of personal information. The government must keep data adequately secure.

FAIR INFORMATION PRACTICES (FIPs)

In 1973, the U.S. Department of Health, Education & Welfare (HEW) issued the highly influential report, *Records, Computers, and the Rights of Citizens: Report of the Secretary's Advisory Committee on Automated Personal Data Systems* (1973). The report recommended a code of "fair information practices":

- There must be no personal-data recordkeeping systems whose very existence is secret.

- There must be a way for an individual to find out what information about him is in a record and how it is used.

- There must be a way for an individual to prevent information about him that was obtained for one purpose from being used or made available for other purposes without his consent.

- There must be a way for an individual to correct or amend a record of identifiable information about him.

- Any organization creating, maintaining, using, or disseminating records of identifiable personal data must assure the reliability of the data for their intended use and must take reasonable precautions to prevent misuse of the data.

These FIPs have been embodied throughout U.S. privacy statutes as well as in laws around the world.

COURT RECORDS

Common Law Right to Access Court Records
Under the common law, the U.S. Supreme Court concluded that a right exists, though not an absolute one, to access court records. *Nixon v. Warner Commc'ns, Inc.*, 435 U.S. 589 (1978).

The privacy of court records is generally within the discretion of trial court judges. Courts also have the discretion to seal certain court proceedings or portions of court proceedings from the public.

Protective Orders
Federal Rule of Civil Procedure 26(c) provides that judges may, "for good cause," issue protective orders where disclosure of information gleaned in discovery might cause a party "annoyance, embarrassment, oppression, or undue burden or expense."

Depositions and Interrogatories
"[P]retrial depositions and interrogatories are not public components of a civil trial. Such proceedings were not open to the public at common law, and, in general, they are conducted in private as a matter of modern practice." *Seattle Times Co. v. Rhinehart*, 467 U.S. 20 (1984).

Pseudonymous Litigation
Courts may permit parties to proceed anonymously under special circumstances. "The ultimate test for permitting a plaintiff to proceed anonymously is whether the plaintiff has a substantial privacy right which outweighs the 'customary and constitutionally-embedded presumption of openness in judicial proceedings.' It is the exceptional case in which a plaintiff may proceed under a fictitious name." *Doe v. Frank*, 951 F.2d 320 (11th Cir. 1992), *quoting Doe v. Stegall*, 653 F.2d 180 (5th Cir. 1981).

Juror Privacy
There is a strong presumption that jurors' names be made public, but there is no absolute right of public access to jurors' identities. "[A] judge must find some *unusual* risk to justify keeping jurors' names confidential; it is not enough to point to possibilities that are present in every criminal prosecution." *United States v. Blagojevich*, 612 F.3d 558 (7th Cir. 2010).

The First Amendment Right to Access
The First Amendment requires that certain judicial proceedings be open to the public when: (1) the proceeding "historically has been open to the press and general public" and (2) access "plays a particularly significant role in the functioning of the judicial process and the government as a whole." *Globe Newspaper Co. v. Superior Court*, 457 U.S. 596 (1982).

The First Amendment requires public access to criminal trials, and the government can deny access only if "the denial is necessitated by a compelling governmental interest, and is narrowly tailored to serve that interest." *Id.*

The First Amendment right to access extends to voir dire in criminal cases as well as to pretrial proceedings.

PUBLIC RECORDS

Freedom of Information Act (FOIA)
5 U.S.C. § 552 (1966)

Primary Function: To promote transparency in government by requiring federal agencies to disclose information to people who request it.

Applies to: Any person may request records from federal agencies. Congress is not a federal agency and is therefore not subject to the act. Nor is the president or his advisors.

Exemptions: The Freedom of Information Act contains nine enumerated exemptions to disclosure: (1) classified information; (2) internal personnel rules and practices; (3) information exempted by statute; (4) trade secrets and confidential information; (5) certain litigation materials; (6) "personnel and medical files and similar files the disclosure of which would constitute a clearly unwarranted invasion of personal privacy"; (7) law enforcement records that would interfere with litigation, invade privacy, reveal confidential sources, or endanger people's safety; (8) certain information involved with the supervision of financial institutions, and (9) geological and geophysical data concerning wells. 5 U.S.C. § 552(b).

The Privacy Exemptions: Two of these exemptions explicitly reference privacy concerns:

- Exemption 6 applies to "personnel and medical files and similar files." It has been interpreted broadly to apply beyond personnel and medical information to all types of data.

- Exemption 7(C) exempts law enforcement records from disclosure that "could reasonably be expected to constitute an unwarranted invasion of personal privacy."

When the FOIA otherwise mandates releases of documents, it also requires the redaction of data that would violate privacy, where possible.

Only the government agency can raise Exemptions 6 and 7(C). The individual to whom the information pertains has no right to litigate the issue if the agency does not choose to; nor does the individual have a right to be given notice that her personal information falls within a FOIA request.

Exemption 7(C) has been held to permit more categorical approaches to a decision to withhold information compared to Exemption 6, which typically requires an identification and balancing of relevant interests in disclosure and in privacy. For example, courts will draw a "bright line" and withhold information that identifies third parties in law enforcement records.

Leading Cases

U.S. Dep't of Justice v. Reporters Comm. for Freedom of the Press, 489 U.S. 749 (1989)

Concludes that FBI "rap sheets" (aggregated compilations of publicly available information) about individuals are exempt under Exemption 7(C). The court notes that although the information is in the public domain, "there is a vast difference between the public records that might be found after a diligent search of courthouse files, county archives, and local police stations throughout the country and a computerized summary located in a single clearinghouse of information." This understanding of privacy differs greatly from the way that most courts understand privacy. Typically, courts often conclude that once information is exposed to the public, it can no longer be private.

U.S. Dep't of State v. Wash. Post Co., 456 U.S. 595 (1982)

Under Exemption 6, "similar files" has a "broad, rather than a narrow, meaning" and applies to any information that constitutes "a clearly unwarranted invasion of that person's privacy."

Nat'l Archives & Records Admin. v. Favish, 541 U.S. 157 (2004)

Under FOIA Exemption 7(C), surviving family members have a privacy right "with respect to their close relative's death-scene images."

State Public Records

Common Law Right to Access Public Records

Under the common law, there is "a general right to inspect and copy public records and documents." *Nixon v. Warner Commc'ns, Inc.*, 435 U.S. 589 (1978).

State Freedom of Information Laws

Privacy in records maintained by state agencies is protected under each state's freedom of information law. Most states have some form of exemption for privacy, often patterned after the federal Freedom of Information Act's privacy exemptions. Not all states interpret their privacy exemptions as broadly as the Supreme Court has interpreted FOIA's. Further, certain state FOIAs do not have privacy exemptions.

State Erasure Laws

Some states have laws requiring removal of information from records. For example, Connecticut, Conn. Gen. Stat. § 54-142a, requires the state to erase an individual's arrest from certain official records if he was subsequently found not guilty or pardoned or if the charges are nulled or dismissed. An individual subject to such an erasure is deemed to never have been arrested and may so swear under oath. In *Martin v. Hearst Corp.*, 777 F.3d 546 (2nd Cir. 2015), the court found an erasure statute did not undo the underlying historical facts and require news reports or other publications to erase accounts of a person's arrest. The law did prevent government and courts from relying on erased police, court, or prosecution records in a later trial.

STATE FREEDOM OF INFORMATION STATUTES		
STATE	**OPEN MEETINGS LAW**	**PUBLIC RECORDS LAW**
AL	Ala. Code § 36-12-40 *et seq.*	Ala. Code § 36-25A-1 *et seq.*
AK	Alaska Stat. § 44.62.310 *et seq.*	Alaska Stat. § 40.25.110 *et seq.*
AZ	Ariz. Rev. Stat. Ann. § 38-431 *et seq.*	Ariz. Rev. Stat. Ann. § 39-121 *et seq.*
AR	Ark. Code Ann. § 25-19-101 *et seq.* including § 25-19-105.	Ark. Code Ann. § 25-19-101 *et seq.* including § 25-19-106.
CA	Cal. Gov't Code §§ 54950-54960.5	Cal. Gov't Code §§ 6250-6268
CO	Colo. Rev. Stat. § 24-6-401 *et seq.*	Colo. Rev. Stat. § 24-72-201 *et seq.*
CT	Conn. Gen. Stat. § 1-200 *et seq.*	Conn. Gen. Stat. § 1-200 *et seq.*

DC	D.C. Code §§ 2-571 to 580	D.C. Code §§ 2-531 to 540
DE	Del. Code Ann. tit. 29, § 10001 *et seq.*	Del. Code Ann. tit. 29, § 10001 *et seq.*
FL	Fla. Stat. § 286.011 *et seq.*	Fla. Stat. § 119.01 *et. seq.*
GA	Ga. Code Ann. § 50-14-1	Ga. Code Ann. § 50-18-70
HI	Haw. Rev. Stat. § 92-1 *et seq.*	Haw. Rev. Stat. § 91-1 *et seq.*
ID	Idaho Code Ann. § 67-2341 *et seq.*	Idaho Code Ann. § 9-337 *et seq.*
IL	5 Ill. Comp. Stat. 120/1-7.5 *et seq.*	5 Ill. Comp. Stat. 140/1 *et. seq.*
IN	Ind. Code § 5-14-1.5-1 *et seq.*	Ind. Code § 5-14-3-1 *et seq.*
IA	Iowa Code § 21.1 *et seq.*	Iowa Code § 22.1 *et seq.*
KS	Kan. Stat. Ann. § 75-4317 *et seq.*	Kan. Stat. Ann. § 45-215
KY	Ky. Rev. Stat. Ann. § 61.810	Ky. Rev. Stat. Ann. § 61.870
LA	La. Stat. Ann. § 42:4.1 *et seq.*	La. Stat. Ann. § 44:1 *et seq.*
ME	Me. Rev. Stat. Ann. tit. 1, § 403 *et seq.*	Me. Rev. Stat. Ann. tit. 1, § 402 *et seq.*
MD	Md. Code Ann., State Gov't §10-501 *et seq.*	Md. Code Ann., State Gov't § 10-611 *et seq.*
MA	Mass. Gen. Laws ch. 39, §§ 23-24. Mass. Gen. Laws ch. 30, § 11.	Mass. Gen. Laws ch. 66, § 10
MI	Mich. Comp. Laws § 15.261 *et seq.*	Mich. Comp. Laws § 15.231 *et seq.*
MN	Minn. Stat. § 13.01 *et seq.*	Minn. Stat. § 13.01 *et seq.*
MS	Miss. Code Ann. § 25-4-1 *et seq.*	Miss. Code Ann. § 25-61-1 *et seq.*
MO	Mo. Rev. Stat. § 610.010 *et seq.*	Mo. Rev. Stat. § 610.010 *et seq.*
MT	Mont. Code Ann. § 2-3-201 *et seq.*	Mont. Code Ann. § 2-6-101 *et seq.*
NE	Neb. Rev. Stat. § 84-1409 *et seq.*	Neb. Rev. Stat. § 84-712 *et seq.*
NV	Nev. Rev. Stat. § 241 *et seq.*	Nev. Rev. Stat. § 239 *et seq.*
NH	N.H. Rev. Stat. Ann. § 91-A *et seq.*	N.H. Rev. Stat. Ann. § 01-A *et seq.*
NJ	N.J. Stat. Ann. § 10:4 *et seq.*	N.J. Stat. Ann. § 47:1A-1 *et seq.*
NM	N.M. Stat. Ann. § 10-15-1 *et seq.*	N.M. Stat. Ann. § 14-2-1 *et seq.*
NY	N.Y. Pub. Off. Law §103 *et seq.*	N.Y. Pub. Off. Law § 84 *et seq.*
NC	N.C. Gen. Stat. § 143-318.9	N.C. Gen. Stat. § 132-1
ND	N.D. Cent. Code § 44-04-19 *et seq.*	N.D. Cent. Code § 44-04-18 *et seq.*
OH	Ohio Rev. Code Ann. § 121.22 *et seq.*	Ohio Rev. Code Ann. § 149.43 *et seq.*
OK	Okla. Stat. tit. 25, § 301 *et seq.*	Okla. Stat. tit. 51, § 24A.1 *et seq.*
OR	Or. Rev. Stat. § 192.610 *et seq.*	Or. Rev. Stat. § 192.410 *et seq.*
PA	65 Pa. Cons. Stat. § 261 *et. seq.*	65 Pa. Cons. Stat. § 66.1 *et seq.*
RI	R.I. Gen. Laws § 42-46-1	R.I. Gen. Laws § 38-2-1

STATE FREEDOM OF INFORMATION STATUTES

SC	S.C. Code Ann. § 30-4-60	S.C. Code Ann. §30-4-10
SD	S.D. Codified Laws § 1-25-1 *et seq.*	S.D. Codified Laws § 1-27-1 *et seq.*
TN	Tenn. Code Ann. § 8-44-102 *et seq.*	Tenn. Code Ann. §10-7-503 *et seq.*
TX	Tex. Gov't Code Ann. § 551.001	Tex. Gov't Code Ann. § 552.001
UT	Utah Code Ann. § 52-4-1 *et-seq.*	Utah Code Ann. § 63-2-101 *et seq.*
VT	Vt. Stat. Ann. tit. 1, § 310 *et seq.*	Vt. Stat. Ann. tit. 1, § 315 *et seq.*
VA	Va. Code Ann. §§ 2.2-3707 to 3712	Va. Code Ann. §§ 2.2-3704 to 3706
WA	Wash. Rev. Code § 42.30.010 *et seq.*	Wash. Rev. Code § 42.56 *et seq.*
WV	W. Va. Code § 6-9A-1 *et seq.*	W. Va. Code § 29B-1-1 *et seq.*
WI	Wis. Stat. § 19.81 *et seq.*	Wis. Stat. § 19.31 *et seq.*
WY	Wyo. Stat. Ann. § 16-4-201 *et seq.*	Wyo. Stat. Ann. § 16-4-201 *et seq.*

Source: National Freedom of Information Coalition.

http://www.nfoic.org/state-freedom-of-information-laws

The Constitution and Personal Data in Public Records

Prohibited: Establishing post-access restrictions on the disclosure or use of information that is publicly available. Once the information is made available to the public, a state cannot restrict use.

Permitted: Making a record available on *the condition* that certain information is not disclosed or used in a certain manner.

Fla. Star v. B.J.F., 491 U.S. 524 (1989)

"[W]here a newspaper publishes truthful information which it has lawfully obtained, punishment may lawfully be imposed, if at all, only when narrowly tailored to a state interest of the highest order."

L.A. Police Dep't v. United Reporting Publ'g Corp., 528 U.S. 32 (1999)

A state can make the disclosure of certain public records contingent upon a requester agreeing to refrain from disclosing that information for commercial or other purposes. Such a restriction does not trigger the First Amendment because it is "nothing more than a governmental denial of access to information in its possession."

Ostergren v. Cuccinelli, 615 F.3d 263 (4th Cir. 2010)

A law criminalizing the intentional communication of another person's Social Security number (SSN) violated the First Amendment because the law was not narrowly tailored to achieve its goal. The state made records publicly available without redacting SSNs, and taking measures to redact SSNs would be a narrower way of achieving the government interest in protecting the privacy of SSNs.

When Does the Constitution Limit the Government from Disclosing Personal Information?

Disclosure of personal information in public records can trigger the constitutional right to information privacy in *Whalen v. Roe*, 429 U.S. 589 (1977)—"the individual interest in avoiding disclosure of personal matters." Courts will balance the need for disclosure against the privacy interests of the individuals. *See Paul P. v. Verniero*, 170 F.3d 396 (3d Cir. 1999) (Megan's law information); *Kallstrom v. City of Columbus*, 136 F.3d 1055 (6th Cir. 1998) (personal data of police officers).

Critical Infrastructure Information Act of 2002 (CIIA)
6 U.S.C. § 131 *et seq.*

Primary Function: This law creates new safeguards to prevent governmental disclosure of certain kinds of information by crafting a new FOIA exemption.

Applies to: "Critical infrastructure" is a term that refers to systems and assets vital to the United States. The Critical Infrastructure Information Act (CIIA) covers information about these systems and assets that is not customarily in the public domain and is given to the Department of Homeland Security and accompanied by an express statement indicating an expectation of protection from disclosure.

Exemptions from Disclosure: Under the CIIA, critical infrastructure information is exempt from disclosure under FOIA. Unlike FOIA, which permits rather than requires the withholding of information pursuant to its nine exemptions, the CIIA also requires that covered information voluntarily submitted to DHS not be disclosed under FOIA.

PRIVACY RIGHTS IN GOVERNMENT RECORDS

The Privacy Act of 1974
5 U.S.C. § 552a

Primary Function: To regulate the collection, use, and disclosure of personal data by federal agencies.

Applies to: Federal agencies. Does not apply to businesses, private-sector organizations, courts, or state or local governments. Although state and local agencies are not covered by the Privacy Act, the exception to this rule concerns the act's rules for use of the Social Security number.

Protects Citizens and Lawfully Admitted Aliens: The Privacy Act applies only to "a citizen of the United States or an alien lawfully admitted for permanent residence." 5 U.S.C. § 552a(a)(2). In contrast, the FOIA applies more broadly to "any person." 5 U.S.C. § 552(a)(3).

Information Protected: Applies only to a "record" contained within a "system of records." A record must be identifiable to an individual. 5 U.S.C. § 552a(a)(4). The record must be kept as part of a "system of records," which is a group of records retrievable by people's names or other identifying information. 5 U.S.C. § 552a(a)(5).

The Department of Justice has observed, "The highly technical 'system of records' definition is perhaps the single most important Privacy Act concept, because (with some exceptions ...) it makes coverage under the Act dependent upon the method of *retrieval* of the record rather than its substantive content." Office of Privacy & Civil Liberties, U.S. Dep't of Justice, *Overview of the Privacy Act of 1974* (2015).

Limits on Disclosure: Pursuant to the Privacy Act: "No agency shall disclose any record which is contained in a system of records by any means of communication to any person, or to another agency, except pursuant to a written request by, or with prior written consent of, the individual to whom the record pertains." 5 U.S.C. § 552a(b).

Limited Data Collection and Retention: Agencies shall maintain "only such information about an individual as is relevant and necessary to accomplish a purpose of the agency required to be accomplished by statute or by executive order of the President." 5 U.S.C. § 552a(e)(1).

Notice: Agencies shall inform individuals who make a request about how their personal information will be used. Agencies must publish in the *Federal Register* notices about the systems of records they maintain. 5 U.S.C. §§ 552a(e)(3)-(4).

Data Security: Agencies must also "establish appropriate administrative, technical, and physical safeguards to insure the security and confidentiality of records." 5 U.S.C. § 552a(e)(10).

Right to Access and Correct Records: Upon request, individuals can review their records and can ask that the agency correct any inaccuracies in their records. 5 U.S.C. § 552a(d).

Social Security Number (SSN) Usage: The Privacy Act prohibits "any Federal, State, or local government agency" from denying any individual "any right, benefit, or privilege provided by law because" of a refusal to disclosure her SSN. 5 U.S.C. § 552a note (Disclosure of Social Security Number). This provision applies beyond federal agencies. It does not apply, however, to any disclosure that is required by federal statute or disclosures of an SSN that have occurred before January 1, 1975, "if such disclosure was required under statute or regulation adopted prior to such date to verify the identity of an individual."

Enforcement: Civil action and/or injunction. 5 U.S.C. § 552a(g). If the agency "acted in a manner which was intentional or willful," it shall be liable for "actual damages sustained by the individual as a result of the refusal or failure, but in no case shall a person entitled to recovery receive less than the sum of $1,000" and costs and attorney fees. 5 U.S.C. § 552a(g)(4).

Exceptions: The Privacy Act has a number of exceptions for records not covered by the requirements of the statute. These exceptions include, among other things: (1) records for law enforcement and prosecution purposes, (2) records required to be disclosed under FOIA, (3) records disclosed for any "routine use" if disclosure is "compatible" with the purpose for which the agency collected the information, (4) disclosure of records to the Census Bureau, (5) disclosure "to a person pursuant to a showing of compelling circumstances affecting the health or safety of an individual," (6) disclosure to Congress, (7) disclosure to the comptroller general, (8) disclosure pursuant to a court order, and (9) disclosure to a credit reporting agency. 5 U.S.C. § 552a(b).

Establishing a Violation of the Privacy Act

To establish a violation of the Privacy Act, a plaintiff must prove:

1. The information is a "record" contained "within a system of records."

2. The agency violated its obligations under the act.

3. The violation was "willful or intentional."

4. The plaintiff suffered actual damages.

Leading Cases

Doe v. Chao, 540 U.S. 614 (2004)

The Privacy Act provides for "actual damages sustained by the individual as a result of the refusal or failure [to follow the Privacy Act], but in no case shall a person entitled to recovery receive less than the sum of $1,000." The court held that this provision means that plaintiffs must first prove actual damages to qualify for a minimum statutory award of $1,000. The court reasoned that the words "entitled to recovery" meant that only people entitled to recover actual damages could receive the liquidated sum of $1,000.

FAA v. Cooper, 132 S.Ct. 1441 (2012)

"Actual damages" under the Privacy Act does not extend to damages for mental or emotional distress but only to damages for pecuniary harm.

Pippinger v. Rubin, 129 F.3d 519 (10th Cir. 1997)

Disclosure of records does not violate an individual's rights under the "routine use" exception of 5 U.S.C. § 552a(b)(3) if such records were maintained "for the purpose of properly administering" the workplace and its systems.

U.S. Dep't of Defense v. Fed. Labor Relations Auth., 510 U.S. 487 (1994)

The Privacy Act does not apply to information that must be disclosed under FOIA. If a FOIA privacy exemption applies to the information, however, then the Privacy Act would control and require that the government refrain from disclosing the information to third parties.

Albright v. United States, 631 F.2d 915 (D.C. Cir. 1980)

A videotape of a meeting can be a "record" under the Privacy Act if it "contains a means of identifying an individual by picture or voice."

Quinn v. Stone, 978 F.2d 126 (3d Cir. 1992)

Even publicly accessible information is protected against disclosure.

State Privacy Acts

Most states do not have a statute comparable to the federal Privacy Act. California, Massachusetts, Minnesota, New York, and Wisconsin do have such statutes. These states also supplement these omnibus privacy acts for state agencies with more narrowly targeted laws. In the states without such a broad information practices law, there are often narrow laws regulating limited aspects of the state government's use of personal information.

California's Information Practices Act of 1977, Cal. Civ. Code § 1798 et seq.
Establishes a number of fair information practices for state agencies, including limitations on the collection of unnecessary data. Cal. Civ. Code § 1798 et seq., § 1798.3-14. The act requires that agencies maintain in their records only information "relevant and necessary to accomplish a purpose of the agency required or authorized by the California Constitution or statute or mandated by the federal government." Id. It places general limits on secondary limits of information that agencies collect. It also provides numerous statutory exceptions that permit disclosures of such information. § 1798.24. The sharing of data with governmental agencies outside the state government, such as with federal agencies or agencies in other states, can take place in California only when a state or federal law requires that information be transferred. § 1798.24(f). Individuals have a right to inspect and amend their personal information in agency records. § 1798.32.

Massachusetts' Fair Information Practices Act, Mass. Gen. Laws ch. 66A (1975)
Sets requirements for a "holder" of personal information. It defines a "holder" as "an agency which collects, uses, maintains or disseminates personal data or any person or entity which contracts or has an arrangement with an agency." Mass. Gen. Laws ch. 66A, § 1. A holder maintaining personal data must identify one individual responsible for ensuring that the law's requirements are followed. Id. § 2(a). Holders must

"maintain personal data with such accuracy, completeness, timeliness, pertinence and relevance as is necessary to assure fair determination of a data subject's qualifications, character, rights, opportunities or benefits when such determinations are made based upon such data." *Id.* § 2(h). The law also requires that the data subject be notified of "a demand for data made by means of compulsory legal process." Id. § 2(k).

Minnesota Government Data Practices Act, Minn. Stat. § 13.01 *et seq.* (1974)

Establishes statutory obligations and responsibilities for all government entities that collect, process, and disseminate personal information. Minn. Stat. Ann. 13.01 et seq. A state agency must clearly inform the individual about its purposes when collecting personal data as well as the parties authorized by law to receive the data. § 13.04(2). The act allows agencies to share nonpublic data with one another only when such access is specifically authorized or required by state statute or federal law, by the informed consent of the data subject or pursuant to other exceptions. § 13.05(4). Additionally, individuals have a right to access their records. § 13.04(3).

New York's Personal Privacy Protection Act N.Y. Pub. Off. Law §§ 91-99 (1983)

Fair Information Practices for each state agency "that maintains a system of records." N.Y. Pub. Off. Law § 94. These begin with the requirement that an agency "maintain in its records only such personal information which is relevant and necessary to accomplish a purpose of the agency required to be accomplished by statute or executive order, or to implement a program specifically authorized by law." Such records, when used "to make any determination about any data subject," must also be maintained with "accuracy, relevance, timeliness and completeness." Detailed notice of planned use of the information and other relevant issues is to be provided to the data subject at the time of the initial request. Id. § 94(d). State agencies are to provide access to their records to data subjects. Id. § 95. Finally, the act forbids release of personal information unless it falls into one of its exceptions to the general rule barring disclosure. Id. § 96.

Wisconsin's Personal Information Practices Act, Wisc. Stat. §§ 19.62-.80 (1991)

Sets standards for state agencies in their use of personal information. Wisc. Stat. §§ 19.62-.80. These limitations include procedural limits on computer matching. Id. § 19.69. This approach generally tracks that of the federal Computer Matching and Privacy Protection Act (CMPAA). Wisconsin law also forbids state government websites from collecting personally identifiable information from Internet users. Id. § 19.68. It provides an exception, however, for acquisition of IP addresses. It also forbids the state from selling or renting "a record containing an individual's name or address of residence, unless specifically authorized by state law." Id. § 19.71.

State Statutes Regulating Government Website Privacy Policies

AZ	Ariz. Rev. Stat. Ann. §§ 41-4151 to 41-4152
AR	Ark. Code Ann. § 25-1-114
CA	Cal. Govt. Code § 11019.9
CO	Colo. Rev. Stat. §§ 24-72-501 to 24-72-502
DE	Del. Code Ann. tit. 29, § 9017C *et seq.*
IA	Iowa Code § 22.11
IL	5 Ill. Comp. Stat. § 177/15
ME	Me. Rev. Stat. Ann. tit. 1, §§ 541-542
MI	2003 Mich Pub. Acts 83
MN	Minn. Stat. § 13.15
MT	Mont. Code Ann. §§ 2-17-550 to - 553
NY	N.Y . State Tech. Law §§ 201-207
SC	S.C. Code Ann. § 30-2-40
TX	Tex. Gov't Code Ann. § 10-2054.126
UT	Utah Code Ann. §§ 63D-2-101 to -104
VA	Va. Code Ann. §§ 2.2-3800 to -3803

Computer Matching and Privacy Protection Act of 1988 (CMPPA), 5 U.S.C. § 552a(o) *et seq.*

The CMPPA amends the Privacy Act to establish procedures for federal agencies engaging in computer matching of records. The CMPPA does not restrict matching programs; instead, it requires agencies to promulgate procedures and provide notice prior to matching. Agencies desiring to implement a matching program must establish a data integrity board and obtain approval from this board. The Office of Management and Budget (OMB) oversees matching programs.

DNA Databases

DNA Identification Act of 1994
42 U.S.C. §§ 14131-14135
The DNA Identification Act establishes rules for the FBI's index of DNA identification records, called the Combined DNA Index System (CODIS). The database consists of DNA samples from people convicted of a crime or charged with a crime, as well as samples recovered from crime scenes. The statute also sets out the information to be contained in this index and the circumstances under which the data is to be disclosed to other agencies and individuals. 43 U.S.C. § 14133(b)(1)(A)-(C). DNA

records can be expunged from CODIS if the conviction that led to inclusion in the index is overturned or the arrest that resulted in inclusion results in dismissed charges or acquittal. *Id.* § 14132(d).

Leading Cases

U.S. v. Kincade, 379 F.3d 813 (9th Cir. 2004)
The government may store a parolee's DNA and subject the parolee to a blood test without violating the Fourth Amendment, which prohibits unreasonable searches and seizures.

Maryland v. King, 133 S. Ct. 1958 (2013)
Following an arrest supported by probable cause for a serious offense, the government may bring the suspect to the station to be detained in custody and also take and analyze a cheek swab of the arrestee's DNA without violating the Fourth Amendment.

Driver's Privacy Protection Act of 1994 (DPPA)
18 U.S.C. §§ 2721–2725

Primary Function: Regulates the collection, use, and disclosure of motor vehicle records.

Protections: States cannot knowingly disclose personal information in motor vehicle records for a purpose not permitted by the DPPA. 18 U.S.C. § 2721(a). No person can knowingly obtain, use, or disclose personal information from a motor vehicle record for purposes beyond those permitted by the statute. *Id.* § 2724(a).

DPPA: Key Points

- DPPA does not just regulate states—it regulates anyone who obtains, uses, or discloses personal data from motor vehicle records.
- Even if data is properly obtained under the DPPA, the statute can be violated if data is later used or disclosed improperly.

Exclusions: The DPPA defines "personal information" as data "that identifies an individual," but it specifically excludes "information on vehicular accidents, driving violations and driver's status." 18 U.S.C. § 2725(3).

Permissible Uses: DPPA-protected information can be disclosed: (1) for use by any government agency; (2) for motor vehicle safety, theft, recalls, and other related matters; (3) for use by a legitimate business to verify personal data submitted by the individual or to obtain correct information to prevent fraud, pursue litigation, or recover a debt; (4) in connection with litigation or other legal proceeding; (5) for use in research; (6) for use by insurers for fraud investigation or underwriting; (7) to provide notice to owners of towed or impounded vehicles; (8) for use by a licensed private investigator; (9) for use by an employer to verify information relating to a holder of a commercial driver's license; (10) for use in the operation of private toll transportation facilities; (11) with the express consent of the person to whom the information pertains; (12) for bulk distribution for surveys, marketing, and solicitation with express consent of the person to whom the information pertains; (13) for use by any requester after obtaining the express consent of the person to whom the information pertains or (14) for any other use specifically authorized by state law if such use involves motor vehicle operation or public safety. 18 U.S.C. § 2721(b).

Opt In: In order to disclose a driver's personal information for marketing or other restricted uses, the driver must affirmatively indicate her consent (opt in). 18 U.S.C. § 2721(b), (d).

Enforcement: Civil liability and criminal fines. Private right of action when a person "knowingly obtains, discloses or uses personal information from a motor vehicle record for a purpose not permitted under this chapter." 18 U.S.C. § 2724.

Leading Cases

Reno v. Condon, 528 U.S. 141 (2000)
DPPA is a valid exercise of Congress's Commerce Clause powers because personal identifying information is a thing in interstate commerce.

Kehoe v. Fid. Fed. Bank & Trust, 421 F.3d 1209 (11th Cir. 2005)
"A plaintiff need not prove a measure of actual damages to recover liquidated damages under the DPPA, and certainly need not prove actual damages to recover the other types of remedies listed in § 2724(b)."

Pichler v. UNITE, 542 F.3d 380 (3d Cir. 2008)
For civil liability, a defendant does not need to know that its obtaining, use, or disclosure of information is prohibited by DPPA; acting "knowingly" only requires knowledge of the obtaining, use, or disclosure, not its impermissibility.

Senne v. Village of Palatine, 695 F.3d 597 (7th Cir. 2012)
Placement of personal data from DMV records such as sex, age, height, weight, and home address on parking citations left on cars in public violated DPPA. The disclosure of the data on the citation did not fall under DPPA's exceptions for carrying out law enforcement agency functions or for use in connection with any legal proceedings. The disclosure of the data was more than the minimum necessary to achieve the law enforcement purpose.

Identification Records and Requirements

Leading Cases

Kolender v. Lawson, 461 U.S. 352 (1983)
A law requiring any person who "loiters or wanders . . . without apparent reason or business" to "identify himself and to account for his presence when requested by any peace officer to do so" was struck down as unconstitutionally vague.

Carey v. Nev. Gaming Control Bd., 279 F.3d 873 (9th Cir. 2002)
Statutes requiring individuals detained by officials to identify themselves or face criminal sanctions were struck down as violating the Fourth Amendment because the statutes did not require probable cause or any type of suspicion on the part of the officials.

Hiibel v. Sixth Judicial Dist. Court, 542 U.S. 177 (2004)
Upholding a Nevada statute permitting officers to stop and to request the name of an individual based on reasonable and articulable suspicion of criminal involvement. This statute did not violate the Fourth Amendment.

Social Security Numbers

The closest thing that the United States has to a national identifier is the Social Security number (SSN). A nine-digit identifier, the SSN was created in 1936 as part of the Social Security System.

Section 7 of the Privacy Act of 1974 prohibits any governmental agency from denying any right, benefit, or privilege merely because an individual refused to disclose his or her SSN.

Several states have passed laws providing special protections against the use and disclosure of SSNs.

Leading Cases

Greidinger v. Davis, 988 F.2d 1344 (4th Cir. 1993)
Virginia statute requiring disclosure of voters' SSNs was not narrowly tailored to advance a compelling state interest.

State ex rel. Beacon Journal Publ'g Co. v. City of Akron, 640 N.E.2d 164 (Ohio 1994)
SSNs were not considered "public records" for the purposes of Ohio's Public Records Act.

City of Kirkland v. Sheehan, No. 01-2-09513-7 SEA, 2001 WL 1751590 (Wash. Super. Ct. May 10, 2001)
Disclosure of police officers' personal data was protected under the First Amendment, except for the disclosure of SSNs.

REAL ID Act of 2005, Pub. L. No. 109-13 (codified as amended in scattered sections of 8 U.S.C.)
This law seeks to prevent the fraudulent issuance or use of official state identification documents. It does so by prohibiting federal agencies from accepting for official purposes state-issued driver's licenses and ID cards that do not meet certain mandated standards. The REAL ID Act assigns the task of establishing these standards to the Department of Homeland Security (DHS). Among the resulting standards are that

Privacy Law Fundamentals

a state driver's license or ID must incorporate anti-counterfeit technology. A state must also verify the applicant's identity pursuant to DHS requirements and conduct background checks on those employees who issue these identity documents.

Final Phase of REAL ID Implementation
On January 22, 2016, the DHS announced the schedule for the final phase of implementation of the REAL ID act. At the time of the announcement, only 23 states were fully in compliance with the REAL ID Act. DHS had granted 27 states and territories extensions because of their demonstration of steps taken toward compliance. Six states and territories were noncompliant and without extensions. These were Illinois, Minnesota, Missouri, New Mexico, Washington, and American Samoa.

DHS's new REAL ID requirements: effective January 22, 2018, air travelers with driver's licenses or ID cards not meeting the REAL ID Act requirements will be required to present an alternative identification form, such as a passport, before boarding.

GOVERNMENT PRIVACY AND SECURITY MANAGEMENT

E-Government Act of 2002
44 U.S.C. § 208
Section 208 of the E-Government Act requires all federal agencies to conduct a Privacy Impact Assessment (PIA) whenever they develop a new technology involving the collection, use, or disclosure of personal data. Under applicable OMB guidance for implementing the E-Government Act, PIAs are to identify and evaluate potential threats to individual privacy, identify appropriate risk mitigation measures, and explain the rationale behind the final design choice.

Federal Information Security Management Act of 2002 (FISMA)
44 U.S.C. § 3541
Enacted as part of the E-Government Act, FISMA aims to provide a "comprehensive framework" for data security to protect federal information systems. Federal agencies must designate a chief information officer (CIO), develop an information security program, and evaluate the effectiveness of information security policies and practices.

Office of Mgmt. & Budget
Circular No. A-130 (2016)
In its Circular A-130, the OMB sets policy and provides guidance on information technology management for federal executive agencies. Before the Obama Administration issued this update to it in July 2016, Circular A-130 had last been revised in 2000. This update focused on such areas as cyber-security, information governance, privacy, security, and open data. Perhaps most crucially, Circular A-130 calls for strong data governance by the Federal Government to proactively identify risks to privacy and security and to identify and test practical solutions to risk.

FOR FURTHER REFERENCE

Treatises

Office of Info. Policy, U.S. Dep't of Justice, *Guide to the Freedom of Information Act* (2016)
Comprehensive and highly useful guide to FOIA, available on the DOJ's website.

Office of Privacy & Civil Liberties, U.S. Dep't of Justice, *Overview of the Privacy Act of 1974* (2015)
Comprehensive and highly useful guide to the Privacy Act, available on the DOJ's website.

Richard J. Pierce, *Administrative Law Treatise* (5th ed., 2015)
Leading administrative law treatise features detailed analysis of FOIA and other open government acts.

Jacob A. Stein & Glenn A. Mitchell, *Administrative Law* (2016)
The third volume of this multivolume treatise examines the FOIA and Privacy Act.

Books

James B. Jacobs, *The Eternal Criminal Record* (2015)
Examines problems with current criminal recordkeeping.

Articles and Other Sources

Kenneth A. Bamberger & Deirdre K. Mulligan, *Privacy Decisionmaking in Administrative Agencies,* **75 U. Chi. L. Rev. 75 (2008)**
Explores the different paths taken for the development of PIAs by the Department of Homeland Security and the Department of State.

Anthony T. Kronman, *The Privacy Exemption to the Freedom of Information Act,* **9 J. Legal Stud. 727 (1980)**
Classic article about FOIA and privacy.

Erin Murphy, *License, Registration, Cheek Swab: DNA Testing and the Divided Court,* **127 Harv. L. Rev. 161 (2013)**
Criticizes *Maryland v. King,* 133 S. Ct. 1958 (2013), and argues that the Supreme Court broadly embraced expansive forensic DNA testing without meaningful oversight.

Erin Murphy, *The Mismatch Between Twenty-First-Century Forensic Evidence and Our Antiquated Criminal Justice System,* **87 S. Cal. L. Rev. 633 (2014)**
Argues that the adversarial process is ill suited to twenty-first-century evidence—such as location tracking, biometrics, digital forensics, and other database-driven techniques.

Priscilla M. Regan, *Legislating Privacy: Technology, Social Values, and Public Policy* **(1995)**
Background of congressional enactment of leading privacy laws, including the Privacy Act of 1974.

Daniel J. Solove, *Access and Aggregation: Public Records, Privacy, and the Constitution,* **86 Minn. L. Rev. 1137 (2002)**
Examines the tension between transparency and privacy in the context of public records.

Lior Jacob Strahilevitz, *Pseudonymous Litigation,* **77 U. Chi. L. Rev. 1239 (2010)**
Argues that in certain instances it will be optimal for the legal system to permit a party to litigate to final judgment using a pseudonym and only then to consider revealing the litigant's identity at the conclusion of proceedings.

Peter A. Winn, *Online Court Records: Balancing Judicial Accountability and Privacy in an Age of Electronic Information,* **79 Wash. L. Rev. 307 (2004)**
Numerous new privacy issues are being raised as court records are digitized and made accessible online.

CHAPTER 8

Financial Data

ESSENTIAL POINTS

The Financial Services Industry

- The applicable regulation of financial information turns on the legal category in which the data falls or the industry that processes the information. For example, the Fair Credit Reporting Act applies to "any consumer reporting agency" that furnishes a "consumer report." The Gramm-Leach-Bliley Act applies to all financial institutions.

- Tort regulations, such as breach of confidentiality and negligence, can set common law standards for the processing and storage of personal information.

- A special federal statute, Internal Revenue Code § 6103, regulates access to federal tax return information. This law provides for numerous exceptions to the general rule of tax return confidentiality.

- Many important regulations for financial information occur at the state level.

- As in other areas of information privacy, California has its own regulations in place for financial information. Its SB1 requires opt-in sharing for financial institutions that share data with nonaffiliated companies. Vermont has issued a similar rule.

Fair Credit Reporting Act of 1970 (FCRA)
15 U.S.C. §§ 1681 *et seq.*

Primary Function: To regulate the consumer reporting industry and provide privacy rights in consumer reports.

Scope: FCRA applies to "any consumer reporting agency" that furnishes a "consumer report." 15 U.S.C. § 1681b(a).

Key Definitions: The key definitions under FCRA are what constitutes a "consumer report" and what constitutes a "consumer reporting agency" (CRA):

1. *Consumer Report:* A "consumer report" is any communication by a consumer reporting agency relating to a consumer's creditworthiness, reputation, and character that is for the purpose of determining eligibility for credit, insurance, employment, or other authorized purposes under § 1681b (see permissible uses of credit reports below). 15 U.S.C. § 1681a(d).

2. *Consumer Reporting Agency:* A "consumer reporting agency" is any person who regularly assembles or evaluates consumer credit information for the purpose of furnishing consumer reports to third parties. 15 U.S.C. § 1681a(f).

FCRA Applicability Is Determined by the Purpose of Original Collection: Courts have held that "even if a report is used or expected to be used for a non-consumer purpose, it may still fall within the definition of a consumer report if it contains information that was originally collected by a consumer reporting agency with the expectation that it would be used for a consumer purpose." *Ippolito v. WNS, Inc.*, 864 F.2d 440 (7th Cir. 1988); *Bakker v. McKinnon*, 152 F.3d 1007 (8th Cir. 1998).

Permissible Uses of Consumer Reports: A consumer reporting agency can furnish a consumer report only for certain uses. These uses also define FCRA's applicability—if any entity collects information for these purposes in order to provide it to others, then it becomes a consumer reporting agency. Permissible purposes include: (1) providing it in response to a court order or grand jury subpoena; (2) providing it to the person to whom the report pertains; (3) providing it to a "person which [the agency] has reason to believe" intends to use the information in connection with (a) the extension of credit to a consumer, (b) employment purposes, (c) insurance underwriting, (d) licensing or the conferral of government benefits, (e) assessment of credit risks associated with an existing credit obligation or (f) a "legitimate business need" when engaging in "a business transaction involving the consumer"; (4) providing it to establish a person's capacity to pay child support; (5) providing it to an agency administering a state plan for use to set initial or modified child support award; or (6) providing it to the FDIC or National Credit Union Administration. 15 U.S.C. § 1681b(a).

Employment Purposes: When an employer or potential employer seeks a consumer report for employment purposes, she must first disclose in writing to the consumer that a consumer report may be obtained, and the consumer must authorize in writing that the report can be obtained. The person seeking the report from a consumer reporting agency must certify that she obtained the consent of the individual and that she will not use the information in violation of any equal employment opportunity law or regulation. 15 U.S.C. § 1681b(b). If the person who obtained the report takes adverse action based in any way on the report, she must provide the consumer with a copy of the report and a description of the consumer's rights under the FCRA. *Id.*

Government Access: Pursuant to the FCRA, "a consumer reporting agency may furnish identifying information respecting any customer, limited to his name, address, former addresses, places of employment, or former places of employment, to a governmental agency." 15 U.S.C. § 1681f.

The Consumer Financial Protection Bureau

The Dodd-Frank Act of 2010 assigned a new federal agency, the Consumer Financial Protection Bureau (CFPB), primary federal authority for enforcement and rule making regarding the FCRA. The CFPB is an independent agency located within the Federal Reserve. It is also funded by the Federal Reserve.

The Dodd-Frank Act also creates a Consumer Financial Civil Penalty Fund to receive civil penalties obtained by the CFPB for violations of consumer financial protection statutes. The fund is to be used to pay victims of these violations and to support financial literacy and consumer education programs.

The Dodd-Frank Act gives the CFPB broad rule-making authority to "administer and carry out the purposes and objectives of" FCRA and "to prevent evasions thereof." 12 U.S.C. § 5512(b)(1). It also has broad powers of supervision and examination of financial institutions in the market for consumer financial products or services. Finally, the CFPB has enforcement powers over FCRA and a number of other consumer protection laws, including the Electronic Funds Transfer Act, the Fair Debt Collection Practices Act and certain sections of the Gramm-Leach-Bliley Act.

Under the Dodd-Frank Act, however, the FTC retains rule-making authority regarding the Disposal Rule, the Red Flags Rule, and the Gramm-Leach-Bliley Act's Safeguards Rule. The FTC also retains power to carry out certain kinds of investigations and shares power with the CFPB to enforce consumer protection laws with regard to nonbank financial institutions.

CFPB & FTC, *Memorandum of Understanding (MOU) Between the Consumer Financial Protection Bureau and the Federal Trade Commission* (**Jan. 20, 2012**) MOU jointly issued by FTC and CFPB in light of the grant of FCRA enforcement power to CFPB in the Dodd-Frank Act. The agencies have agreed to meet regularly to coordinate enforcement actions, inform the other agency before initiating enforcement actions to avoid duplicative enforcement efforts, consult on rulemaking and guidance initiatives, cooperate on consumer education efforts, and share consumer complaints.

Limitations on Information Contained in Consumer Reports: Consumer reporting agencies are excluded from providing certain information in consumer reports. 15 U.S.C. § 1681c(a)-(b).

CREDIT REPORTING LIMITS		
	WHEN DISCLOSURE IS PROHIBITED	WHEN DISCLOSURE IS ALWAYS ALLOWED
Bankruptcy Proceedings	> 10 years old	Credit transaction > $150,000
Suits and Judgments	> 7 years old	Life Insurance Policy > $150,000
Paid Tax Liens	> 7 years old	Employment Salary > $75,000
Criminal Records	> 7 years old	

Investigative Consumer Reports: An "investigative consumer report" is "a consumer report or portion thereof in which information on a consumer's character, general reputation, personal characteristics, or mode of living is obtained through personal interviews with neighbors, friends, or associates." 15 U.S.C. § 1681a(e). Consumers must be notified about the preparation of these reports. If the report contains any adverse information about a person gleaned from interviews with neighbors, friends or associates, the agency must take reasonable steps to corroborate that information "from an additional source that has independent and direct knowledge of the information" or ensure that "the person interviewed is the best possible source of the information." 15 U.S.C. § 1681d(d)(4).

Accuracy: "Whenever a consumer reporting agency prepares a consumer report it shall follow reasonable procedures to assure maximum possible accuracy of the information concerning the individual about whom the report relates." § 1681e(b).

Disclosures to the Consumer: The FCRA requires that consumer reporting agencies, upon request of the consumer, disclose, among other things, "[a]ll information in the consumer's file at the time of the request, except ... any information concerning credit scores or any other risk scores or predictors relating to the consumer" as well as the sources of the information and a list of each person who procured a consumer report. 15 U.S.C. § 1681g.

Procedures in Case of Disputed Accuracy: Consumers can dispute the completeness or accuracy of information in their file. The agency must reinvestigate free of charge. 15 U.S.C. § 1681i(a)(1). Errors must be fixed promptly. "If the reinvestigation does not resolve the dispute, the consumer may file a brief statement setting forth the nature of the dispute." 15 U.S.C. § 1681i(b). In any subsequent consumer report, the agency must "clearly note" that the information in question "is disputed by the consumer" and provide the consumer's statement. 15 U.S.C. § 1681i(c).

Requirements on Users of Consumer Reports: If a user of a consumer report takes any adverse action on a consumer based in any way on the report, the user shall provide notice of the adverse action to the consumer, information for the consumer to contact the consumer reporting agency that prepared the report and notice of the consumer's right to obtain a free copy of the report and to dispute its accuracy. 15 U.S.C. § 1681m(a).

Civil Liability: A person who "willfully fails to comply with any requirement" of the FCRA is liable to the consumer for actual damages or damages between $100 and $1,000, as well as punitive damages and attorneys' fees and costs. 15 U.S.C. § 1681n. Negligent failure to comply with any requirement of the FCRA results in liability to the consumer for actual damages as well as attorneys' fees and costs. *Id.* The FTC also has the power to enforce the FCRA.

One-Call Fraud Alerts: When a consumer alerts one consumer reporting agency of potential fraud, that agency must notify the other consumer reporting agencies. 15 U.S.C. § 1681c-1.

Business Transaction Data: Victims of identity theft can require creditors to disclose information about the fraudulent transactions carried out in the victim's name. 15 U.S.C. § 1681g(e)(1).

Block of Identity Theft Information: FCRA allows identity theft victims to block the reporting of information related to the identity theft. 15 U.S.C. § 1681c-2.

Free Consumer Reports: Consumer reporting agencies must provide a free consumer report once a year at the request of a consumer. Consumers can obtain their reports at http://annualcreditreport.com.

Statute of Limitations: FCRA's statute of limitation extends to two years after the date when the plaintiff discovers the violation or five years after the date of the violation, whichever occurs earlier.

Enforcement: FCRA creates liability for willfully or negligently failing to comply with its requirements:

1. *Willful Violations:* People can recover actual damages or statutory damages between $100 and $1,000 for willful violations, plus punitive damages and attorneys' fees and costs. 15 U.S.C. § 1681n. "Willful" means that one intentionally commits an act "in conscious disregard for the rights of others." In *Safeco Ins. Co. of Am. v. Burr,* 551 U.S. 47 (2007), the Supreme Court held that acting in "reckless disregard" of a consumer's rights under FCRA was sufficient to establish willfulness.

2. *Negligent Violations:* People can recover actual damages as a result of negligent violations plus attorneys' fees and costs. 15 U.S.C. § 1681o.

Qualified Immunity: FCRA provides for civil liability for willful and negligent noncompliance. 15 U.S.C. §§ 1681n-1681o. Beyond these provisions in FCRA, "no consumer may bring any action or proceeding in the nature of defamation, invasion of privacy, or negligence with respect to the reporting of information against any consumer reporting agency, any user of information, or any person who furnishes information to a consumer reporting agency, based on information disclosed pursuant to [FCRA]." The only exception to this immunity is for "false information furnished with malice or willful intent to injure such consumer." § 1681h(e).

Preemption: After amendment through the Fair and Accurate Credit Transactions Act of 2003 (FACTA), FCRA has complicated measures in place for preemption. Sometimes it preempts state laws for certain kinds of subject matters. 15 USC § 1681t(b). At other times, FCRA preempts only for certain required conduct. *Id.* § 1681t(b)(5). This kind of preemption restricts the assignment of federal power only to the behavior mandated. For example, FACTA requires consumer reporting agencies to place fraud alerts on consumer credit files under certain circumstances. Beyond this conduct preemption, however, it allows states to engage in further regulation regarding the larger subject area, which is identity theft.

FCRA: Keys to Compliance

1. FCRA applies only to a "consumer reporting agency" that furnishes a "consumer report." Many uses of financial information fall outside its jurisdictional scope.

2. Important restrictions are placed on certain kinds of information by FCRA simply because of the age of the underlying information.

3. Once a consumer report contains certain kinds of information relating to the consumer's character and gained through interviews, the credit reporting agency must meet additional safeguards.

4. The overall touchstone of FCRA is to follow "reasonable procedures to assure maximum possible accuracy of the information" about the concerned individual.

Leading Cases

Spokeo, Inc. v. Robins, 136 S. Ct. 1540 (2016)
Not all FCRA violations qualify for standing, despite congressional intent for the statute to create a private cause of action. To demonstrate the necessary "injury in fact" from the dissemination of false information, plaintiffs must also show a "concrete harm." The concrete harm need not be "tangible," and a sufficient risk of real harm may qualify, but a "bare procedural violation" is insufficient.

Dun & Bradstreet, Inc. v. Greenmoss Builders, Inc., 472 U.S. 749 (1985)

A consumer reporting agency reporting on an individual is engaging in "speech on matters of purely private concern" and its report receives lesser First Amendment protection than other forms of speech. All forms of damages (compensatory, presumed, and punitive) are available without showing "actual malice."

Sarver v. Experian Info. Sols., 390 F.3d 969 (7th Cir. 2004)

Seventh Circuit finds that FCRA does not require each credit reporting agency to examine each credit report for "anomalous information" in order for its procedures to be considered reasonable. Such an examination is not needed in the "absence of notice of prevalent unreliable information from a reporting lender."

Dennis v. BEH-1, LLC, 520 F.3d 1066 (9th Cir. 2008)

Ninth Circuit finds that a credit reporting agency can be liable under FCRA when it overlooks or misinterprets documents in a court file. After the plaintiff notified the credit reporting agency of the error in its report, the credit reporting agency failed to follow reasonable procedures by incorrectly interpreting a registry entry in a court's file and a legal document of which it had received a copy. The Ninth Circuit stated, "This case illustrates how important it is for Experian, a company that traffics in the reputation of ordinary people, to train its employees to understand the legal significance of the documents they rely upon."

Sloane v. Equifax Info. Servs., LLC, 510 F.3d 495 (4th Cir. 2007)

Equifax failed to correct errors in Sloane's credit report 21 months after she had reported them. The Fourth Circuit upholds the verdict that Equifax violated FCRA by negligently failing to, among other things, "follow reasonable procedures designed to assure maximum accuracy on her consumer credit report" and "failing to conduct a reasonable investigation to determine whether disputed information in her credit report was inaccurate."

Sweet v. LinkedIn Corp., No. 5:14-cv-04531-PSG, 2015 WL 1744254 (N.D. Cal. Apr. 14, 2015)

LinkedIn's "References Searches" feature, which allowed employers to find people with whom a prospective employee may have worked, did not qualify as a FCRA "consumer report." The report's contents were entirely derived from self-provided information, which is exempted under the statute. Moreover, the district court found that LinkedIn did not qualify under FCRA as a "consumer reporting agency"; the contested feature was only furthering the user's "information-sharing objectives."

FTC FCRA Enforcement Actions

United States v. Teletrack, Inc., No. 11-cv-2060 (N.D. Ga. June 24, 2011)

Teletrack sold credit reports to various lenders and created a database of information gleaned from this business. It then sold the database to marketers. The FTC charged that Teletrack violated FCRA because marketing was not a "permissible purpose" under FCRA. The settlement included a $1.8 million penalty.

***United States v. Spokeo*, No. 2:12-cv-05001-MMM-SH (N.D. Cal. June 19, 2012)**
Spokeo, a data broker, settled with the FTC for marketing consumer profiles to
employers without complying with FCRA. FCRA's scope is based on the way data
is used. It limits the use of data even in the context of determinations of eligibility
for employment. FCRA's applicability turns on the way the data is marketed and on
the amount used by entities that typically use data to evaluate employment eligibility. The FTC did not accept as valid Spokeo's disclaimer that it was not a consumer
reporting agency. Spokeo agreed to pay $800,000 to settle the FTC charges.

***United States v. HireRight Sols., Inc.*, No. 1:12-cv-01313 (D.D.C. Aug. 8, 2012)**
HireRight, an employment background screening company, is subject to FCRA
because its reports are "consumer reports." HireRight did not follow many FCRA
requirements. In its settlement with the FTC, it agreed to pay a $2.6 million penalty.

***United States v. TeleCheck Servs., Inc.*, No. 1:14-cv-00062 (D.D.C. Jan. 17, 2014)**
TeleCheck is a leading check authorization service company. It provides recommendations to merchants as to whether or not to accept checks from consumers.
In its complaint, the FTC argued that the check authorization recommendations of
TeleCheck were consumer reports under the FCRA. Although its practices were
regulated by this statute, TeleCheck violated FCRA by failing to follow its procedures
for disputed information, including reinvestigations of the information and providing FCRA-required notice to consumers. It was also alleged to have failed to follow
reasonable procedures to assure the maximum possible accuracy of the information
that it provided to merchants. TeleCheck agreed to a $3.5 million penalty, the second
largest obtained by the FTC in an FRCA case. TeleCheck also agreed to follow all
FCRA requirements, including those for reinvestigations of disputes and notice to
consumers.

***United States v. Certegy Check Servs., Inc.*, No. 1:13-cv-01247
(D.D.C. Aug. 15, 2013)**
According to the FTC's complaint, Certegy, a leading check authorization service
company, was also a consumer reporting agent (CRA) under the FCRA. Moreover,
the FTC alleged that Certegy was also a "nationwide specialty consumer reporting
agency" with additional responsibilities under the FCRA section 603(x). Certegy
violated the Fair Credit Reporting Act by failing: (1) to follow proper reasonable
procedures to assure maximum possible accuracy of consumers' report information;
(2) to reinvestigate disputed information; and (3) to provide consumers with an
annual file disclosure as required by law. Certegy agreed to a $3.5 million civil penalty
and to follow required procedures for tracking the handling of customer disputes and
correcting inaccuracies in a credit report.

***In re Filiquarian Publ'g, LLC*, FTC No. C-4401 (Apr. 30, 2013)**
This settlement was the first FCRA case involving mobile apps. Filiquarian, Choice
Level, and CEO Linsk (respondents) were responsible for a mobile app that com-
piled and sold criminal record reports from specific states. It advertised its service as

allowing individuals to conduct a "quick criminal background check for convictions" in specific states. It also had provided a disclaimer in its "terms and conditions" stating that its products were not to be considered "screening products" for employment, credit, and certain other purposes. Its disclaimer also stated that the company was not compliant with FCRA and that any person using its product for FCRA purposes would assume sole responsibility for compliance with this statute and any other applicable laws. Despite this disclaimer, the FTC alleged that Filiquarian was a consumer reporting agency and had violated the law by failing to comply with required FCRA procedures. Its disclaimers could not be used to avoid FCRA liability because the company had advertised that its reports could be used by customers for employment purposes and could expect such use of its reports. Under the terms of the settlement, the respondents agreed to follow the FCRA and only to furnish reports to persons who have a "permissible purpose" under the statute and "maintain reasonable procedures to assure the maximum possible accuracy" of information.

THE USE AND DISCLOSURE OF FINANCIAL INFORMATION

Gramm-Leach-Bliley Act of 1999 (GLBA)
15 U.S.C. §§ 6801–6809

Primary Function: To facilitate data sharing among financial institutions and their affiliates while protecting customer privacy.

Applies to: All financial institutions.

Key Definition—Nonpublic Personal Information: The privacy provisions of the GLBA apply only to "nonpublic personal information" that consists of "personally identifiable financial information." 15 U.S.C. § 6809(4).

Sharing of Information with Affiliated Companies: Financial institutions can share nonpublic personal information with affiliates. Customers must be provided notice via a general privacy policy. No right to opt out. 15 U.S.C. § 6802(a).

Sharing of Information with Third Parties: Financial institutions can share nonpublic personal information with nonaffiliated companies only if they first provide individuals with the ability to opt out of the disclosure. 15 U.S.C. § 6802(b). The financial institution must have a contract with the third party requiring it to maintain the confidentiality of the information. These provisions do not apply to disclosures to consumer reporting agencies.

Limits on Disclosure: Financial institutions cannot disclose (other than to consumer reporting agencies) account numbers or credit card numbers for use in direct marketing. 15 U.S.C. § 6802(d).

Privacy Notices: The GLBA requires that financial institutions inform customers of their privacy policies. 15 U.S.C. § 6803(a).

Security: Financial institutions "shall develop, implement, and maintain a comprehensive information security program." 16 C.F.R. § 314.3(a).

Preemption: The GLBA does not preempt state laws that provide greater privacy protection. 15 U.S.C. § 6807(b).

The Safeguards Rule: As part of its role implementing GLBA, the FTC issued the Safeguards Rule. 16 C.F.R. pt. 314. This regulation requires financial institutions that fall under the FTC's jurisdiction to establish administrative, technical, and physical information safeguards. These companies must develop a comprehensive written information security program, and one that appropriately responds to the company's size and complexity, the nature and scope of its activities, and the sensitivity of the customer data that it handles. The Safeguards Rule also requires designation of an employee or employees to coordinate the company's information security program, which can encourage introduction of a chief privacy officer position at organizations that do not yet have one. 16 C.F.R. § 314.4.

Consumer Financial Protection Bureau (CFPB) and FTC: The Dodd-Frank Act, which created the CFPB, also assigned that agency broad enforcement powers over a series of "enumerated consumer laws," including the GLBA. It preserved a continuing FTC role, however, for GLBA's provisions concerning a financial institution's use and protection of nonpublic consumer information. 15 U.S.C. §§ 6802-6809. The CFPB also has authority to make determinations as to whether or not a state law is preempted.

Amendment to the Annual Privacy Notice Requirement Under Gramm-Leach-Bliley Act (Regulation P), 79 Fed. Reg. 64,057 (CFPB Oct. 28, 2014) (codified at 12 C.F.R. pt. 1016)

The CFPB amended Regulation P to allow certain financial institutions that meet its new requirements to post privacy policies on their website rather than engage in an annual mailing of such privacy policies to their customers. Financial institutions must still mail annual notices, however, to any customer who requests them by telephone. To be eligible for this alternative method of providing notice, the financial institution must (1) not have information sharing practices that trigger opt-out rights under GLBA; (2) not have included in its annual privacy notice the notice and opt-out rights of FCRA section 603; (3) not share information with an affiliate and previously provided notice and opt-out rights pursuant to FCR section 624 in the annual notice; (4) have information in the privacy notice that has not changed since the last notice was sent; and (5) utilize the model form provided in Regulation P. This CFPB Rule is not applicable to an entity that is subject to the GLBA regulations of the FTC, the Securities and Exchange Commission, or the Commodities Futures Trading Commission.

CFPB Enforcement Actions

In re Dwolla, Inc., **CFPB No. 2016-CFPB-0007 (Mar. 2, 2016)**
This consent order stemmed from the first CFPB action related to data security.
An online payment platform, Dwolla allows members to transfer funds to other
members. The company advertised that its data-security practices "exceed[ed]" or
"surpass[ed] industry security standards." It also claimed that members' "information
is securely encrypted and stored." Among other things, the CFPB found that Dwolla
did not reasonably protect consumer data, did not encrypt all sensitive information,
and did not exceed industry standards. The CFPB alleged that the company engaged
in "deceptive acts or practices." Dwolla agreed to a $100,000 civil penalty, to comply
with all statutory requirements in the future, and to implement numerous improvements in its data-security practices.

Right to Financial Privacy Act of 1978 (RFPA)
12 U.S.C. §§ 3401–3422

Primary Function: To protect customer records at financial institutions from federal
government access.

Scope: RFPA covers all financial institutions, but only protects customer records
from the federal government. 12 U.S.C. § 3401.

Key Definition—Financial Record: The RFPA's protection extends to "financial
records," which consists of "an original of, a copy of, or information known to have
been derived from, any record held by the financial institution pertaining to a customer's relationship with the financial institution." 12 U.S.C. § 3401(2).

Permissible Federal Access to Financial Records: A financial institution may only disclose financial records to a federal government authority if the records are reasonably
described and one of the following conditions is met: (1) the customer adequately
authorizes the disclosure; (2) it is in response to an adequate administrative subpoena or summons; (3) it is in response to an adequate search warrant; (4) it is in
response to an adequate judicial subpoena; or (5) it is in response to a formal written
request authorized by regulations.

Certification of Authority: The federal authority seeking disclosure must certify in
writing that it has complied with the statutory requirements necessary for the request
to be adequate before the financial institution may release financial records. 12 U.S.C.
§ 3403(b).

Protection Against Forced Authorization: Financial institutions are prohibited from
requiring customer authorization for disclosure of financial records as a condition of
doing business. 12 U.S.C. § 3404(b).

Exceptions: The RFPA does not protect financial records from disclosure when the federal government has specific statutory authority to obtain the records, such as pursuant to an Internal Revenue Code proceeding. 12 U.S.C. § 3413.

Leading Cases

***Young v. U.S. Dep't of Justice*, 882 F.2d 633 (2d Cir. 1989)**
A person's status as "government authority" depends on the capacity in which the person makes the request for financial information. The RFPA does not apply to a court-appointed commissioner.

***In re Duque*, 177 B.R. 397 (Bankr. S.D. Fla. 1994)**
RFPA does not limit a trustee's right to discovery; it is well established that the RFPA only restricts federal governmental agencies.

***Lopez v. First Union Nat'l Bank of Fla.*, 129 F.3d 1186 (11th Cir. 1997)**
RFPA's provision permitting disclosure to law enforcement of information pertaining to possible violations of law does not extend to disclosure of actual financial records. The provision limits disclosure to the account holder's name and "the nature of any suspected illegal activity."

Bank Secrecy Act of 1970 (BSA)
31 U.S.C. § 5311 *et seq.*

Primary Function: Requires financial institutions to assist federal government agencies to prevent money laundering and terrorist financing by detecting and reporting potentially suspicious activity.

Scope: BSA applies to financial institutions.

BSA Regulations Require Financial Institutions to Submit Reports: Financial institutions are required to submit numerous reports, including (1) a Currency Transaction Report (CTR) for any transaction in currency over $10,000. 31 C.F.R. 1010.311; and (2) a Suspicious Activity Report (SAR) for any "suspicious transaction relevant to a possible violation of law or regulation." 31 C.F.R. 1020.320. This includes any transaction over $5,000 that the bank has reason to suspect: (1) "involves funds derived from illegal activities or is intended or conducted in order to hide or disguise" such funds; (2) the activity is structured to avoid BSA requirements; or (3) has no "apparent lawful purpose" in which the customer would ordinarily engage. 31 C.F.R. 1020(a)(2).

BSA Recordkeeping Requirements: Financial institutions are required to keep records that are deemed to have "a high degree of usefulness in criminal, tax, or regulatory investigations or proceedings." 31 C.F.R. 1010.401. Among other things, this includes extensions of credit over $10,000, and any advice given regarding a transaction in currency over $10,000 to a foreign entity. 31 C.F.R. 1040.410.

The Financial Crimes Enforcement Network: A bureau of the U.S. Department of the Treasury, the Financial Crimes Enforcement Network (FinCEN) has regulatory authority under the BSA. The Secretary of Treasury, whom the BSA authorizes to issue regulations, delegated to FinCEN the authority to implement, administer, and enforce the BSA and its regulations. FinCEN also has congressionally delegated responsibilities to collect, store, protect, and disseminate data filed under the BSA's reporting requirements.

Torts and Financial Privacy

Breach of Confidentiality Tort
A bank can be liable to a customer when it has a duty to maintain the confidentiality of the customer's information and it breaches that duty. For example, in *Peterson v. Idaho First National Bank,* 367 P.2d 284 (Idaho 1961), the court held that a bank could be sued for breach of confidentiality for disclosing customer information because "it is an implied term of the contract between the banker and his customer that the banker will not divulge to third persons, without the consent of the customer, express or implied, either the state of the customer's account or any of his transactions with the bank, or any information relating to the customer acquired through the keeping of his account."

Several other jurisdictions have held likewise. *See, e.g., Barnett Bank of W. Fla. v. Hooper,* 498 So. 2d 923 (Fla. 1986); *Indiana Nat'l Bank v. Chapman,* 482 N.E.2d 474 (Ind. Ct. App. 1985); *Suburban Trust Co. v. Waller,* 408 A.2d 758 (Md. Ct. Spec. App. 1979); *Richfield Bank & Trust Co. v. Sjogren,* 244 N.W.2d 648 (Minn. 1976); *McGuire v. Shubert,* 722 A.2d 1087 (Pa. Super. Ct. 1998).

Negligence
The tort of negligence requires that a plaintiff prove, among other elements, a duty of care that the defendant owed to the plaintiff, and conduct by the defendant that falls below the applicable standard of care, i.e., that breaches that duty. In general, the defendant's required duty of conduct is that of "reasonable care" under the circumstances. In *Wolfe v. MBNA America Bank,* 485 F. Supp. 2d 874 (W.D. Tenn. 2007), the district court found that the defendant bank had "a duty to verify the authenticity and accuracy of a credit account application before issuing a credit card." This duty did not involve an obligation to prevent all identity theft, but rather one "to implement reasonable and cost-effective verification methods that can prevent criminals, in some instances, from obtaining a credit card with a stolen identity."

A different result was reached in *Huggins v. Citibank, N.A.,* 585 S.E.2d 275 (S.C. 2003), where the South Carolina Supreme Court found no duty between a credit card–issuing bank and a victim of identity theft. The Huggins court placed significant weight on the lack of an established prior relationship between the bank and the plaintiff, who was not a customer of the defendant bank.

State Financial Statutes

Vermont's Privacy of Consumer Financial and Health Information Regulation, 21-010-16 Vt. Code R. IH-2001-01 (2001)
Requires opt-in for financial institutions sharing data with nonaffiliated companies.

California Financial Information Privacy Act (SB1), Cal. Fin. Code §§ 4050–4060
Requires opt-in for financial institutions sharing data with nonaffiliated companies. Permits financial institutions to offer incentives or discounts for people to opt in.

California's SB1 and FCRA Preemption

Financial institutions challenged SB1, arguing that it was preempted by FCRA. In *American Bankers Ass'n v. Gould,* 412 F.3d 1081 (9th Cir. 2005), the court concluded that "SB1 is preempted [by FCRA] to the extent that it applies to information shared between affiliates concerning consumers' 'credit worthiness, credit standing, credit capacity, character, general reputation, personal characteristics, or mode of living' that is used, expected to be used, or collected for the purpose of establishing eligibility for 'credit or insurance,' employment, or other authorized purpose."

In a later opinion, *American Bankers Ass'n v. Lockyer,* 541 F.3d 1214 (9th Cir. 2008), the Ninth Circuit held that SB1 had valid non-preempted applications pertaining to the sharing of non-consumer report information by affiliates. SB1 remains valid when narrowed to exclude the regulation of consumer report information from its reach.

TAX PRIVACY

**Internal Revenue Code
26 U.S.C. §§ 6103, 7216 (1976)**

Primary Function: To protect confidentiality of tax information.

Confidentiality: Prior to the Tax Reform Act of 1976, federal tax returns were considered "public records," but ones available only upon order of the president and rules and regulations prescribed by the secretary of the treasury. The Tax Reform Act changed this previous default of publicity for tax information to one of confidentiality that could be altered only through statutory disclosure permissions. Only an explicit legal authorization can trump the general mandate of confidentiality of tax return information.

Permissible Disclosures: There are many legal authorizations for disclosure of tax information, such as: (1) to Congress if the head of a congressional committee makes a written request to the IRS; (2) to the president and executive branch employees if the president issues a written request "signed by him personally"; (3) to the Department of Treasury and Department of Justice for purposes of tax administration, such as for use in judicial or administrative tax proceedings; (4) pursuant to an ex parte order from a federal district judge or magistrate to federal officials who are preparing for a proceeding pertaining to "the enforcement of a specifically designated federal criminal statute (not involving tax administration) to which the United States … may be a party"; (5) to inform appropriate officials for investigations of terrorist activities; (6) to various parties in an emergency situation; and (7) to child support enforcement agencies in the states. 26 U.S.C. § 6103.

Restrictions on Tax Preparers: The Internal Revenue Code, 26 U.S.C. § 7216, prohibits anyone preparing tax returns from knowingly or recklessly disclosing any data furnished for the preparation of the return or using such data for any purpose beyond preparing the return. Violations are punished as a misdemeanor, with a fine of up to $1,000 and up to one year of imprisonment, along with paying the costs of prosecution.

IDENTITY THEFT

Identity Theft Assumption and Deterrence Act of 1998
18 U.S.C. § 1028
The act makes it a federal crime to "knowingly transfer or use, without lawful authority, a means of identification of another person with the intent to commit, or to aid or abet, any unlawful activity that constitutes a violation of federal law, or that constitutes a felony under any applicable state or local law."

State Identity Theft Statutes
The vast majority of states have statutes concerning identity theft, often focusing primarily on criminalizing it. *See, e.g.,* Ariz. Rev. Stat. Ann. § 13-2008(D); Cal. Penal Code § 530.5(a); Fla. Stat. § 817.568. Many states punish identity theft based on the dollar value of the things the thief wrongfully took.

California has enacted numerous innovative provisions to combat identity theft. These include:

Cal. Civil Code § 1748.95
Victims can obtain the fraudulent applications that the identity thief made as well as a record of the thief's transactions in the victim's name.

Cal. Civ. Code § 1788.18
Assists victims in stopping debt collectors from continuing to try to collect debts that the thief created.

Cal. Civ. Code § 1785.15.3(b)
Requires consumer credit reporting agencies to furnish identity theft victims, upon request, with up to 12 free copies of their credit files during a consecutive 12-month period.

Leading Cases

Wolfe v. MBNA Am. Bank, **485 F. Supp. 2d 874 (W.D. Tenn. 2007)**
The plaintiff sued a bank that issued a credit card in his name to an identity thief. The court held that the duty to verify the information contained in a credit card application required only "reasonable and cost-effective verification methods that can prevent criminals, in some instances, from obtaining a credit card with a stolen identity." That issue is one for the trier of fact.

Huggins v. Citibank, N.A., **585 S.E.2d 275 (S.C. 2003)**
The relationship between credit card issuers and potential victims of identity theft was far too attenuated to rise to the level of duty between them. There can be no negligence in tort without a duty running from the defendant to the plaintiff.

GOVERNMENT ACCESS TO FINANCIAL INFORMATION
See Chapter 7

FOR FURTHER REFERENCE

Treatises

L. Richard Fischer, *The Law of Financial Privacy* (2004)

IRS, *Disclosure & Privacy Law Reference Guide* (2012)
Analysis of the chief disclosure laws that affect the IRS, including the applicable aspects of the Internal Revenue Code, FOIA, and the Privacy Act. This guide also considers litigation privileges and disclosures for nontax criminal purposes.

Articles and Other Sources

David H. Carpenter, Cong. Research Serv., *The Dodd-Frank Wall Street Reform and Consumer Protection Act: Title X, The Consumer Financial Protection Bureau* (July 21, 2010)
Discusses the power of the Consumer Financial Protection Bureau to enforce a variety of consumer protection statutes.

Elizabeth D. De Armond, *Frothy Chaos: Modern Data Warehousing and Old-Fashioned Defamation,* 41 Val. U. L. Rev. 1061 (2007)
A critique of FCRA preemption and duties to consumers under FCRA.

Evan Hendricks, *Credit Scores & Credit Reports: How the System Really Works, What You Can Do* (2007)
An accessible introduction to how the credit reporting system functions.

Chris Jay Hoofnagle, *Identity Theft: Making the Known Unknowns Known*, 21 Harv. J. L. & Tech. 97 (2007)
Argues for a reporting requirement on financial institutions about identity theft incidents.

M. Maureen Murphy, Cong. Research Serv., *Privacy Protection for Customer Financial Information* (Jan. 14, 2014)
Analyzes the Dodd-Frank Act's changes to the administration and enforcement of FCRA, GLBA, and other statutes.

Paul M. Schwartz, *The Future of Tax Privacy*, 61 Nat'l Tax J. 883 (2008)
Explores the history of tax privacy, current rules, and likely impact of issues such as data security on the future development of existing statutory regulation.

Paul M. Schwartz & Edward J. Janger, *The Gramm-Leach-Bliley Act, Information Privacy, and the Limits of Default Rules*, 86 Minn. L. Rev. 1219 (2002)
Criticism of GLBA's privacy safeguards as failing both to reflect majority preferences and to provide consumers with adequate information.

Daniel J. Solove, *Identity Theft, Privacy, and the Architecture of Vulnerability*, 54 Hastings L.J. 1227 (2003)
Argues that identity theft can be better prevented by regulating the way financial institutions handle personal data.

Peter P. Swire, *The Surprising Virtues of the New Financial Privacy Law*, 86 Minn. L. Rev. 1263 (2002)
Praises GLBA's privacy protections as addressing legitimate industry concerns about excessive costs and legal barricades to needed information.

CHAPTER 9

Consumer Data

ESSENTIAL POINTS

- A series of targeted, sectoral information privacy laws governs the use of business records in different settings.

- Federal laws regulating business data and consumer privacy offer different kinds of protections. Among the ways these safeguards vary are: (1) opt-out rules versus opt-in rules, (2) preemption of state law, and (3) the existence of a private right of action for violations.

- The FTC has played an important role in policing the privacy practices of companies.

- Numerous federal statutes provide for liquidated damages in the case of privacy violations.

- Damages are often difficult for plaintiffs to establish when businesses misuse or improperly disclose personal data.

- With a few exceptions, courts generally sustain privacy regulations under the First Amendment when the law requires opt-in rules or when it enables consumers to restrict the marketing solicitations they receive.

- In the few cases decided thus far, many courts have rejected breach of contract claims when companies violate their privacy policies. These holdings have been based primarily on two rationales: (1) privacy policies are notices, not contracts, and (2) the plaintiffs failed to establish damages.

PERSONALLY IDENTIFIABLE INFORMATION

Personally identifiable information (PII) is one of the most central concepts in privacy regulation. It defines the scope and boundaries of a large range of privacy statutes and regulations. Numerous federal statutes turn on this distinction. Similarly, many state statutes also rely on PII as a jurisdictional trigger. These laws all share the same basic assumption—that in the absence of PII, there is no privacy harm. Thus, privacy regulation focuses on the collection, use, and disclosure of PII, and leaves non-PII unregulated.

Approaches to Defining PII

In the United States, there are three predominant approaches to defining PII in various laws and regulations:

1. **The Tautological Approach.** Defines PII as any information that identifies a person. Example: VPPA

2. **The Nonpublic Approach.** Defines PII as any nonpublic personal information or as non-aggregate data. Examples: GLBA, Cable Act

3. **The Specific-Types Approach.** Defines PII by listing specific types of data that constitutes PII. Examples: COPPA, many state data security breach notification laws

Source: Paul M. Schwartz & Daniel J. Solove, *The PII Problem: Privacy and a New Concept of Personally Identifiable Information*, 86 N.Y.U. L. Rev. 1814 (2011)

Leading Cases

Pineda v. Williams-Sonoma Stores, Inc., 246 P.3d 612 (Cal. 2011)
California's Song–Beverly Act prohibits merchants who accept credit cards from collecting a cardholder's "personal identification information" when transacting business with her. More specifically, it prohibits retailers from requesting or requiring "as a condition to accepting the credit card" that a cardholder provide "any personal identification information upon the credit card transaction form or otherwise." Cal. Civ. Code § 1747.08(a)(1). The critical language in the act defines PII as "information concerning the cardholder, other than information set forth on the credit card, and including, but not limited to, the cardholder's address and telephone number." In *Pineda*, the California Supreme Court analyzed the statutory language and legislative history of the act and found that both demonstrated a legislative intent to include a zip code as part of the "cardholder's address." In other words, that statutory category included "not only a complete address, but also its components."

Apple Inc. v. Superior Court, 292 P.3d 883 (Cal. 2013)

Online digital media retailer did not violate provision of the Song-Beverly Credit Card Act prohibiting merchants from requesting and recording "personal identification information" concerning the cardholder. The California Supreme Court found that the overall statutory scheme of the Song-Beverly Act indicated a legislative desire to balance privacy protection and fraud protection. For electronically downloadable products, online merchants faced limitations on their anti-fraud activities that brick-and-mortar retailers did not face for their own anti-fraud activities. The California Court was unwilling to assume that the Legislature that enacted Song-Beverly in 1990 would have extended its prohibitions to electronically downloadable products.

Injury and Standing

Standing

An overarching issue in privacy cases is whether the privacy violation caused any harm. Plaintiffs must typically allege a cognizable injury in order to have a viable cause of action. In federal courts, in order to have standing, the plaintiff must show that:

1. it has suffered an "injury in fact" that is (a) concrete and particularized and (b) actual or imminent, not conjectural or hypothetical;

2. the injury is fairly traceable to the challenged action of the defendant; and

3. it is likely, as opposed to merely speculative, that the injury will be redressed by a favorable decision.

Leading Cases

Spokeo, Inc. v. Robins, 136 S. Ct. 1540 (2016)

Not all FCRA violations qualify for standing, despite congressional intent for the statute to create a private cause of action. To demonstrate the necessary "injury in fact" from the dissemination of false information, plaintiffs must also show a "concrete harm." The concrete harm need not be "tangible," and a sufficient risk of real harm may qualify, but a "bare procedural violation" is insufficient.

Friends of the Earth, Inc. v. Laidlaw Envtl. Servs. (TOC), Inc., 528 U.S. 167 (2000)

If a plaintiff cannot establish standing, then a plaintiff's lawsuit cannot proceed forward in federal court.

Clapper v. Amnesty Int'l USA, 133 S. Ct. 1138 (2013)

Although this is a case involving a constitutional challenge to the Foreign Intelligence Surveillance Act (FISA), it has relevance for standing in consumer privacy cases. The U.S. Supreme Court held that plaintiffs failed to allege a legally cognizable injury when they challenged a provision of FISA that permits the government to engage in surveillance of their communications. The plaintiffs claimed that there was an "objectively reasonable likelihood" that their communications would be monitored, and as a result, they had to take "costly and burdensome measures to protect the confidentiality of their international communications." The Supreme Court concluded that the plaintiffs were speculating and that "allegations of possible future injury are not sufficient" to establish an injury. According to the Court, "fears of hypothetical future harm" cannot justify the countermeasures the plaintiffs took. "Enterprising" litigants could establish an injury "simply by making an expenditure based on a nonparanoid fear."

***In re Google Inc. Cookie Placement Consumer Privacy Litig.*, 988 F. Supp. 2d 434 (D. Del. 2013), *aff'd in part and vacated in part*, 806 F.3d 125 (3d Cir. 2015), *petition for cert filed*, (U.S. Mar. 14, 2016) (No. 15-1141)**
Plaintiffs alleged that Google "'tricked' their Apple Safari and/or Internet Explorer browsers into accepting cookies, which then allowed defendants to display targeted advertising." The court held that the plaintiffs couldn't prove a harm because they couldn't demonstrate that Google interfered with their ability to "monetize" their personal data.

***Resnick v. AvMed, Inc.*, 693 F.3d 1317 (11th Cir. 2012)**
Plaintiffs sufficiently pleaded an injury-in-fact by alleging a sufficient nexus between data breach and theft of their identify. Allegation was that the same sensitive information stored on stolen laptops was used by thieves to open bank accounts in plaintiffs' names.

***Perkins v. LinkedIn Corp.*, 53 F.Supp.3d 1190 (N.D. Cal. 2014)**
Class action suit alleging LinkedIn accessed user email accounts and sent correspondence without permission. The court found that the social networking site's users had consented to this usage but had not agreed to follow-up emails LinkedIn sent. The parties entered a settlement wherein LinkedIn agreed to pay $13 million in damages and $3.25 million in legal fees.

TORT LAW

The privacy torts have thus far *not* provided a good fit for addressing complaints about improper collection, use or disclosure of personal data by businesses. The breach of confidentiality tort has not been used in this manner. Negligence has sometimes been recognized as a viable cause of action to protect consumer privacy, but significant precedent does not exist in this area.

Leading Cases

***Dwyer v. Am. Express Co.*, 652 N.E.2d 1351 (Ill. App. Ct. 1995)**
American Express sold cardholder information to marketers. Cardholders did not have an action for intrusion upon seclusion because they had voluntarily exposed their information to American Express. They lacked a cause of action for appropriation of name or likeness because "an individual name has value only when it is associated with one of defendants' lists."

Shibley v. Time, Inc., 341 N.E.2d 337 (Ohio Ct. App. 1975)

Plaintiff sued the publishers of magazines for selling subscription lists to direct-mail advertising businesses. There was no liability for public disclosure of private facts because the sale of the lists did not "cause mental suffering, shame or humiliation to a person of ordinary sensibilities." The appropriation tort was not available because the defendant had not used the plaintiff's name or likeness to endorse a product.

Remsburg v. Docusearch, Inc., 816 A.2d 1001 (N.H. 2003)

A database company released the victim's address and other personal information to a man who hunted her down and murdered her. The court held that if a private investigator or information broker discloses information to a client and creates a foreseeable risk of criminal misconduct against the third person whose information was disclosed, there is a duty to exercise reasonable care not to subject the third person to an unreasonable risk of harm. Due to the risks posed by stalking and identity theft, the threat of criminal misconduct was sufficiently foreseeable that an investigator had a duty to exercise reasonable care in disclosing a third person's personal information. Few other courts have found such a duty.

Fraley v. Facebook, Inc., 830 F. Supp. 2d 785 (N.D. Cal. 2011)

This case concerned a Facebook feature called "Sponsored Stories." Plaintiffs alleged a "coherent theory of how they were economically injured by the misappropriation of their names, photographs, and likenesses for use in paid commercial endorsements targeted not at themselves, but at *other* consumers, without their consent." Their "personalized endorsement" of products and services to their friends "has a concrete, provable value." In a subsequent order, Judge Richard Seeborg rejected a proposed settlement of the case. *Fraley v. Facebook, Inc.*, No. C 11-1726 RS, 2012 WL 5838198 (N.D. Cal. Aug. 17, 2012). In his order, Judge Seeborg requested more information about the scope of the injunctive relief to which Facebook agreed. In August 2013, the court approved a $20 million settlement with Facebook. Court held that the plaintiffs successfully stated a claim for misappropriation under Cal. Civ. Code § 3344.

CONTRACT AND PROMISSORY ESTOPPEL

Contract and promissory estoppel appear highly relevant as causes of action to remedy the improper collection, use, or disclosure of personal data, because many companies have privacy policies that make promises about privacy that consumers rely upon. In the few cases decided thus far, however, courts have not been receptive to these theories.

Breach of Contract

To establish a breach of contract claim, a plaintiff must prove:

1. The existence of a contract

2. Breach of the contract

3. Damages that flow from the breach

Promissory Estoppel

Under the doctrine of promissory estoppel, a "promise which the promisor should reasonably expect to induce action or forbearance on the part of the promisee or a third person and which does induce such action or forbearance is binding if injustice can be avoided only by enforcement of the promise. The remedy granted for breach may be limited as justice requires." Restatement (Second) of Contracts § 90 (1981).

Are Privacy Policies Contracts?

Thus far, only a few courts have addressed this question, and they have uniformly held that privacy policies are not contracts. These courts view privacy policies as mere notices of a company's practices. Cases have also failed because plaintiffs have not established contractual damages. Examples:

Dyer v. Nw. Airlines Corps., 334 F. Supp. 2d 1196 (D.N.D. 2004)

Breach of contract claim against Northwest Airlines for disclosing passenger records to the government in violation of its privacy policy. The court held that "broad statements of company policy do not generally give rise to contract claims." The court also noted that the plaintiffs failed to allege they had read or relied upon the privacy policy or that they suffered any "contractual damages arising out of the alleged breach."

In re Jet Blue Airways Corp. Privacy Litig., 379 F. Supp. 2d 299 (E.D.N.Y. 2005)

Plaintiffs sued Jet Blue Airlines for breach of contract for sharing passenger records with the government. The court granted Jet Blue's motion to dismiss because plaintiffs failed to prove damages. It stated: "There is ... no support for the proposition that an individual passenger's personal information has or had any compensable value in the economy at large."

Liability for Third-Party Apps?

In re iPhone Application Litig., 844 F. Supp. 2d 1040 (N.D. Cal. 2012)

The court denied Apple's motion to dismiss two state law claims against it based on a class action against Apple for the practices of third-party apps. Despite Apple's Privacy Policy and Terms of Use, which disclaimed liability from third-party conduct, the court concluded that Apple's promise to protect consumer privacy encompasses data it provides to third parties. This general promise overrode the disclaimer of liability. The court recognized that increased security risks and lessened device resources (storage, battery life, and bandwidth) from third-party apps could constitute concrete injuries.

FTC ENFORCEMENT OF SECTION 5 OF THE FTC ACT

FTC Act: Since 1998, the FTC has been bringing enforcement actions against companies for privacy and data security practices that the FTC deems to be in violation of Section 5 of the Federal Trade Commission Act (FTC Act), 15 U.S.C. § 45. The FTC Act prohibits "unfair or deceptive acts or practices in or affecting commerce." In some instances, the actions of a company can be both deceptive and unfair.

Deception: A deceptive act or practice is a material "representation, omission or practice that is likely to mislead the consumer acting reasonably in the circumstances, to the consumer's detriment." Letter from James C. Miller III, Chairman, FTC, to Hon. John D. Dingell, Chairman, Comm. on Energy & Commerce (Oct. 14, 1983).

Unfairness: The FTC Act classifies a trade practice as unfair if it "causes or is likely to cause substantial injury to consumers which is not reasonably avoidable by consumers themselves and is not outweighed by countervailing benefits to consumers or to competition." 15 U.S.C. § 45(n).

The Types of Cases Brought: Early FTC actions involved charging companies that violated the promises made in their privacy policy with engaging in a deceptive practice. In the ensuing years, the FTC has found violations of the FTC Act beyond broken promises in privacy policies. Most cases brought by the FTC have settled.

Enforcement: The FTC can obtain injunctive remedies. The FTC Act does not provide for private causes of action; only the FTC can enforce it. The FTC does not have the ability to issue fines for violations of Section 5, but the FTC can issue fines up to $16,000 for each violation when companies violate a consent decree previously entered into for a violation of Section 5.

FTC Jurisdiction: Section 5 gives the FTC a broad authority to regulate most companies. However, several types of financial institutions, airlines, telecommunications carriers, and other types of entities are exempt from Section 5. In addition to its Section 5 authority, the FTC has regulatory authority from a number of statutes.

Statutes Granting Enforcement Authority to the FTC

- Federal Trade Commission Act (FTC Act)
- Children's Online Privacy Protection Act (COPPA)
- Gramm-Leach-Bliley Act (GLBA)
- Telemarketing and Consumer Fraud Abuse Prevention Act (TCFAPA)
- Fair Credit Reporting Act (FCRA)

Leading Cases

FTC v. Wyndham Worldwide Corp., 799 F.3d 236 (3d Cir. 2015)

Affirmed the FTC's authority to bring actions against companies with inadequate data protection practices. The FTC had pursued a suit against Wyndham, a chain of hospitality suites, alleging a string of data breaches at the company resulted from insufficient security measures. The Third Circuit held that a company's failure to maintain reasonable and appropriate data security could constitute "unfair practices" under Section 5 of the FTC Act. Additionally, the court concluded that prior FTC guidelines and actions provided fair notice that Wyndham's conduct fell within the agency's statutory authority.

Leading Enforcement Actions

In re Liberty Fin. Cos., FTC No. C-3891 (Aug. 12, 1999)

Website for children and teen investors falsely promised that personal data collected in a survey would be kept anonymous, but it was kept in an identifiable form. Liberty Financial settled with the FTC, agreeing to refrain from making future misrepresentations, to post a privacy notice on its website, and to obtain parental consent prior to gathering personal data from children.

FTC v. Toysmart.com, LLC, No. 00-11341-RGS, 2000 WL 34016434 (D. Mass. July 21, 2000)

An Internet toy retailer went bankrupt and planned to sell its customer database to pay back creditors. This action violated its privacy policy, which stated that customer data "is never shared with a third party." The FTC charged this behavior was a deceptive practice. Toysmart and the FTC settled, agreeing that the bankruptcy court had to approve the buyer and that the buyer would be limited in how it could use the information.

FTC v. ReverseAuction.com, Inc., No. 00-0032, 2000 U.S. Dist. LEXIS 20761 (Jan. 10, 2000)

ReverseAuction.com improperly obtained personal information from eBay customers and used it to e-mail them to promote its own auction website. Their e-mail falsely stated to the recipients that their eBay user IDs would expire soon. The FTC charged that ReverseAuction's practice was both unfair and deceptive. ReverseAuction settled, agreeing to be barred from making future misrepresentations and to notify the customers and correct the falsehood.

In re Gateway Learning Corp., FTC No. C-4120 (Sept. 10, 2004)

When Gateway Learning Corp. collected personal information from its consumers, its privacy policy stated that it would not sell, rent, or loan personal information to third parties unless people consented. Subsequently, Gateway altered its privacy policy to allow the renting of personal information to third parties without informing customers or obtaining their consent. The FTC alleged this practice was unfair, and Gateway settled, agreeing to avoid making deceptive claims or retroactively changing its privacy policy without consumer consent. Gateway agreed to pay $4,608, the amount it earned from renting the information.

In re Vision I Properties, LLC, FTC No. C-4135 (Apr. 19, 2005)

Vision I Properties licensed shopping cart software and provided related services to small online retail merchants. The company's software created customizable shopping cart pages for client merchants' websites. The resulting pages resided on websites managed by Vision I Properties, but resembled the other pages on its client merchants' websites. Vision I Properties violated the privacy promises of some of these client merchants as stated in their websites; it rented consumers' personal information collected through its shopping cart software. This personal information was then used by third parties to send direct mail and make telemarketing calls to consumers. For the FTC, it was reasonable for consumers to rely on merchants' privacy policies. Moreover, Vision I Properties did not adequately inform merchants of its information sharing. Vision I settled, agreeing to cease selling the data, to provide better notice and to disgorge $9,101 of profits.

In re Sears Holdings Mgmt. Corp., FTC No. C-4264 (Aug. 31, 2009)

Sears invited website users to "participate in exciting, engaging and on-going interactions—always on your terms and always by your choice." Customers were paid to participate and had to download software that would track their Internet browsing. A long user license agreement informed users of the extensiveness of the tracking. The FTC alleged Sears engaged in a deceptive practice by failing to adequately disclose the extent of the tracking. The settlement requires Sears to destroy all data collected and to clearly disclose the scope of the tracking before the software is installed and apart from the user license agreement.

In re Facebook, Inc., FTC No. C-4365 (July 27, 2012)

The FTC charged that Facebook's changes to its privacy policy in December 2009 resulted in data about its users being exposed to the public. The FTC alleged both deception (failing to properly notify people) and unfairness (making a retroactive material change to its privacy policies without consumer consent). The FTC also alleged that Facebook had not adhered to the Safe Harbor principles regarding notice and choice. The settlement requires Facebook to develop and maintain a "comprehensive privacy program."

In re Google Inc., FTC No. C-4336 (Oct. 13, 2011)

Google Buzz violated the FTC Act and Safe Harbor by suggesting that Gmail users could choose whether to join Buzz, but then enrolling some people who had not wanted to join Buzz in certain Buzz features. The FTC required Google to institute a "comprehensive privacy program." This was the first case involving a Safe Harbor violation and the requirement that a company develop a comprehensive privacy program.

United States v. Google Inc., No. CV 12-04177 SI, 2012 WL 5833994 (N.D. Cal. Nov. 16, 2012)

Google agreed to pay a $22.5 million fine to the FTC based on the charge that, in violation of its promises, it placed a tracking cookie on the computers of Safari users. This practice violated the October 2011 settlement with the FTC that Google not misrepresent the extent to which it provided users control over their data.

In re MySpace LLC, FTC No. C-4369 (Aug. 30, 2012)

"Constructive sharing"—sharing non-PII with third parties that can be used by third parties to access PII—without indicating it to users is a "deceptive act or practice" under the FTC Act as well as a violation of Safe Harbor. If non-PII is shared with third parties, and that non-PII can be used by the third parties to obtain PII, then a business is not accurate in stating that it does not share PII with third parties. Consistent with other recent cases, the FTC required MySpace to implement a comprehensive privacy program.

In re Epic Marketplace, Inc., FTC No. C-4389 (Mar. 13, 2013)

A behavioral advertising company, Epic engaged in "history sniffing." This practice involves a company accessing a user's browsing history to determine whether the user had previously visited a webpage. Epic then used this information within interest segments, including such sensitive categories as "Incontinence," "Arthritis," and "Pregnancy—Fertility Getting Pregnant." Once placed in such categories, the consumer would receive targeted ads based on this classification. The FTC settlement prohibited Epic from engaging in history sniffing and from misrepresenting its practices. It was also required to delete any information collected using history sniffing.

In re DesignerWare, LLC, FTC No. C-4390 (Apr. 11, 2013)

The FTC brought this action against seven rent-to-own companies (and a software company and others) for spying on consumers from computers they were renting. Without knowledge of the customers, software on the computer (called "Detective Mode") took screenshots of confidential and personal information, logged customers' computer keystrokes, and in certain cases, took webcam pictures of people in their own homes. The FTC settlement includes 20 years of auditing and a prohibition on the use of GPS information without consumer consent and notice. Information improperly gathered from consumers cannot be used by the companies to collect on accounts.

In re Aaron's, Inc., FTC No. C-4442 (Mar. 10, 2014)

A follow-up to the *DesignerWare* and related settlements. Although Aaron's own stores did not license or use the contested DesignerWare product, Aaron's knew that some of its franchisees had done so. It also knew, according to the FTC's complaint, that "Detective Mode captured confidential and personal information from consumer computer users without notice to those users." Under the terms of the FTC settlement, Aaron's will be prohibited from utilizing "monitoring technology to gather data or information from or about a consumer from any computer rented to a consumer." The order also prohibits it from "[r]eceiving, storing, or communicating" data gathered from a computer rented to a consumer using monitoring technology.

In re Goldenshores Techs., LLC, FTC No. C-4446 (Mar. 31, 2014)

A company offered "Brightest Flashlight Free," a popular Android mobile application. Users had downloaded it tens of millions of times. The flashlight app transmitted user geolocation data and persistent device identifiers from Android mobile devices to third parties, including advertising networks. The FTC alleged that Brightest Flashlight's Privacy Policy did not adequately disclose this fact. Although the EULA presented a choice to "Accept" or "Refuse" the terms of the Agreement, the app was already collecting and sending information to third parties before a consumer was presented with this choice. The settlement required improved notice and also for "just-in-time" notice and affirmative consent when geolocation data is collected.

FTC v. T-Mobile USA, Inc., No. 2:14-cv-00967-JLR (W.D. Wash. Dec. 19, 2014)

Suit alleging T-Mobile improperly billed customers for unwanted third-party services like horoscopes and celebrity gossip. T-Mobile alleged to have essentially hidden these charges from consumers by placing them in extensive phone bills. T-Mobile and the FTC entered a $90 million settlement agreement, including fines in all states and refunds for affected customers.

In re Snapchat, Inc., FTC No. C-450 (Dec. 23, 2014)

Mobile app Snapchat allows users to share photos and videos that will automatically be deleted after several seconds. In 2014, Snapchat suffered data breaches involving usernames and passwords. The FTC brought a suit against the company, alleging Snapchat users were deceived by a privacy policy that promised less protection than actually provided. In their settlement with the FTC, Snapchat agreed to strengthen privacy and security measures, to provide users with an accurate description of these measures, and to be monitored by an independent privacy professional for 20 years.

In re GMR Transcription Servs., FTC No. C-4482 (Aug. 14, 2014)

Settlement involved allegations that a medical transcription company outsourced services to a third party without adequately checking that it could implement reasonable security measures.

In re Accretive Health, Inc., FTC No. C-4432 (Feb. 5, 2014)

A company providing medical billing and revenue management services to hospitals put consumers' personal information at risk by, among other things, transporting laptops with sensitive data in a way that made them vulnerable to theft. The FTC also said the company gave access to personal information to employees who didn't need it to do their jobs.

In re Craig Brittain, FTC No. C-4564 (Dec. 28, 2015)

Craig Brittain allegedly operated a "revenge porn" website and deceptively acquired and posted nude images of women. Subsequently, he demanded that the victims pay fees to have the content removed. After the FTC pursued an action against him, Brittain entered into a settlement prohibiting him from publicly sharing any nude content without the express consent of the subjects. The settlement also required the deletion of all previously published content on Brittain's website.

In re Payments MD, LLC, FTC No. C-4505 (Jan. 27, 2015)

PaymentsMD provided a billing platform for medical care providers, allowing patients to pay bills online. The FTC alleged that PaymentsMD deceptively collected consumer health information by contacting various health insurance companies, pharmacies, medical offices, and labs without informing consumers.

As a result of an FTC order, PaymentsMD must destroy all this collected information; the order also prohibits the company from engaging in similarly deceptive collection and use of consumers' personal information.

In re RadioShack, Corp., 550 B.R. 700 (Bankr. D. Del. 2016)

RadioShack intended to sell their customer database during bankruptcy proceedings. Referring to *In re Toysmart*, the FTC urged the bankruptcy court to protect consumer data through limiting the sale and use of data to ensure RadioShack's privacy promises were honored. RadioShack subsequently entered into an agreement with state attorney generals that limited the company purchaser's access to RadioShack's customer database. The bankruptcy court ultimately approved the sale.

In re Nomi Techs., Inc., FTC No. C-4538 (Aug. 28, 2015)

Nomi Technologies allegedly misled consumers through statements published on the company website falsely indicating that consumers could opt-out of in-store mobile device tracking. The FTC order prohibits Nomi from misleading consumers regarding how their data is collected, processed, used, and shared on any type of electronic device. Furthermore, Nomi may not misrepresent the extent to which consumers will receive notification about the company's privacy practices. Strong dissents in this matter from Commissioners Maureen Ollhausen and Joshua Wright.

In re ASUSTeK Comput., Inc., FTC No. C-4587 (July 18, 2016)

ASUSTeK, a Taiwan-based computer hardware maker, sold routers and cloud services, advertising that these products included multiple security features that would protect customer's computers from viruses and other types of unauthorized access. In fact, ASUSTeK's product possessed security weaknesses that exposed and compromised thousands of consumers' personal information. The FTC's order requires the company to establish and maintain a security program that will be subject to independent audits for the next 20 years.

FTC v. Sitesearch Corp., No. CV-14-02750-PHX-NVW (D. Ariz. Dec. 11, 2015)

The FTC brought an action against data brokers that gathered loan applications that consumers had submitted through payday loan sites. These companies allegedly provided third-party scammers with consumers' sensitive personal information, allowing scammers to withdraw money from the consumers' accounts. A settlement now prohibits these companies from providing further sensitive information to third parties and also requires the destruction of previously collected data. The order also includes a $5.7 million suspended judgment against defendants and a $4.1 million default judgment against Sitesearch.

Triggers for FTC Complaints

These are the types of privacy practices that will trigger FTC complaints:

- *Inadequate Security.* Promising but failing to provide adequate security. No data security breach needs to occur and no data needs to be lost. *See In re Microsoft Corp.*, FTC No. C-4069 (Dec. 20, 2002); *In re Guess?, Inc.*, FTC No. C-4091 (July 30, 2003).

- *Security Gaffes and Failure to Train.* Suffering a data security breach due to negligence or failure to properly train employees about adequate security practices. *In re Eli Lilly & Co.*, FTC No. C-4047 (May 8, 2002).

- *Broken Promises.* Failing to adhere to promises made in a privacy policy. *In re Liberty Fin. Cos.*, FTC No. C-3891 (Aug. 12, 1999). Selling customer data at a bankruptcy proceeding when a privacy policy states that data will not be shared with third parties. *FTC v. Toysmart.com, LLC*, No. 00-11341-RGS, 2000 WL 34016434 (D. Mass. July 21, 2000).

- *Retroactive Privacy Policy Changes.* Altering a privacy policy to allow more disclosure of personal information without acquiring people's consent to the change. *In re Gateway Learning Corp.*, FTC No. C-4120 (Sept. 10, 2004).

- *Deceptive Data Collection.* Collecting data about people deceptively, even if they are not visiting or using the company's website. *FTC v. ReverseAuction.com, Inc.*, No. 00-0032, 2000 U.S. Dist. LEXIS 20761 (Jan. 10, 2000).

- *Inadequate Disclosure of Extent of Data Gathering.* Failing to clearly and conspicuously inform users about the extensiveness of Internet browsing tracking by software. *In re Sears Holdings Mgmt. Corp.*, FTC No. C-4264 (Aug. 31, 2009).

FTC Consent Decrees

FTC consent decrees often contain at least some of the following elements:

- prohibition on the activities in violation of the FTC Act

- steps to remediate the problematic activities, such as software patches or notice to consumers

- deletion of wrongfully-obtained consumer data

- modifications to privacy policies

- establishment of a comprehensive privacy program, including risk assessment, appointment of a person to coordinate the program, and employee training, among other things

- biennial assessment reports by independent auditors

- recordkeeping to facilitate FTC enforcement of the order

| FTC Consent Decrees |

- obligation to alert the FTC of any material changes in the company that might affect compliance obligations (such as mergers or bankruptcy filings)
- a 20-year compliance period

CFPB ENFORCEMENT

In re Dwolla, Inc., CFPB No. 2016-CFPB-0007 (Mar. 2, 2016)
The CFPB brought its first data security enforcement action against Dwolla, Inc. Dwolla claimed to operate an online payment service "above industry standards," but the CFPB alleged the company's online payment system was unsafe. The order sets a $100,000 penalty and requires the company to establish and implement a written data security program including proper employee training and regular data security risk assessments.

FEDERAL STATUTES: ENTERTAINMENT RECORDS

Cable Communications Policy Act of 1984 (CCPA)
47 U.S.C. § 551

Primary Function: To protect the privacy of cable subscribers.

Applies to: Cable operators and service providers. 47 U.S.C. § 551(a)(1).

Notice and Access: Requires cable service providers to notify subscribers of the nature and uses of personal information collected. Subscribers must have access to their personal data held by cable operators.

Limitations on Data Collection: Cable operators "shall not use the cable system to collect personally identifiable information concerning any subscriber without the prior written or electronic consent of the subscriber concerned." 47 U.S.C. § 551(b)(1).

Opt-In: Cable operators cannot disclose personally identifiable information about any subscriber without the subscriber's consent. 47 U.S.C. § 551(c)(1).

Opt-Out: Cable operators may disclose subscriber names and addresses if "the cable operator has provided the subscriber the opportunity to prohibit or limit such disclosure." 47 U.S.C. § 551(c)(2).

Exceptions: Disclosure permitted when necessary for a "legitimate business activity" or pursuant to a court order if the subscriber is notified. 47 U.S.C. § 551 (c)(2).

Data Destruction: Cable operators must destroy personal data if the information is no longer necessary for the purpose for which it was collected. 47 U.S.C. § 551(e).

Government Access to Cable Information: The government can obtain cable subscriber data pursuant to a court order justified by "clear and convincing evidence" the subscriber is "reasonably suspected of engaging in criminal activity and that the information sought would be material evidence in the case." The subscriber must be notified and allowed to challenge the order. 47 U.S.C. § 551(h).

Enforcement: Private cause of action and actual damages, with a minimum of $1,000 or $100 for each day of the violation, whichever is higher. Punitive damages and attorneys' fees. 47 U.S.C. § 551(f).

Leading Case

Kilmas v. Comcast Cable Commc'ns, Inc., 465 F.3d 271 (6th Cir. 2006)
The Sixth Circuit held that the Cable Act did not apply to a cable company's alleged collection of IP-URL linkage information. The plain language of the Cable Act precluded application of its privacy protections to the cable company's offering of broadband Internet service. As the Sixth Circuit observed, "[B]roadband Internet service delivered via cable is *not* 'cable services'" in the sense of the Cable Act.

Video Privacy Protection Act of 1988 (VPPA)
18 U.S.C. §§ 2710-2711

Primary Function: To protect the privacy of video watching.

Applies to: Covers any "video tape service provider"—"any person, engaged in the business, in or affecting interstate or foreign commerce, of rental, sale, or delivery of prerecorded video cassette tapes or similar audio visual materials." 18 U.S.C. § 2710(a)(4). It covers DVDs and online delivery of videos.

Opt-In: Videotape service providers cannot knowingly disclose personal information without the individual's written consent. 18 U.S.C. § 2710(2)(B).

Opt-Out: Videotape service providers can disclose the names and addresses of consumers if the consumer has been given the right to opt out, and the disclosure does not identify information about the videos the consumer rents. 18 U.S.C. § 2710(b)(2)(D). "[T]he subject matter of such materials may be disclosed if the disclosure is for the exclusive use of marketing goods and services directly to the consumer." 18 U.S.C. § 2710(b)(2)(D)(ii).

Destruction of Records: Records of personal information must be destroyed as soon as practicable. 18 U.S.C. § 2710(e).

Exceptions: VPPA contains several exceptions, such as permitting videotape providers to disclose "to any person if the disclosure is incident to the ordinary course of business of the video tape service provider." 18 U.S.C. § 2710(b)(2)(E).

Government Access: Permits disclosure to a law enforcement agency pursuant to a warrant, court order or subpoena. 18 U.S.C. § 2710(b)(2)(C).

Preemption: VPPA does not block states from enacting statutes that are more protective of privacy. 18 U.S.C. § 2710(f).

Enforcement: Private cause of action when a videotape service provider "knowingly discloses ... personally identifiable information concerning any consumer of such provider." 18 U.S.C. § 2710(b)(1). Actual damages and liquidated damages in the amount of $2,500. Punitive damages, attorneys' fees, equitable and injunctive relief. 18 U.S.C. § 2710(c). The VPPA also includes a statutory exclusionary rule that prevents the admission into evidence of any information obtained in violation of the statute. 18 U.S.C. § 2710(d).

Video Privacy Protection Act Amendments Act of 2012
Pub. L. No. 112-258, 126 Stat. 2414 (codified as amended at 18 U.S.C. § 2710)
Permitting a videotape service provider to obtain the consumer's informed, written consent through the Internet. Such consent is valid for a period of up to two years or until consent is withdrawn.

Leading Cases

Austin-Spearman v. AMC Network Entm't, LLC., 98 F. Supp. 3d 662 (S.D.N.Y. 2015)
AMC Networks allegedly violated the VPPA by sharing user's video-streaming history collected from their website with a social network. The court ruled that these claims were sufficient to constitute an injury-in-fact, required for Article III standing. However, the plaintiff failed to establish that she was a registered user or had any other relationship with the website; the court consequently held she was not a "consumer" protected by the VPPA.

Eichenberger v. ESPN, Inc., No. C14–463 TSZ, 2015 WL 7252985 (W.D. Wash. May 7, 2015)
Class action suit against ESPN alleging that the network's Roku streaming app improperly shared consumer's PII, such as streaming behavior, with third parties. The information given to third parties combined unique Roku serial number with information previously collected about that consumer. The unique serial number of a Roku device was held not to constitute PII under the VPPA.

Locklear v. Dow Jones & Co., 101 F. Supp. 3d 1312 (N.D. Ga. 2015), *abrogated by Ellis v. Cartoon Network, Inc.,* 803 F.3d 1251 (11th Cir. 2015)
Another court reached a conclusion similar to the *Eichenberger* decision, holding that a device's unique serial number was not PII under the VPPA.

Ellis v. The Cartoon Network, Inc., 803 F.3d 1251 (11th Cir. 2015)

The Cartoon Network offered free mobile app services that allowed consumers to stream freely available content. A consumer alleged that the company violated the VPPA by disclosing mobile device identification numbers and records about the viewed content with data-analytics companies. The court held that an individual who uses a free mobile app to view freely available content does not qualify as a "subscriber" and consequently is not a "consumer" under the VPPA.

Yershov v. Gannett Satellite Info. Network, Inc., 820 F.3d 482 (1st Cir. 2016)

Newspaper publisher Gannett Satellite offered a mobile app and allegedly disclosed personal information to third-party data-analytics companies, including the unique identifier number of consumers' mobile devices, GPS locations, and content viewed through the app. While the Eleventh Circuit agreed with the district court that this type of information qualifies as PII under the VPPA, it reversed the lower court's dismissal on the grounds that the complaint adequately alleged that the plaintiff was a "consumer" for purposes of the VPPA.

Robinson v. Disney Online, 152 F. Supp. 3d 176 (S.D.N.Y. 2015)

Users of Disney's digital streaming service brought a class action, alleging that the corporation violated the VPPA by disclosing and sharing PII with a third-party data analytics company. The court ruled that encrypted serial numbers of consumer devices did not constitute PII under the VPPA. The serial number itself identified only a specific device, not a specific person.

In re Hulu Privacy Litig., No. C 11-03764 LB, 2014 WL 1724344 (N.D. Cal. Apr. 28, 2014)

Class action brought by viewers of Hulu's online video content alleged that Hulu wrongfully disclosed to third parties their video viewing selections and other data linked to their unique identifiers. The court held that the classification of information as PII under VPPA does not require disclosure of a person's actual name—all that is required is "identification of a specific person tied to a specific transaction." Anonymized IDs alone are not PII "but context could render it not anonymous and the equivalent of the identification of a specific person." Certain disclosures made by Hulu were thus not PII but other disclosures, such as sending cookies that could "show the Hulu user's identity on Facebook" would constitute the disclosure of PII. To be liable under VPPA, Hulu would have to know that it was "transmitting both an identifier and the person's video watching information," and facts remained in dispute about intent, and thus Hulu's motion to dismiss was denied.

In re Hulu Privacy Litig., No. C 11-03764 LB, 2012 WL 3282960 (N.D. Cal. Aug. 10, 2012)

Hulu, an online provider of streaming video, was a "video tape service provider" under VPPA because the definition of a "video tape service provider" regulates "any person, engaged in the business … of rental, sale, or delivery of prerecorded video cassette tapes or similar audio visual materials." The term "similar" is deliberately broad and "designed to include new technologies for pre-recorded video content."

Sterk v. Redbox Automated Retail, LLC, 672 F.3d 535 (7th Cir. 2012)
Damages are not available under VPPA for simply failing to destroy old records.
There must be a subsequent disclosure for there to be an injury and damages.

FEDERAL STATUTES: MARKETING

Telecommunications Act of 1996
47 U.S.C. § 222

Primary Function: The Telecommunications Act requires a telecommunications
carrier "to protect the confidentiality of proprietary information of, and relating to …
customers."

CPNI: The act establishes the important legal category of "customer proprietary
network information" (CPNI). 47 U.S.C. § 222(c). It places certain kinds of restrictions on the use, disclosure of, and access to CPNI. In a nutshell, a telecommunications carrier does not need customer approval to use and disclose CPNI to provide
or market offerings among the categories of service to which the customer already
subscribes from the carrier. Unless it meets certain exceptions provided in the regulations, a carrier must obtain opt-in consent from a customer before sharing CPNI with
joint venture partners and independent contractors for marketing purposes.

In *U.S. West, Inc. v. Federal Communications Commission,* 182 F.3d 1224 (10th Cir.
1999), U.S. West had objected to FCC regulations, enacted pursuant to the Telecommunications Act, which required an opt-in rule for use of a customer's CPNI for marketing purposes. The Tenth Circuit found that this aspect of the CPNI regulations
violated the First Amendment. The FCC had failed to demonstrate a real harm to
customer privacy that the regulation prevented and also failed to adequately consider
a less restrictive alternative, namely an opt-out strategy.

The FCC responded to the *U.S. West* decision at length in its 2007 CPNI Order
and rejected its holdings. Specifically, the FCC declared that the Tenth Circuit in
that case based its decision "on a different record than the one compiled here" and in
particular on premises that were no longer valid. First, there was now ample evidence
of disclosure of CPNI and the adverse effects it could have on customers. Second,
there was now substantial evidence that an opt-out strategy would not adequately
protect customer privacy "because most customers either do not read or do not
understand carriers' opt-out notices." *In re Implementation of the Telecommunications
Act of 1996,* FCC No. 07-22 ¶ 44 (April 2, 2007). The FCC also stated that requiring opt-in consent from customers before sharing CPNI with joint venture partners
and independent contractors for marketing purposes would pass First Amendment
scrutiny. *Id.* at ¶ 45.

Telephone Consumer Protection Act of 1991 (TCPA)
47 U.S.C. § 227

Primary Function: Permits people to stop unwanted telemarketing calls.

Key Provisions: Authorizes the federal Do Not Call Registry, where people can sign up their numbers if they do not wish to receive telemarketing calls. Does not apply to charitable or political calls. 47 U.S.C. § 227(c)(3). Prohibits marketers from calling residences and using prerecorded messages without the consent of the called party. *Id.* § 227(b)(1)(B). The TCPA prohibits the use of a fax, computer, or other device to send an unsolicited advertisement to a fax machine.

Enforcement: Permits individuals to sue a telemarketer in small claims court for an actual loss of up to $500 (whichever is greater) for each call received after requesting to be placed on its Do Not Call list. States may initiate actions against telemarketers "engaging in a pattern or practice of telephone calls or other transmissions to residents of that state" in violation of the TCPA. 47 U.S.C. § 227(f)(1). If a telemarketer has acted "willfully or knowingly," then damages are trebled.

Leading Cases

Palm Beach Golf Center-Boca, Inc. v. John G. Sarris, D.D.S., P.A., 781 F.3d 1245 (11th Cir. 2015)

Eleventh Circuit ruled transmission of junk faxes conferred Article III standing, even if the faxes in question were unseen by recipients. The court contended that rendering a plaintiff's fax machine unavailable for a period of time constituted an injury-in-fact.

Gager v. Dell Fin. Servs., LLC, 727 F.3d 265 (3rd Cir. 2013)

Consumer brought action against creditor, alleging that creditor violated the TCPA by calling her through an automated telephone dialing system after prior express consent to be contacted had been revoked. The Third Circuit held that a contractual relationship between consumer and creditor does not exempt the creditor from TCPA requirements and that the creditor violated the TCPA.

Chesbro v. Best Buy Stores, 705 F.3d 913 (9th Cir. 2012)

The TCPA generally prohibits robocalls to residential phone lines without prior consent. Calls that do not adversely affect privacy and do not transmit unsolicited ads are exempt. Yet, FCC regulations under TCPA do not exempt from regulation "dual-purpose" robocalls, which inquire about customer satisfaction plus market goods or services. As a result, the FCC determined that the TCPA prohibits "dual-purpose" robocalls. Best Buy made robocalls to follow up on customer purchases, but the calls discussed a rewards program for points to be redeemed for other Best Buy purchases. The court deemed them "dual-purpose" calls subject to the TCPA because the reward points were designed to entice customers to Best Buy stores to make future purchases.

Controlling the Assault of Non-Solicited Pornography and Marketing Act of 2003 (CAN-SPAM)
15 U.S.C. §§ 7701-7713

Primary Function: To regulate commercial e-mail.

Applies to: Commercial e-mail—a "message the primary purpose of which is the commercial advertisement or promotion of a commercial product or service."

Restrictions: Prohibits the knowing sending of commercial messages with the intent to deceive or mislead recipients.

Opt-Out: The CAN-SPAM Act also requires that a valid opt-out option be made available to e-mail recipients. To make opt-out possible, the act requires senders of commercial e-mail to contain a return address "clearly and conspicuously displayed." 15 U.S.C. § 7704(a)(3)(A).

Enforcement: No private right of action. Enforced by the FTC and other agencies. Violations are deemed an "unfair or deceptive act or practice." 15 U.S.C. § 7706(a). State attorneys general can bring actions for damages suffered by the state's residents as well as injunctive and equitable relief. Criminal penalties against predatory and abusive commercial e-mail. 15 U.S.C. § 7703.

Preemption: Preempts state regulation that "expressly regulates the use of electronic mail to send commercial messages, except to the extent that any such statute, regulation, or rule prohibits falsity or deception in any portion [of the e-mail message]." 15 U.S.C. § 7707(b).

State Anti-Spam Laws: At least 20 states have anti-spam statutes.

International Approaches: Most other countries favor an opt-in approach as a legal response to commercial unsolicited emails and may provide for strong administrative penalties as well as a private right of action. The EU E-Privacy Directive requires prior consent. In German law, prior express consent requires a process termed "double opt-in," meaning a consumer has to agree to receive commercial emails by checking a box and then again opt-in in by clicking on a link contained in the first email received after enrollment. Canada's Anti-Spam Law (CASL) requires opt-in consent, and provides for high monetary penalties as well as a private right of action. For more on CASL, see Chapter 13.

FCC Enforcement
The FCC has increased its enforcement of privacy matters and has handed out large fines. Collaborating with other agencies, the FCC has collected more than $365 million through its settlements, including punitive fines and refunds to consumers.

FCC, *Privacy Guidelines for ISPs* (2016)
Privacy guidelines issued for ISPs, providing three separate categories for using and sharing information. The guidelines also provide ISP customers with increased transparency and power regarding their personal information.

In re Cellco P'ship, **FCC No. EB-TCD-14-00017601 (Mar. 7, 2016)**
Verizon Wireless had previously added unique identifier headers, or "supercookies,"
into customers' mobile Internet traffic without notification or consent. According
to an FCC suit, these "supercookies" were employed from 2012 to 2014. A settlement between the parties included a $1.35 million fine and required the adoption a
three-year compliance plan. Verizon agreed to notify consumers about tracking and
targeting practices, and the company now needs consumer consent in order to share
supercookie information with third parties.

In re AT&T Servs., Inc., **FCC No. EB-TCD-14-00016243 (Apr. 8, 2015)**
AT&T's overseas workers stole personal information from 280,000 customers. In a
settlement with the FCC, AT&T agreed to pay a $25 million fine for violating their
statutory duty under the Communications Act to reasonably secure and protect their
customer data. The FCC noted this failure also constituted "an unjust and unreasonable practice in violation of the Communications Act."

In re TerraCom, Inc., **FCC No. EB-TCD-13-00009175 (July 9, 2015)**
TerraCom and YourTel exposed consumers' sensitive information to unauthorized
individuals when its data storage vendors utilized servers without any encryption
or password protection. As a result, the FCC issued an order to the companies that
set out a $3.5 million penalty. The companies were also required to implement a
comprehensive information security program, a data breach response plan, enhanced
employee training, and regular privacy risk assessments. The FCC's order mandated
that the two parties designate a certified privacy professional at a senior corporate
manager level and to provide compliance reports with the FCC.

In re Cox Commc'ns, Inc., **FCC No. EB-IHD-14-00017829 (Nov. 5, 2015)**
FCC data security enforcement action against a cable provider following a data
breach and subsequent allegations of unreasonable data security practices. The FCC
also alleged that Cox failed to notify law enforcement authorities of the security
breaches in a timely fashion. Cox entered into a consent decree that included a
$595,000 civil penalty and required enhanced security practices including oversight
of vendors, privacy risk assessments, a written compliance program, training of employees, and notification issued to affected consumers.

FEDERAL STATUTES: INTERNET USE AND ELECTRONIC COMMUNICATIONS

Children's Online Privacy Protection Act of 1998 (COPPA)
15 U.S.C. §§ 6501-6506

Primary Function: Regulates the collection and use of children's information by
Internet websites by requiring parental consent.

Applies to: Websites that collect personal information from children under age 13. 15 U.S.C. § 6502(1). More specifically, it applies to:

1. "[A]n operator of a website or online service directed to children." 15 U.S.C. § 6502(a)(1).

2. "[A]ny operator that has actual knowledge that it is collecting personal information from a child." 15 U.S.C. § 6502(a)(1).

Personal Information: FTC amendments to the COPPA rule in 2013 expanded the definition of "personal information" to clearly include persistent identifiers, such as IP addresses and mobile device IDs, that recognize users over time and across different online services. As a result, behavioral advertising on child-directed online services now requires parental notice and consent.

Notice: Children's websites must post privacy policies describing "what information is collected from children by the operator, how the operator uses such information, and the operator's disclosure practices for such information." 15 U.S.C. § 6502(b)(1)(A)(i).

Opt-In: Children's websites must "obtain verifiable parental consent for the collection, use, or disclosure of personal information from children." 15 U.S.C. § 6502(b)(1)(A)(ii). Websites cannot condition a child's participation in a game or receipt of a prize on the disclosure of more personal information than is necessary to participate in that activity. 15 U.S.C. § 6502(b)(1)(C).

Third-Party Ad Networks, Plug-Ins, and Apps: Pursuant to the FTC's amended COPPA rule in 2013, both websites and mobile apps will be held strictly liable for collection by third-party ad networks and plug-in providers absent parental notice and consent. Additionally, third-party social plug-ins and ad networks must comply with COPPA themselves if they have actual knowledge that they are collecting personal information from children under the age of 13.

Enforcement: Violations of COPPA are "treated as a violation of a rule defining an unfair or deceptive act or practice" under the FTCA. The FTC enforces the law and can impose fines. There is no private cause of action for violations of COPPA. States can bring civil actions for violations of COPPA in the interests of their citizens to obtain injunctions and damages. 15 U.S.C. § 6504.

Preemption: COPPA preempts state law. 15 U.S.C. § 6502(d).

Safe Harbor: If an operator follows self-regulatory guidelines issued by marketing or online industry groups that are approved by the FTC, then the COPPA requirements will be deemed satisfied. 15 U.S.C. § 6503.

FTC COPPA Enforcement Actions

United States v. Bigmailbox.com, Inc., **No. 01-605-A (E.D. Va. Apr. 19, 2001)**
Website targeted to young girls collected names, addresses, and other information, despite stating in its privacy policy that such data would not be collected without verifiable parental consent. Settlement with FTC for $35,000.

United States v. Ohio Art Co., **No. 3:02CV7203 (N.D. Ohio Apr. 19, 2002)**
(the "Etch-A-Sketch Case")
The Ohio Art Company collected information from children for a contest to win an Etch-A-Sketch. To obtain parental permission, the company asked children to "get your parent or guardian's permission first." This was inadequate. Moreover, the company collected more information than reasonably necessary. Settlement with FTC for $35,000.

United States v. Mrs. Fields Famous Brands, Inc., **No. 2:03CV205-JTG**
(D. Utah Feb. 26, 2003)
The company collected information from 84,000 children for a birthday club without obtaining parental consent. Settlement with FTC for $100,000.

United States v. Hershey Foods Corp., **No. 4:CV03-350 (M.D. Pa. Feb. 26, 2003)**
Hershey offered an online parental consent form but did not ensure parents filled it out. The company still collected personal data even if the form was not completed. This was an inadequate way of obtaining parental consent. Settlement with FTC for $85,000.

United States v. Bonzi Software, Inc., **No. CV-04-1048 RJK (Ex)**
(C.D. Cal. Feb. 17, 2004)
Software company had users provide their birth date when registering software. Although the site was not directed to children, Bonzi had actual knowledge children were using its software. Bonzi thus had to comply with COPPA, and it did not. Settlement with FTC for $75,000.

United States v. UMG Recordings, Inc., **No. CV-04-1050 JFW (Ex)**
(C.D. Cal. Feb. 17, 2004)
UMG notified parents *after* collecting children's data. Notice had to be given beforehand. Settlement with FTC for $85,000.

United States v. Xanga.com, Inc., **No. 06-CIV-6853(SHS) (S.D.N.Y. Sept. 7, 2006)**
Social network website allowed children under 13 years old to create profiles. Had actual knowledge children were under this age but failed to obtain parental consent. Settlement with FTC for $1 million.

United States v. Industrious Kid, Inc., No. 3:08-cv-00639-SI (N.D. Cal. Mar. 6, 2008)

Social network website directed at children 8 to 14 years old allowed them to create profiles and upload information. Profiles could not be viewed by others until parents completed the registration process. This ran afoul of COPPA because the website maintained the information prior to receiving parental consent. Settlement with FTC for $130,000.

United States v. Sony BMG Music Entm't, No. 1:08-cv-10730-LAK (S.D.N.Y. Dec. 15, 2008)

Sony had actual knowledge that some of its user fan pages were created by children. Falsely stated in its privacy policy that children were not allowed to participate. Settlement with FTC for $1 million.

United States v. Iconix Brand Grp., No. 1:09-cv-08864-MGC (S.D.N.Y. Nov. 5, 2009)

Knowingly collected information from children without obtaining parental consent. Settlement with FTC for $250,000.

United States v. W3 Innovations, LLC, No. 5:11-cv-03958-PSG (N.D. Cal. Sept. 8, 2011)

In the FTC's first mobile app case, it settled with W-3 Innovations LLC for a violation of COPPA. The app collected children's personal data and allowed children to post personal data on public message boards. The company did not provide a notice or require parental consent. It also failed to provide a privacy policy.

United States v. Playdom, Inc., No. 8:11-cv-00724-AG (ANx) (C.D. Cal. May 24, 2011)

Playdom, an operator of online "virtual worlds," violated COPPA by collecting children's ages and e-mail addresses during registration. Children could publish personal data publicly on profile pages, and Playdom failed to provide proper notice or obtain parental consent. Additionally, the company violated the FTC Act because its privacy policy falsely stated that the company prohibited children under age 13 from posting personal data on the Internet. As part of its settlement, Playdom agreed to pay $3 million, which is the largest civil penalty ever assessed for a violation of the FTC's COPPA rule

United States v. RockYou, Inc., No. 3:12-cv-01487-SI (N.D. Cal. Mar. 28, 2012)

RockYou, a social gaming site, allowed users to create slide shows with their photos. To save these slide shows, users had to enter an e-mail address and password as well as birth date. Although it collected data from children under 13, the company did not comply with COPPA. This settlement action also alleged that flaws in RockYou's game site had exposed 32 e-mail addresses and passwords to hackers.

United States v. Path, Inc., No. 3:13-cv-00448-RS (N.D.Cal. Feb. 8, 2013)
Social networking app involved users uploading personal data to a journal that they could share with friends in the Path network. The app collected birth date information during user registration, including about 3,000 children under the age of 13. Parental consent was not obtained. The settlement requires Path to pay an $800,000 penalty, to establish a comprehensive privacy program, and be audited every other year for the next 20 years.

In re Apple Inc., FTC No. C-4444 (Mar. 25, 2014)
Apple failed to notify parents that by entering a password they were approving 15 minutes of unlimited purchases their children could make when using apps. FTC settlement required Apple to obtain express informed consent before billing them, and consumers who consent to future charges must be allowed to withdraw consent at any time. Apple must provide refunds to consumers, for a minimum total of $32.5 million.

United States v. LAI Sys., LLC, No. 2:15-cv-9691 (W.D. Cal. Dec. 17, 2015) and
United States v. Retro Dreamer, No. 5:15-cv-2569 (E.D. Cal. Dec. 17, 2015)
Multiple apps directed at children create by LAI Systems and Retro Dreamer failed to notify parents regarding information practices and also failed to obtain parental consent prior to allowing third-party advertisers to use persistent personal identifiers. Furthermore, LAI Systems did not notify ad networks that their apps collected children's PII. The FTC settlement requires LAI and Retro Dreamer to pay a combined total of $360,000 in penalties and to enact policies that comply with the modified COPPA rules.
Note: The settlements with the FTC also involved other requirements, typically an agreement not to violate COPPA in the future and extensive compliance monitoring for up to two decades.

> ## Complying with COPPA
>
> According to the FTC's website, a company's compliance with COPPA requires the following:
>
> 1. Post a clear and comprehensive privacy policy on the company's website describing its information practices for children's personal information;
>
> 2. Provide direct notice to parents and obtain verifiable parental consent, with limited exceptions, before collecting personal information from children;
>
> 3. Give parents the choice of consenting to the operator's collection and internal use of a child's information, but prohibiting the operator from disclosing that information to third parties;

Complying with COPPA

4. Provide parents access to their child's personal information to review and/or have the information deleted;

5. Give parents the opportunity to prevent further use or online collection of a child's personal information;

6. Maintain the confidentiality, security and integrity of information they collect from children.

Source: FTC, COPPA FAQs, http://www.ftc.gov/privacy/coppafaqs.shtm (Mar. 2015)

How to Determine if a Website (or a Portion of It) Is Directed at Children

In its regulations, 16 C.F.R. § 312.2, the FTC provides several factors that it will consider:

- Subject matter
- Visual and audio content
- Age of models
- Language or other characteristics of the site
- Empirical evidence regarding audience composition
- Evidence regarding the intended audience
- Whether a site uses animated characters
- Whether the site has child-oriented activities and incentives

Electronic Communications Privacy Act of 1986 (ECPA)
18 U.S.C. §§ 2510-3127

In several cases, plaintiffs have attempted to use the Electronic Communications Privacy Act (ECPA) to prevent certain kinds of information collection, use and disclosure by commercial entities. ECPA consists of three acts: (1) the Wiretap Act, 18 U.S.C. §§ 2510–2522, which regulates the interception of communications; (2) the Stored Communications Act (SCA), 18 U.S.C. §§ 2701–2711, which regulates communications in storage and ISP subscriber records; and (3) the Pen Register Act, 18 U.S.C. §§ 3121–3127, which regulates the use of pen register and trap and trace devices.

The attempts to use ECPA to regulate commercial entities using personal information primarily seek to use the Wiretap Act or the SCA. In most cases, ECPA does not apply because of user consent. See *In re Pharmatrak, Inc. Privacy Litig.*, 329 F.3d 9 (1st Cir. 2003); *In re DoubleClick Inc. Privacy Litig.*, 154 F. Supp. 2d 497 (S.D.N.Y. 2001); *Dyer v. Nw. Airlines Corps.*, 334 F. Supp. 2d 1196 (D.N.D. 2004).

However, in *Campbell v. Facebook Inc.*, 77 F.Supp.3d 836 (N.D. Cal. 2014), plaintiffs alleged that Facebook scanned users' private messages for targeted advertising purposes. The court held that consumers of Facebook's website neither expressly nor implicitly consented to the alleged interception of their private messages. Facebook's disclosure that it may use information about users for data analysis was not specific enough to constitute valid consent, nor did it provide adequate notice regarding the private communications text-scanning.

Computer Fraud and Abuse Act (CFAA)
18 U.S.C. § 1030 (1984)

Primary Function: To prevent unauthorized access to computers.

Applies to: Any "protected computer" (used in interstate commerce or communications). Due to this broad definition, the act generally will apply to any computer connected to the Internet.

Criminal Penalties: The CFAA creates seven crimes. Among these offenses, it imposes criminal penalties when a person or entity "intentionally accesses a computer without authorization or exceeds authorized access, and thereby obtains ... information from any protected computer." 18 U.S.C. § 1030(a)(2)(c). It prohibits knowingly transmitting "a program, information, code, or command" or "intentionally access[ing] a protected computer without authorization" that causes damage to a protected computer. 18 U.S.C. § 1030(5). Punishments range from fines to imprisonment for up to 20 years depending on the provision violated.

Damage: Some of the provisions of CFAA require causing "damage," which means "any impairment to the integrity or availability of data, a program, a system or information." 18 U.S.C. § 1030(e). In many provisions in the CFAA, the damage must exceed $5,000 in a one-year period.

Civil Remedies: "Any person who suffers damage or loss by reason of a violation of this section may maintain a civil action against the violator to obtain compensatory damages or injunctive relief or other equitable relief." 18 U.S.C. § 1030(g). "Damage" must cause a loss "aggregating at least $5,000 in value" during any one-year period to one or more individuals. 18 U.S.C. § 1030(c).

Exceeding Authorized Access: Many provisions in the CFAA can be violated not just by unauthorized access, but also when one "exceeds authorized access." To "exceed authorized access" means "to access a computer with authorization and to use such access to obtain or alter information in the computer that the accesser is not entitled so to obtain or alter." 18 U.S.C. § 1030(e)(6).

Leading Cases

United States v. Drew, 259 F.R.D. 449 (C.D. Cal. 2009)

A woman who created a fake MySpace profile to harass a young girl (ultimately resulting in her suicide) was charged with exceeding authorization because MySpace's terms of service prohibited creating fictitious profiles. The court held that such an interpretation of the CFAA would transform it "into an overwhelmingly overbroad enactment that would convert a multitude of otherwise innocent Internet users into misdemeanant criminals."

LVRC Holdings LLC v. Brekka, 581 F.3d 1127 (9th Cir. 2009)

An employee who e-mailed files to himself from a workplace computer right before he was to leave the office did not access the computer without authorization since he originally had permission to use the computer. Although some courts have reached contrary conclusions (see Citrin below), this decision reflects the majority view among courts that have examined this issue.

Int'l Airport Ctrs., LLC v. Citrin, 440 F.3d 418 (7th Cir. 2006)

An employee accesses a computer without authorization in violation of the CFAA when he accesses it in breach of a duty of loyalty to the company. This court represents the minority view.

United States v. Steele, 595 Fed. Appx. 208 (4th Cir. 2014)

Adhering to its narrow construction of the CFAA, the Fourth Circuit upheld a defendant's criminal conviction after he accessed his former employer's servers. The decision distinguished this case from others limiting CFAA liability by noting that termination of employment ends authorized access regardless of whether or not the employer changed its server's password.

Is the CFAA Too Broad and Vague?

The CFAA was originally an anti-hacking statute, but its definitions of accessing a computer without authorization or exceeding authorization can be quite broad and vague under some interpretations. Under the theory expressed by the government in United States v. Drew, 259 F.R.D. 449 (C.D. Cal. 2009), every time people violate a website's terms of service, they may be committing a federal crime.

FEDERAL STATUTES: OVERVIEW

SCOPE OF FEDERAL STATUTE COVERAGE

REGULATED	NOT REGULATED*
Federal agency records (Privacy Act)	State agency records
State DMV records (DPPA)	Property records
Cable TV records (CCPA)	Library records
Video rental records (VPPA)	Supermarket purchase records
Medical records (HIPAA)	Bookstore records
Bank records (RFPA, GLB)	Department store records
Consumer reporting agency records (FCRA)	Internet websites (adult Web surfers)
Internet websites (kid Web surfers) (COPPA)	
ISP records (ECPA)	

*By not regulated, we mean not covered by a specific federal statute. Records may still be regulated by the FTC to the extent that a company makes promises in its privacy policy.

FEDERAL STATUTES AND PRIVATE RIGHTS OF ACTION

STATUTES *WITH* PRIVATE RIGHTS OF ACTION	STATUTES *WITHOUT* PRIVATE RIGHTS OF ACTION
Cable Communications Policy Act (CCPA) 47 U.S.C. § 551(f)	Children's Online Privacy Protection Act (COPPA) 15 U.S.C. §§ 6501-6506
CAN-SPAM Act 15 U.S.C. § 7706(g) (allows actions by ISPs, but not individuals)	Family Educational Rights and Privacy Act (FERPA) 20 U.S.C. § 1232g
Drivers Privacy Protection Act (DPPA) 18 U.S.C. § 2724	Federal Trade Commission Act (FTC Act) 15 U.S.C. §§ 41, 45, 46, 571, 57b, 57b-1
Employee Polygraph Protection Act (EPPA) 29 U.S.C. § 2005(c)	Gramm-Leach-Bliley Act (GLBA) 15 U.S.C. §§ 6801-6809, 6821-6827
Fair Credit Reporting Act (FCRA) 15 U.S.C. § 1681n (willful violations) 15 U.S.C. § 1681o (negligent violations)	Health Insurance Portability and Accountability Act (HIPAA) 45 C.F.R. 164

FEDERAL STATUTES AND PRIVATE RIGHTS OF ACTION

Foreign Intelligence Surveillance Act (FISA) 18 U.S.C. § 1810 (improper disclosure/ use of electronic surveillance) 18 U.S.C. § 1828 (improper physical search or disclosure/use)	Pen Register Act 18 U.S.C. §§ 3121-3123
Privacy Act 5 U.S.C. § 552a(g)(1)	
Privacy Protection Act (PPA) 42 U.S.C. § 2000aa-6(a)	
Right to Financial Privacy Act (RFPA) 12 U.S.C. § 3417	
Stored Communications Act (SCA) 18 U.S.C. § 2707 (against others) 18 U.S.C. § 2712 (against U.S.)	
Telephone Consumer Protection Act (TCPA) 47 U.S.C. § 227(c)(5)	
Video Privacy Protection Act (VPPA) 18 U.S.C. § 2710(c)	
Wiretap Act 18 U.S.C. § 2520	

FEDERAL STATUTES AND LIQUIDATED DAMAGES

Statutes *with* Liquidated Damages
No Proof of Actual Damages Required

Cable Communications Policy Act (CCPA)
47 U.S.C. § 551(f)
"actual damages but not less than liquidated damages computed at the rate of $100 a day for each day of violation or $1,000, whichever is higher"

CAN-SPAM Act
15 U.S.C. § 7706(g) (ISPs only)
Multiply the number of violations times $100 or $25 depending upon the nature of the violation.

Drivers Privacy Protection Act (DPPA)
18 U.S.C. § 2724
"actual damages, but not less than liquidated damages in the amount of $2,500"

Fair Credit Reporting Act (FCRA)
15 U.S.C. § 1681n (willful violations)
"any actual damages sustained by the consumer as a result of the failure or damages of not less than $100 and not more than $1,000"

Privacy Law Fundamentals

15 U.S.C. § 1671o (negligent violations)
only actual damages allowed; no liquidated damages

Foreign Intelligence Surveillance Act (FISA)
50 U.S.C. § 1810 (improper disclosure/use of electronic surveillance)
"actual damages, but not less than liquidated damages of $1,000 or $100 per day for each day of violation, whichever is greater"

18 U.S.C. § 1828 (improper physical search or disclosure/use)
"actual damages, but not less than liquidated damages of $1,000 or $100 per day for each day of violation, whichever is greater"

Privacy Protection Act (PPA)
42 U.S.C. § 2000aa-6(f)
"actual damages but not less than liquidated damages of $1,000"

Right to Financial Privacy Act (RFPA)
12 U.S.C. § 3417
"(1) $100 without regard to the volume of records involved; (2) any actual damages sustained by the customer as a result of the disclosure"

Stored Communications Act (SCA)
18 U.S.C. § 2707 (against others)
"actual damages but not less than liquidated damages of $1,000"

18 U.S.C. § 2712 (against U.S.)
"actual damages, but not less than $10,000, whichever amount is greater"

Telephone Consumer Protection Act (TCPA)
47 U.S.C. § 227(c)(5)
"recover for actual monetary loss from such a violation, or to receive up to $500 in damages for each such violation, whichever is greater"

Video Privacy Protection Act (VPPA)
18 U.S.C. § 2710(c)
"actual damages but not less than liquidated damages in an amount of $2,500"

Wiretap Act
18 U.S.C. § 2520
"the court may assess as damages whichever is the greater of (A) the sum of the actual damages suffered by the plaintiff and any profits made by the violator as a result of the violation; or (B) statutory damages of whichever is the greater of $100 a day for each day of violation or $10,000"

Statutes *with* Liquidated Damages
Proof of Actual Damages Required

Privacy Act
5 U.S.C. § 552a
"actual damages sustained by the individual as a result of the refusal or failure, but in no case shall a person entitled to recovery receive less than the sum of $1,000"

Doe v. Chao, 540 U.S. 614 (2004), concluded that the phrase "entitled to recover" required that plaintiffs be entitled to recover actual damages before receiving liquidated damages.

Stored Communications Act (SCA)
18 U.S.C. § 2707 (against others)
"The court may assess as damages in a civil action under this section the sum of the actual damages suffered by the plaintiff and any profits made by the violator as a result of the violation, but in no case shall a person entitled to recover receive less than the sum of $1,000."

Statutes *without* Liquidated Damages
Employee Polygraph Protection Act (EPPA)
29 U.S.C. § 2005(c)

FEDERAL STATUTES AND CRIMINAL PENALTIES

STATUTES WITH CRIMINAL PENALTIES	STATUTES WITHOUT CRIMINAL PENALTIES
CAN-SPAM Act 15 U.S.C. §§ 7703-7704 (for certain fraudulent e-mail practices)	Cable Communications Policy Act (CCPA) 47 U.S.C. § 521, 551-552
Computer Fraud and Abuse Act (CFAA) 18 U.S.C. § 1030(c)	Children's Online Privacy Protection Act (COPPA) 15 U.S.C. §§ 6501-6505
Drivers Privacy Protection Act (DPPA) 18 U.S.C. § 2723	Employee Polygraph Protection Act (EPPA) 29 U.S.C. §§ 2001-2009
Fair Credit Reporting Act (FCRA) 15 U.S.C. § 1681q (for knowingly obtaining consumer data under false pretenses)	Family Educational Rights and Privacy Act (FERPA) 20 U.S.C. § 1232g
Foreign Intelligence Surveillance Act (FISA) 50 U.S.C. § 1809 (improper use and disclosure of electronic surveillance) 50 U.S.C. § 1827 (improper physical search or disclosure/use)	Privacy Protection Act (PPA) 42 U.S.C. FERPA 20 U.S.C. § 2000aa
Gramm-Leach-Bliley Act (GLBA) 15 U.S.C. § 6823 (only for obtaining customer information by false pretenses)	Right to Financial Privacy Act (RFPA) 12 U.S.C. §§ 3401-3422
Health Insurance Portability and Accountability Act (HIPAA) 42 U.S.C. § 1320d-6(a)	Video Privacy Protection Act (VPPA) 18 U.S.C. § 2710
Pen Register Act 18 U.S.C. § 3123(d)	

FEDERAL STATUTES AND CRIMINAL PENALTIES

Privacy Act 5 U.S.C. § 552a(i)	
Stored Communications Act (SCA) 18 U.S.C. § 2701(b)	
Telephone Consumer Protection Act (TCPA) 47 U.S.C. § 227	
Wiretap Act 18 U.S.C. § 2511(4)	

FEDERAL STATUTES: ENFORCEMENT

STATUTE	Private Cause of Action	Liqui-dated Damages	Atty Fees & Costs	Punitive Damages	Equitable Reme-dies	Gov't Agency Enforce-ment*	State AG Enforce-ment	Criminal Penalties
Cable Communications Policy Act	Yes	Yes	Yes	Yes	No	No	No	No
CAN-SPAM Act	Yes (ISPs only)	Yes	Yes	Yes	Yes	FTC and other agencies	Yes	Yes
Children's Online Privacy Protection Act (COPPA)	No	N/A	N/A	N/A	N/A	FTC	Yes	Yes
Computer Fraud and Abuse Act (CFAA)	Yes	No	No	No	Yes	DOJ	No	Yes
Drivers Privacy Protection Act (DPPA)	Yes	Yes	Yes	Yes	Yes	No	No	Yes
Employee Polygraph Protection Act (EPPA)	Yes	No	Yes	No	No	Labor Dept.	No	No
Fair Credit Reporting Act (FCRA)	Yes	Yes	Yes	Yes Willful Viola-tions	No	FTC and other agencies	Yes	Yes
Family Education Rights and Privacy Act (FERPA)	No	No	N/A	N/A	N/A	Dep't of Educa-tion	No	No

Federal Trade Commission Act (FTCA)	No	No	N/A	N/A	N/A	FTC	No	Yes
Foreign Intelligence Surveillance Act (FISA)	Yes	Yes	Yes	Yes	No	No	No	Yes
Gramm-Leach-Bliley Act (GLBA)	No	N/A	N/A	N/A	N/A	FTC and other agencies	No	Yes
Health Insurance Portability and Accountability Act (HIPAA)	No	N/A	N/A	N/A	N/A	HHS	Yes	Yes
Pen Register Act	No	N/A	N/A	N/A	N/A	No	No	Yes
Privacy Act	Yes	Yes	Yes	No	Yes	No	No	Yes
Privacy Protection Act (PPA)	Yes	Yes	Yes	No	No	No	No	No
Right to Financial Privacy Act (RFPA)	Yes	Yes	Yes	Yes	Yes	No	No	No
Stored Communications Act (SCA)	Yes	Yes	Yes	Yes	Yes	No	No	Yes
Telephone Consumer Protection Act (TCPA)	Yes	Yes	Yes	Yes*	No	FCC	Yes	Yes
Video Privacy Protection Act (VPPA)	Yes	Yes	Yes	Yes**	Yes	No	No	No
Wiretap Act	Yes	Yes	Yes	Yes	Yes	No	No	Yes

* Treble damages for willful or knowing violations.

**The DOJ enforces statutes with criminal violations.

FEDERAL STATUTES AND PREEMPTION

NAME OF FEDERAL STATUTE	DOES THE STATUTE CONTAIN A PREEMP-TION CLAUSE?	SUMMARY OF PREEMPTION CLAUSE	TEXT OF PREEMPTION CLAUSE
CAN-SPAM Act 15 U.S.C. § 7707	YES	Preempts any state law that "prohibits falsity or deception in any portion of a commercial electronic mail message or information attached thereto." Does not preempt state law that is not specific to e-mail or other state laws to the extent that they relate to computer crime or fraud. Does not preempt COPPA or any federal criminal law. Does not impact the FTC's ability to bring enforcement actions under the FTC act. Does not have any "effect on policies of providers of Internet access service."	(a) Federal law (1) Nothing in this chapter shall be construed to impair the enforcement of section 223 or 231 of Title 47, chapter 71 (relating to obscenity) or 110 (relating to sexual exploitation of children) of Title 18, or any other Federal criminal statute. (2) Nothing in this chapter shall be construed to affect in any way the Commission's authority to bring enforcement actions under FTC Act for materially false or deceptive representations or unfair practices in commercial electronic mail messages. (b) State law (1) In general This chapter supersedes any statute, regulation, or rule of a State or political subdivision of a State that expressly regulates the use of electronic mail to send commercial messages, except to the extent that any such statute, regulation, or rule prohibits falsity or deception in any portion of a commercial electronic mail message or information attached thereto. (2) State law not specific to electronic mail This chapter shall not be construed to preempt the applicability of— (A) State laws that are not specific to electronic mail, including State trespass, contract, or tort law; or (B) other State laws to the extent that those laws relate to acts of fraud or computer crime. (c) No effect on policies of providers of Internet access service Nothing in this chapter shall be construed to have any effect on the lawfulness or unlawfulness, under any other provision of law, of the adoption, implementation, or enforcement by a provider of Internet access service of a policy of declining to transmit, route, relay, handle, or store certain types of electronic mail messages. d) Inconsistent State law No State or local government may impose any liability for commercial activities or actions by operators in interstate or foreign commerce in connection with an activity or action described in this chapter that is inconsistent with the treatment of those activities or actions under this section.

NAME OF FEDERAL STATUTE	DOES THE STATUTE CONTAIN A PREEMP-TION CLAUSE?	SUMMARY OF PREEMPTION CLAUSE	TEXT OF PREEMPTION CLAUSE
Children's Online Privacy Protection Act (COPPA) 15 U.S.C. § 6502(d)	YES	State and local governments cannot impose liability for the operators of websites or online services that direct their services towards children or know that children are using their services.	
Fair Credit Reporting Act (FCRA) 15 U.S.C. § 1681t	YES	Only preempts state laws that relate to the collection, distribution, or use of consumer information to the extent that they are inconsistent with the statute, and only to the extent of the inconsistency. Subject to numerous exceptions.	"(a) In general Except as provided in subsections (b) and (c) of this section, this subchapter does not annul, alter, affect, or exempt any person subject to the provisions of this subchapter from complying with the laws of any State with respect to the collection, distribution, or use of any information on consumers, or for the prevention or mitigation of identity theft, except to the extent that those laws are inconsistent with any provision of this subchapter, and then only to the extent of the inconsistency. (b) General exceptions No requirement or prohibition may be imposed under the laws of any State— (1) with respect to any subject matter regulated under— (A) subsection (c) or (e) of section 1681b of this title, relating to the prescreening of consumer reports; (B) section 1681i of this title, relating to the time by which a consumer reporting agency must take any action, including the provision of notification to a consumer or other person, in any procedure related to the disputed accuracy of information in a consumer's file, except that this subparagraph shall not apply to any State law in effect on September 30, 1996; (C) subsections (a) and (b) of section 1681m of this title, relating to the duties of a person who takes any adverse action with respect to a consumer;"

FEDERAL STATUTES AND PREEMPTION

NAME OF FEDERAL STATUTE	DOES THE STATUTE CONTAIN A PREEMP- TION CLAUSE?	SUMMARY OF PREEMPTION CLAUSE	TEXT OF PREEMPTION CLAUSE
			(D) section 1681m(d) of this title, relating to the duties of persons who use a consumer report of a consumer in connection with any credit or insurance transaction that is not initiated by the consumer and that consists of a firm offer of credit or insurance;
			(E) section 1681c of this title, relating to information contained in consumer reports, except that this subparagraph shall not apply to any State law in effect on September 30, 1996;
			(F) section 1681s-2 of this title, relating to the responsibilities of persons who furnish information to consumer reporting agencies, except that this paragraph shall not apply—
			(i) with respect to section 54A(a) of chapter 93 of the Massachusetts Annotated Laws (as in effect on September 30, 1996); or
			(ii) with respect to section 1785.25(a) of the California Civil Code (as in effect on September 30, 1996);
			(G) section 1681g(e) of this title, relating to information available to victims under section 1681g(e) of this title;
			(H) section 1681s-3 of this title, relating to the exchange and use of information to make a solicitation for marketing purposes; or
			(I) section 1681m(h) of this title, relating to the duties of users of consumer reports to provide notice with respect to terms in certain credit transactions;
			(2) with respect to the exchange of information among persons affiliated by common ownership or common corporate control, except that this paragraph shall not apply with respect to subsection (a) or (c) (1) of section 2480e of title 9, Vermont Statutes Annotated (as in effect on September 30, 1996);
			(3) with respect to the disclosures required to be made under subsection (c), (d), (e), or (g) of section 1681g of this title, or subsection (f) of section 1681g of this title relating to the disclosure of credit scores for credit granting purposes, except that this paragraph—
			(A) shall not apply with respect to sections 1785.10, 1785.16, and 1785.20.2 of the California Civil Code (as in effect on December 4, 2003) and section 1785.15 through section 1785.15.2 of such Code (as in effect on such date);
			(F) subsections (e), (f), and (g) of section 1681m of this title;

FEDERAL STATUTES AND PREEMPTION

NAME OF FEDERAL STATUTE	DOES THE STATUTE CONTAIN A PREEMP-TION CLAUSE?	SUMMARY OF PREEMPTION CLAUSE	TEXT OF PREEMPTION CLAUSE
			(B) shall not apply with respect to sections 5-3-106(2) and 212-14.3-104.3 of the Colorado Revised Statutes (as in effect on December 4, 2003); and (C) shall not be construed as limiting, annulling, affecting, or superseding any provision of the laws of any State regulating the use in an insurance activity, or regulating disclosures concerning such use, of a credit-based insurance score of a consumer by any person engaged in the business of insurance; (4) with respect to the frequency of any disclosure under section 1681j(a) of this title, except that this paragraph shall not apply— (A) with respect to section 12-14.3-105(1)(d) of the Colorado Revised Statutes (as in effect on December 4, 2003); (B) with respect to section 10-1-393(29)(C) of the Georgia Code (as in effect on December 4, 2003); (C) with respect to section 1316.2 of title 10 of the Maine Revised Statutes (as in effect on December 4, 2003); (D) with respect to sections 14-1209(a)(1) and 14-1209(b)(1)(i) of the Commercial Law Article of the Code of Maryland (as in effect on December 4, 2003); (E) with respect to section 59(d) and section 59(e) of chapter 93 of the General Laws of Massachusetts (as in effect December 4, 2003); (F) with respect to section 56:11-37.10(a)(1) of the New Jersey Revised Statutes (as in effect on December 4, 2003); or (G) with respect to section 2480c(a)(1) of title 9 of the Vermont Statutes Annotated (as in effect on December 4, 2003); or (5) with respect to the conduct required by the specific provisions of— (A) section 1681c(g) of this title; (B) section 1681c-1 of this title; (C) section 1681c-2 of this title; (D) section 1681g(a)(1)(A) of this title; (E) section 1681j(a) of this title;

FEDERAL STATUTES AND PREEMPTION

NAME OF FEDERAL STATUTE	DOES THE STATUTE CONTAIN A PREEMPTION CLAUSE?	SUMMARY OF PREEMPTION CLAUSE	TEXT OF PREEMPTION CLAUSE
			(G) section 1681s(f) of this title; (H) section 1681s-2(a)(6) of this title; or (I) section 1681w of this title. (c) "Firm offer of credit or insurance" defined Notwithstanding any definition of the term "firm offer of credit or insurance" (or any equivalent term) under the laws of any State, the definition of that term contained in section 1681a(l) of this title shall be construed to apply in the enforcement and interpretation of the laws of any State governing consumer reports. (d) Limitations Subsections (b) and (c) of this section do not affect any settlement, agreement, or consent judgment between any State Attorney General and any consumer reporting agency in effect on September 30, 1996."
Privacy Protection Act (PPA) 42 U.S.C. § 2000aa-6(d)	YES	If a citizen has a cause of action against the United States under this statute, pursuit of that cause of action comes at the exclusion of all other potential claims.	Exclusive nature of remedy The remedy provided by subsection (a)(1) of this section against the United States, a State, or any other governmental unit is exclusive of any other civil action or proceeding for conduct constituting a violation of this chapter, against the officer or employee whose violation gave rise to the claim, or against the estate of such officer or employee.
Cable Communications Policy Act (CCPA) 47 U.S.C. §§ 521, 551-552	NO	No preemption clause.	

FEDERAL STATUTES AND PREEMPTION

NAME OF FEDERAL STATUTE	DOES THE STATUTE CONTAIN A PREEMPTION CLAUSE?	SUMMARY OF PREEMPTION CLAUSE	TEXT OF PREEMPTION CLAUSE
Employee Polygraph Protection Act (EPPA) 29 U.S.C. §§ 2001-2009	NO	No preemption clause.	
Gramm–Leach–Bliley Act (GLBA) 15 U.S.C. §§ 6801-6809, 6821-6827	NO	No preemption clause.	
Health Insurance Portability and Accountability Act (HIPPA) 45 C.F.R. 164	NO	No preemption clause.	
Pen Register Act 18 U.S.C. §§ 3121-3123	NO	No preemption clause.	
Stored Communications Act (SCA) 18 U.S.C. §§ 2701-2712	NO	No preemption clause.	

FEDERAL STATUTES AND PREEMPTION

NAME OF FEDERAL STATUTE	DOES THE STATUTE CONTAIN A PREEMPTION CLAUSE?	SUMMARY OF PREEMPTION CLAUSE	TEXT OF PREEMPTION CLAUSE
Telephone Consumer Protection Act (TCPA) 47 U.S.C. § 227	NO	No preemption clause.	
Wiretap Act 18 U.S.C. §§ 2510-2522	NO	No preemption clause.	

FEDERAL STATUTES AND OPT-IN/OPT-OUT

OPT-IN RIGHTS	BREACH OF CONFIDENTIALITY
Cable Communications Policy Act (CCPA) 47 U.S.C. § 551(c)(1) (for PII except names and addresses)	Cable Communications Policy Act (CCPA) 47 U.S.C. § 551(c)(2) (names and addresses)
Children's Online Privacy Protection Act (COPPA) 15 U.S.C. § 6502(b)	CAN-SPAM Act 15 U.S.C. § 7704(a)(3)
Driver's Privacy Protection Act (DPPA) 18 U.S.C. § 2721(b), (d)	Gramm-Leach-Bliley Act (GLBA) 15 U.S.C. § 6802(b) (for disclosures to nonaffiliates)
Fair Credit Reporting Act (FCRA) 15 U.S.C. § 1681b (for uses beyond permissible uses)	Family Educational Rights and Privacy Act (FERPA) 20 U.S.C. § 1232g(b)(1) ("directory information"—name, address, telephone listing, date and place of birth, activities, degrees, awards, etc.)
Family Educational Rights and Privacy Act (FERPA) 20 U.S.C. § 1232g(b)(1) (all PII except "directory information")	Telephone Consumer Protection Act (TCPA) 47 U.S.C. § 227
Health Insurance Portability and Accountability Act (HIPAA) 45 C.F.R. § 164.508(a) (all uses and disclosures beyond those for treatment, payment, or healthcare operations)	Video Privacy Protection Act (VPPA) 18 U.S.C. § 2710(2)(D) (names/ addresses and subject matter of videos for marketing)
Privacy Act 5 U.S.C. § 552a(b) (for disclosures)	
Video Privacy Protection Act (VPPA) 18 U.S.C. § 2710(2)(B) (all PII, especially video titles, except names/ addresses)	

STATE STATUTES

Unfair and Deceptive Acts and Practices Acts (UDAP Acts)

The FTCA is enforced exclusively by the FTC, but there are unfair-and-deceptive-acts-and-practices acts (UDAP Acts) (also termed "mini-FTC Acts") in most states. Many of these statutes not only enable a state attorney general to bring actions but also provide a private cause of action to consumers. Several of these laws have provisions for statutory minimum damages, punitive damages, and attorneys' fees.

Privacy Law Fundamentals

In interpreting these laws, many state courts have been heavily influenced by FTCA jurisprudence.

Many states create private rights of actions under their UDAP Acts. The states vary, however, in the scope of illegal action covered, the kinds of plaintiffs permitted to seek redress, and the recovery permitted.

Examples:

Unfair Competition Law, Cal. Bus. & Prof. Code § 17200
California's Unfair Competition Law ("UCL") covers a broad range of conduct, permits only certain kinds of relief, and permits only certain plaintiffs to bring suit. It is a powerful tool for plaintiffs, because it permits private suits for a violation of law, civil or criminal, that would on its own grant no private right of action or enforcement.

Deceptive and Unlawful Practices Act, N.Y. Gen. Bus. Law § 349
Compared to California, New York's consumer protection statute allows equitable remedies for a more limited private right of action. It requires a showing that the deceptive practice is aimed at consumers, was deceptive or misleading in a material way, and that plaintiff was consequently injured. While plaintiffs must show actual harm, they need not show pecuniary harm.

Radio Frequency Identification (RFID)
Many states have laws restricting the use of RFID devices. Several of these laws pertain to the government's use of RFID in driver's licenses, but some of the statutes restrict private-sector uses as well.

State Statutes Regulating Private-Sector Use of RFID	
CA	Cal. Civil Code § 52.7 (S.B. 31); Cal. Civil Code §§ 1798.79 to 1798.795
NV	Nev. Rev. Stat. §§ 205.461-.4675 (SB 125)
NH	N.H. Rev. Stat. Ann. § 236.130
ND	N.D. Cent. Code § 12.1-15-06
OK	Okla. Stat. tit. 1, § 1-1430
RI	R.I. Gen. Laws §§ 42-153-1 to 42-153-4
WA	Wash. Rev. Code §§ 9A.58.020, 19.300.010 *et seq.*
WI	Wis. Stat. § 146.25

Illustrative statutes include:

California, Cal. Civil Code §§ 1798.79 and 52.7
Prohibits establishing a connection with an RFID tag to access stored information without explicit consent from the tag's owner. Cal. Civ. Code §§ 52.7, 1798.79. California law also forbids forced implantation of RFID tags. Cal. Civil Code § 52.7.

Nevada, Nev. Rev. Stat. §§ 205.461-.4675 (S.B. 125)
Prohibits capturing, storing, or reading information from a person's "RFID document" for the purposes of knowingly or intentionally committing identity theft or any unlawful act without that person's prior knowledge and consent. The statute defines an RFID document as a document containing data issued to an individual for the primary purpose of establishing identity.

New Hampshire, N.H. Rev. Stat. Ann. § 236.130
Forbids use of surveillance devices, including an RFID device, to identify ownership of a vehicle or identity of a vehicle's occupants.

North Dakota, N.D. Cent. Code § 12.1-15-06
Prohibits required implantation of an RFID device.

Rhode Island, R.I. Gen. Laws §§ 42-153-1 to 42-153-4
Prohibits use of RFID for tracking the movement or identity of any schoolchildren on school grounds or while being transported to or from school grounds or school functions.

Washington, Wash. Rev. Code §§ 9A.58.020, 19.300.010 *et seq.*
Washington law generally prohibits the scanning of an RFID tag by anyone except the business or agency that issued the tag. The statute also provides for numerous exceptions, such as when the scanning is part of a sales transaction that the tag holder initiates or the reading of the tag occurs as part of good-faith security research, experimentation, or scientific research. Wash. Rev. Code § 19.300.010 *et seq.*

Washington also has a criminal prohibition on reading RFID tags to capture information about a person without her knowledge and consent for the purpose of committing fraud, identity theft, or other illegal activity. Wash. Rev. Code § 9A.58.020.

"Eraser" or "Right to Be Forgotten" Laws

California, Calif. Bus. & Prof. Code §§ 22580-22582 (S.B. 568)
(effective Jan. 1, 2015)
California's Privacy Rights for California Minors in the Digital World Act, also called the "eraser" bill, permits minors to remove, or to request and obtain removal of, content or information posted on an Internet Web site, online service, online application, or mobile application. It also prohibits an operator of a Web site or online service directed to minors from marketing or advertising to minors specified products or services that minors are legally prohibited from buying. The law also will prohibit marketing or advertising certain products based on personal information specific to a minor or knowingly using, disclosing, compiling, or allowing a third party to do so.

Marketing

California Online Privacy Protection Act ("CalOPPA")
Cal. Bus. & Prof. Code §§ 22575-22579
CalOPPA applies to owners or operators of commercial websites or online services,

including operators of software and mobile apps, that "collect and maintain PII from website visitors residing in California." Operators must post a noticeable privacy policy on their website that describes the PII being collected and how it will be shared with third parties. Users must be notified about any changes to privacy policies. CalOPPA does not apply to ISPs or similar services that transfer or store PII for third parties.

A 2013 amendment to CalOPPA added "Privacy Rights for California Minors in the Digital World," prohibiting online marketing of certain products to minors. Upon request, operators must remove website content posted by minors if the minor is a registered user. These removal rights must be displayed and explained to minors. CalOPPA does not prohibit companies from conducting online behavioral advertising, but the act requires disclosure about how websites respond to "Do Not Track" signals and third-party information sharing in their privacy policies.

Spyware

Several states have anti-spyware laws.

State Spyware Statutes	
AK	Alaska Stat. §§ 45.45.792, .794, .798; § 45.50.471(51)
AZ	Ariz. Rev. Stat. Ann. §§ 44-7301 to 44-7304
AR	Ark. Code Ann. §§ 4-11-101 to -105, 19-6-301, 19-6-804
CA	Cal. Bus. & Prof. Code §§ 22947-22947.6
GA	Ga. Code Ann. §§ 16-9-152 to -157
IL	720 Ill. Comp. Stat. 5/16D-5.5
IN	Ind. Code § 24-4.8-1 *et seq.*
IA	Iowa Code §§ 715.1-.8
LA	La. Stat. Ann. §§ 51:2006-2014
NV	Nev. Rev. Stat. § 205.4737
NH	N.H. Rev. Stat. Ann. §§ 359-H:1 to 359-H:6
RI	R.I. Gen. Laws §§ 11-52.2-2 to -7
TX	Tex. Bus. & Comm. Code Ann. §§ 324.001-.102
UT	Utah Code Ann. §§ 13-40-101 to 13-40-401
VA	Va. Code Ann. § 18.2-152.4
WA	Wash. Rev. Code §§ 19.270.101-.900
WY	Wyo. Stat. Ann. § 6-3-506, 40-25-101 (2014 H.B. 178, Act 48)
PR	P.R. Laws Ann. tit. 10, §§ 2181-2185

Source: National Conference of State Legislatures, State Spyware Laws, www.ncsl.org/default.aspx?tabid=13452

Illustrative statutes include:

California, Cal. Bus. & Prof. Code §§ 22947-22947.6

California law prohibits an unauthorized user from willfully loading software onto the computer of a California resident and using the software to carry out a number of forbidden activities. These activities include modification of certain settings related to the computer's access to or use of the Internet; collection through intentionally deceptive means of certain types of PII; and preventing, through intentionally deceptive means, an authorized user's reasonable efforts to block the installation of or disabling of software. The law also forbids the taking control of the computer by e-mails or viruses, using the computer to engage in denial-of-service attacks; or allowing multiple, sequential stand-alone advertisements to be opened on the computer in a fashion that blocks a reasonable user from closing the advertisements.

Iowa, Iowa Code §§ 715.1-.8

Prohibits a person who is "not an owner or operator of a computer" from transmitting computer software to a computer "knowingly or with conscious avoidance of actual knowledge," and to use such software for a number of acts, including: (1) modifying through intentionally deceptive means the settings of a computer, (2) collecting through intentionally deceptive means personally identifiable information through a keystroke-logging function and (3) preventing through intentionally deceptive means an owner's or an operator's reasonable efforts to block the installation of, or to disable, computer software by causing computer software that the owner or operator has properly removed or disabled to automatically reinstall or reactivate on the computer.

Texas, Tex. Bus. & Comm. Code Ann. §§ 324.001-.102

Prohibits a series of conduct or activities, including collection or culling of personally identifiable information, unauthorized access to or modifications of computer settings, unauthorized interference with installation or disabling of computer software, and unauthorized creation of, access to, or use of zombies or botnets.

Washington, Wash. Rev. Code §§ 19.270.101-.900

Prohibits the transmission of software to the owner's or operator's computer or software for (1) modifying through intentionally deceptive means the settings of a computer, (2) collecting through intentionally deceptive means personally identifiable information through a keystroke-logging function that records and certain other actions, and (3) preventing through intentionally deceptive means an owner's or an operator's reasonable efforts to block the installation of, or to disable, computer software by causing computer software that the owner or operator has properly removed or disabled to automatically reinstall or reactivate on the computer.

Video Privacy

Several States have enacted laws regulating video privacy protection, in some cases offering more robust protection than the VPPA.

Conn. Gen. Stat. § 53-450

PII in video rental records considered confidential. Sale of PII prohibited. Statute provides for right of action to recover damaged with fines up to $500 for violation of provision.

Del. Code Ann. tit. 11, § 925

Prohibiting videotape distributors from wrongfully disclosing records of videotapes purchased or rented by an individual protected under the statute to any other person unless exemptions apply. Violations are subject to a fine up to $500, imprisonment for not more than six months, or both.

Md. Code Ann., Crim. Law § 3-907

Unless allowed by statute, law prohibits disclosure of any numerical designation used by a videotape distributor to identify the protected individual or any listing of videotapes, disks, or films bought, rented, or borrowed from the videotape distributor. Violation of statute is a misdemeanor and carries penalties including imprisonment not exceeding six months, fines not exceeding $500 for each violation, or both.

N.Y. Gen. Bus. Law §§ 670-675

Protecting against wrongful disclosure of videotape rental and sales records. Violation of statute creates liability for actual damages sustained by consumers up to $500.

R.I. Gen. Laws § 11-18-32

Records are considered confidential, and it is unlawful to reveal or disseminate records that identify names and addresses of individuals with titles or general nature of videos purchased or rented. Violation of provisions punishable by a fine up to $1,000 per violation, by imprisonment up to six months, or both. Injured individual may bring civil action against the violator for actual damages or $250, whichever is greater, for each violation.

Iowa Code § 727.11

Unless expressly allowed in provision or with customer consent, it is unlawful for a video distributor to disclose any information that would reveal the identity of an individual renting a videotape or similar material. Violation is a misdemeanor.

Transparency

California's "Shine the Light" Law, Cal. Civ. Code § 1798.83

This statute permits consumers to obtain from businesses information about the personal data that the businesses disclosed to third parties for direct marketing purposes. People can find out this data as well as the "names and addresses of all of the third parties that received personal information from the business." § 1798.83(a)(2). The law applies to businesses with 20 or more employees. § 1798(c)(1). It does not apply to financial institutions. Companies with privacy policies that allow people to opt out of sharing their data with third parties are exempt. § 1798(c)(2).

FIRST AMENDMENT

Privacy regulation of the collection, use, and disclosure of personal data can come into conflict with the First Amendment.

First Amendment Protection of Commercial Speech: Although commercial speech is constitutionally protected, it has a lower value than regular categories of speech and therefore is entitled to a lesser protection. *Ohralik v. Ohio State Bar Ass'n,* 436 U.S. 447 (1978).

Defining Commercial Speech: The court has defined commercial speech as speech that "proposes a commercial transaction," *Virginia State Board of Pharmacy v. Virginia Citizens Consumer Council, Inc.,* 425 U.S. 748 (1976), and as "expression related solely to the economic interests of the speaker and its audience," *Central Hudson Gas & Electric Corp. v. Public Service Commission of New York,* 447 U.S. 557 (1980). The court later held that neither of these is a requirement to define commercial speech; both are factors to be considered in determining whether speech is commercial. *Bolger v. Youngs Drug Prods. Corp.,* 463 U.S. 60 (1983).

The Central Hudson Test: In *Central Hudson,* 447 U.S. 557 (1980), the court established a four-part test for analyzing the constitutionality of restrictions on commercial speech:

1. Is the speech about lawful activity and not misleading?

2. Is the government interest substantial?

3. Does the regulation directly advance the government interest?

4. Is the regulation "no more extensive than is necessary" to achieve the government interest?

Leading Cases

Rowan v. U.S. Post Office Dep't, 397 U.S. 728 (1970)
The Postal Revenue and Federal Salary Act, 39 U.S.C. § 4009 (1967), allowed people to request that a mailer stop all future mailings. Not a First Amendment violation because the government was not censoring—the individual makes the choice not to receive the mail. "Nothing in the Constitution compels us to listen to or view any unwanted communication."

Mainstream Mktg Servs., Inc. v. FTC, 358 F.3d 1228 (10th Cir. 2004)
The Do Not Call Registry did not violate the First Amendment because it satisfied the *Central Hudson* test. Protecting people's privacy and right not to receive unwanted phone calls in their homes was a substantial government interest. Although the registry does not allow people to block all unwanted calls since it exempts political and charitable calls, it will still be effective and stop many unwanted calls. Thus, it directly advances the government's interest.

U.S. West, Inc. v. FCC, 182 F.3d 1224 (10th Cir. 1999)

FCC order limiting the disclosure and use of customer proprietary network information (CPNI) violated *Central Hudson* because privacy did not rise to a substantial interest. Disclosure and use of CPNI merely caused a "general level of discomfort" and not "undue embarrassment or ridicule." An opt-out would have been a less restrictive alternative to the FCC's opt-in requirement. The FCC later rejected this holding in its 2007 CPNI Order (*see* page 184).

Trans Union Corp. v. FTC, 245 F.3d 809 (D.C. Cir. 2001) (Trans Union I)

The FTC ordered Trans Union to stop selling its targeted marketing lists, claiming the sale violated FCRA. The court concluded privacy was a substantial interest and that although an opt-out was a less restrictive alternative, the First Amendment does not require the least restrictive means (only in cases involving strict scrutiny). See also *Trans Union v. FTC,* 295 F.3d 42 (D.C. Cir. 2002) *(Trans Union II).*

Sorrell v. IMS Health Inc., 564 U.S. 552 (2011)

The U.S. Supreme Court struck down Vermont's Prescription Confidentiality Law as a violation of the First Amendment right to free speech. The Vermont law restricted the sale and marketing use of information that would identify prescribers without their consent. The Court reasoned that the Vermont law "enacts content- and speaker-based restrictions on the sale, disclosure, and use of prescriber-identifying information." According to the Court, the statute made content-based restrictions because it singled out marketing, and the statute made speaker-based restrictions because it focused exclusively on pharmaceutical manufacturers. The Supreme Court stated: "The law on its face burdens disfavored speech by disfavored speakers."

FOR FURTHER REFERENCE

Books

Kenneth A. Bamberger & Deirdre K. Mulligan, *Privacy on the Ground: Driving Corporate Behavior in the United States and Europe* **(2015)**
Comparing U.S. privacy and data security laws and enforcement strategies with those of Europe, finding certain trends towards convergence as well as a distinctive US model of compliance.

Michelle Finneran Dennedy, Jonathan Fox, & Thomas R. Finneran, *The Privacy Engineer's Manifesto: Getting from Policy to Code to QA to Value* **(2014)**
A detailed and concrete discussion about Privacy by Design and how to implement privacy in the development of technology.

Lothar Determann, *California Privacy Law* **(2d ed. 2017)**
Comprehensive analysis of the strict standards of California privacy law.

Chris Jay Hoofnagle, *Federal Trade Commission Privacy Law and Policy* (2016)
Comprehensive examination of the FTC and its modern role as an inventive regulator in the US privacy marketplace. Valuable analysis of the FTC's history—in the privacy area and beyond—to explain its current role and predict where it will go in the future.

Frank Pasquale, *The Black Box Society: The Secret Algorithms That Control Money and Information* (2015)
Argues that the detailed profiles that companies are creating about people have profound implications for their reputations and opportunities as well as for society. The algorithms used to make automated decisions based on personal data re often hidden, and they should be more transparent. The law should also ensure that important decisions be made fairly and in a non-discriminatory manner.

Neil Richards, *Intellectual Privacy: Rethinking Civil Liberties in the Digital Age* (2015)
Argues that surveillance—by both the government and private-sector entities—threatens freedom of speech, belief, and intellectual exploration.

H. Jeff Smith, *Managing Privacy: Information Technology and Corporate America* (1994)
Although dated, this book remains an insightful examination of how various institutions and businesses formulate and implement their privacy policies.

Daniel J. Solove, *The Digital Person: Technology and Privacy in the Information Age* (2004)
Examines the growing collection and use of personal data and proposes how it should be regulated.

Articles and Other Sources

Danielle Keats Citron, *Reservoirs of Danger: The Evolution of Public and Private Law at the Dawn of the Information Age*, 80 S. Cal. L. Rev. 241 (2007)
A provocative argument for strict liability for harms created by the creation and use of computer databases of personal information.

Julie E. Cohen, *Examined Lives: Informational Privacy and the Subject as Object*, 52 Stan. L. Rev. 1373 (2000)
A discussion of the commercialization of personal data, the nature of privacy harms and whether the sale of personal data constitutes speech.

Woodrow Hartzog & Daniel J. Solove, *The Scope and Potential of FTC Data Protection*, 83 Geo. Wash. L. Rev. 2230 (2015)
Arguing that the FTC's statutory authority permits the agency to reach a broader scope of privacy and data security issues than the agency currently pursues.

Chris Jay Hoofnagle & Jan Whittington, *Free: Accounting for the Costs of the Internet's Most Popular Price,* **61 UCLA L. Rev. 606 (2014)**
Suggesting that the FTC should help consumers realize the true nature of online services by clarifying that the consumer's personal information is the basis of a bargain and will be used for secondary purposes.

Jerry Kang, *Information Privacy in Cyberspace Transactions,* **50 Stan. L. Rev. 1193 (1998)**
An early and classic article about how to balance privacy and efficient consumer transactions.

Orin S. Kerr, *Cybercrime's Scope: Interpreting "Access" and "Authorization" in Computer Misuse Statutes,* **78 N.Y.U. L. Rev. 1596 (2003)**
The leading article about the Computer Fraud and Abuse Act and its state statutory analogues.

Joel R. Reidenberg, *Lex Informatica: The Formulation of Information Policy Rules Through Technology,* **76 Tex. L. Rev. 553 (1998)**
Classic article about how technology embedded in design and code can protect privacy.

Joel R. Reidenberg, *Privacy Wrongs in Search of Remedies,* **54 Hastings L.J. 877 (2003)**
A critique of the FTC as the primary enforcer of privacy.

Neil M. Richards, *Reconciling Data Privacy and the First Amendment,* **52 UCLA L. Rev. 1149 (2005)**
A thoughtful argument that the sale and use of computer databases does not constitute "speech" under the First Amendment.

Ira S. Rubinstein & Nathaniel Good, *Privacy by Design: A Counterfactual Analysis of Google and Facebook Privacy Incidents,* **28 Berkeley Tech. L.J. 1333 (2013)**
Carrying out the first comprehensive analysis of engineering and usability principles specifically relevant to privacy. Based on a review of the technical literature, it proposes a small number of relevant principles and illustrates them by reference to ten recent privacy incidents involving Google and Facebook.

Paul M. Schwartz, *Privacy and Preemption,* **118 Yale L.J. 902 (2009)**
Develops a proposal for an optimal dual federal-state system for information privacy law and the role of preemption rules in this system.

Paul M. Schwartz & Daniel J. Solove, *The PII Problem: Privacy and a New Concept of Personally Identifiable Information,* **86 N.Y.U. L. Rev. 1814 (2011)**
Rethinks the concept of PII and discusses how the difficulties in de-identifying data can be addressed.

Daniel J. Solove & Woodrow Hartzog, *The FTC and the New Common Law of Privacy*, 114 Colum. L. Rev. 583 (2014)
Argues that "the FTC's privacy jurisprudence is functionally equivalent to a body of common law." Companies look to these agreements as a quasi-common law for determining best practices, and the structures of these FTC agreements amount to a common law equivalent—and one that is amenable to study.

Jeff Sovern, *Opting In, Opting Out, or No Options at All: The Fight for Control of Personal Information*, 74 Wash. L. Rev. 1033 (1999)
A thorough examination of the pros and cons of both opt-in and opt-out systems.

Jeff Sovern, *Protecting Privacy with Deceptive Trade Practices Legislation*, 69 Fordham L. Rev. 1305 (2001)
Discusses state deceptive trade practice acts.

Daniel J. Solove, *Privacy Self-Management and the Consent Dilemma*, 126 Harv. L. Rev. 1879 (2013)
Current approaches to privacy in law and policy rely on "privacy self-management"—providing people with notice about how their data is being collected and used, and then allowing people a choice about whether or not to consent to such collection and use. Privacy self-management, however, cannot succeed alone because a range of cognitive and structural problems makes it nearly impossible for people to weigh the costs and benefits of various uses of their personal data.

Michael E. Staten & Fred H. Cate, *The Impact of Opt-in Privacy Rules on Retail Markets: A Case Study of MBNA*, 52 Duke L.J. 745 (2003)
A practical illustration of how information privacy regulation affects business practices.

Peter P. Swire, *Trustwrap: The Importance of Legal Rules to Electronic Commerce and Internet Privacy*, 54 Hastings L.J. 847 (2003)
A pragmatic argument about how privacy regulation can enhance rather than impede business interests.

CHAPTER 10

Data Security

ESSENTIAL POINTS

- The vast majority of states have enacted data breach notification statutes. These laws can contain important differences that make multistate notifications complex undertakings.

- The FTC has brought approximately 55 enforcement actions concerning poor security practices.

DATA BREACH NOTIFICATION STATUTES

Rise of the State Statutes

California's Data Security Breach Notification Statute, S.B. 1386 (2002)
This was the first data breach notification law in the United States. Following the well-publicized data security breach at ChoicePoint, which was made public pursuant to this statute, many other states enacted similar data breach notification laws. At present, 47 states have enacted data security breach statutes.

The various statutes can differ in sometimes dramatic, and sometimes subtle, ways. These distinctions complicate the task of carrying out a multistate notification of a data breach. There has also been a discussion of the merits of enacting a federal data breach notification law, but no such bill has been enacted thus far.

State Data Security Breach Notification Statutes
The vast majority of states have data security breach notification statutes. These statutes vary primarily based on the following elements:

1. *Trigger for Notice:* The statutes differ according to when they mandate a notification. Some of the laws require a reasonable belief that information has either been accessed or acquired. These standards are on the pro-notification side of

the continuum, as they require notice when a third party merely has had access to the information. A showing that this third party actually acquired the information—that is, gained control of it—is not necessary under these laws. A large number of states have a narrower trigger for notification by requiring a finding of a risk of misuse or harm to the affected party before mandating disclosure.

2. **Exceptions to Notification:** The most prevalent of the notification exceptions is one based on a finding by the breached entity that there is no reasonable likelihood of harm flowing from the breach. Sometimes such an exception also requires a consultation with law enforcement officials. Other states provide an exception built around a finding that there is no reasonable likelihood of misuse of the breached data.

3. **Parties to Whom Disclosure Is Required:** All states require disclosure to the affected individual and almost all to the owner or licensee of the data. State statutes also frequently require disclosure to credit reporting agencies but generally do so only if 1,000 or more persons are affected by the breach. Some laws also require disclosures to the state attorney general, other state agencies and information brokers.

4. **Enforcement:** Only a minority of state statutes provide a private right of action. In states with such a statutory right, private parties can sue for violations of the state breach notification laws. In the other states, only a state official, typically the state attorney general, can enforce the law. Currently, 32 of the 47 state breach notification statutes lack a private right of action.

State Data Security Breach Notification Laws
(Key to chart on page 207)

Trigger for Notification	Exceptions to Notice	Party to Whom Disclosure Is Required
• Acquisition (AQ)	• Alternative notification: Victim of breach is resident of another state that has its own breach notification law (AN)	
• Access (AC)		• Affected individuals (I)
• Misuse (M)		• Owner or licensee of data (O)
• Risk of misuse (RM)	• No reasonable likelihood of harm (NH)	• Credit reporting agencies if 1,000+ persons affected (CRA)
• Risk of harm (RH)	• No reasonable likelihood of misuse (NM)	
• Risk of identity theft or fraud (RID)	• No breach occurred (NB)	• Information brokers (IB)
• Substantial risk of identity theft or fraud (SRID)	• Required consultation with law enforcement (RC)	• Attorney general (AG)
		• Other state agencies (OA)

STATE DATA SECURITY BREACH NOTIFICATION LAWS

STATE STATUTE	TRIGGER FOR NOTICE	EXCEPTIONS TO NOTICE	PARTY TO WHOM NOTICE IS REQUIRED	PRIVATE RIGHT OF ACTION?
AK Alaska Stat. § 45.48.010 et seq.	AQ	NH	I, CRA, O, AG	Yes
AZ Arz. Rev. Stat. § 44-7501	AQ + AC + RH	NB	I, O	No
AR Ark. Code § 4-110-101 et seq.	AQ	NH	I, O	No
CA Cal. Civ. Code §§ 1798.29, 1798.80 et seq.	AQ		I, O, AG*	Yes
CO Colo. Rev. Stat. § 6-1-716	AQ	NM	I, O, CRA	No
CT Conn. Gen. Stat. § 36a-701b	AC or AQ	NH + RC	I, O, AG	No
DE Del. Code tit. 6, § 12B-101 et seq.	AQ	NM	I, O	No
DC D.C. Code § 28-3851 et seq.	AQ		I, O, CRA	Yes
FL Fla. Stat. § 501.171	AC	NH + RC	I, CRA, AG*	No
GA Ga. Code § 10-1-910, -911, -912; § 46-5-214	AQ		I, CRA (10,000+ only), IB	No
HI Haw. Rev. Stat. § 487N-1 et seq.	M or RM	NH or NM	I, O, CRA, OA	Yes
ID Idaho Code § 28-51-104 et seq	M or RM	NM	I, O, AG	No
IL 815 Ill. Comp. Stat. 530/1 et seq	AQ		I, O, CRA (if data collector is a state agency), AG (250+ only), OA (if data collector is a state agency)	Yes
IN Ind. Code § 4-1-11-1 et seq., § 24-4.9	AQ + M or RID		No	
IA Iowa Code §§ 715C.1, 715C.2	AQ	NH + RC	I, O, AG*	No
KS Kan. Stat. § 50-7a01 et seq.	AC or AQ + RID	NM	I, O, CRA	No
KY KRS § 365.732	AQ + RID	I, O, CRA	No	
LA La. Rev. Stat. Ann. §§ 51:3071 et seq. La. Admin. Code tit. 16, pt. III, § 701	AQ	NH	I, O, AG	Yes
ME Me. Rev. Stat. Ann. tit. 10, § 1347 et seq.	M or RM	NM	I, O, CRA, AG	No
MD Md. Code Com. Law § 14-3501 et seq.	AQ + M or RM	NM	I, O, CRA, AG	Yes

MA Mass. Gen. Laws ch. 93H, § 1 et seq. Mass. Code Regs. § 17.01 et seq.	AQ + SRID or M		I, O, AG, OA	No
MI Mich. Comp. Laws §§ 445.63, 445.72	AC + AQ	NH	I, CRA (unless subject to Gramm-Leach-Bliley Act)	No
MN Minn. Stat. §§ 13.055, 325E.61	AQ		I, O, CRA (500 + only)	Yes
MS Miss. Code § 75-24-29	AQ	NH	I, O	No
MO Mo. Rev. Stat. § 407.1500	AC + AQ	NH	I, O, AG (1,000+ only), CRA	No
MT Mont. Code § 30-14-1701 et seq.	AQ + RH		I, O, AG	No
NE Neb. Rev. Stat. § 87-801 et seq.	AQ + M or RM	NM	I, O, AG	No
NV Nev. Rev. Stat. §§ 603A.010–603A.920	AQ		I, O, CRA	Yes
NH N.H Rev. Stat. § 359-C:19 et seq.	AQ + M or RM or determination of use cannot be made	NM	I, O, CRA (unless subject to Gramm-Leach- Bliley Act), AG, OA	Yes
NJ N.J. Stat. § 56:8-161 et seq.	AC	NM	I, O, CRA, OA	No
NY N.Y. State Tech. Law § 57-A:208 N.Y. Gen. Bus. § 899aa	AQ		I, O, AG, OA, CRA (5,000+ only)	No
NC N.C. Gen. Stat. § 75-60 et seq.	AC + AQ + M or RM	NM	I, O, AG, CRA	Yes
ND N.D. Cent. Code § 51-30-01 et seq.	AQ		I, O, AG (250+ only)	No
OH Ohio Rev. Code §§ 1349.19, 1349.191, 1349.192, 1347.12	AC + AQ + RID	NH	I, O, CRA	No
OK Okla. Stat. tit. 24, § 161 Okla. Stat. tit. 74, § 3113.1	AQ or AC + RID		I, O	No
OR Or. Rev. Stat. § 646A.600 et seq.	AQ	NH	I, O, CRA, AG (250+ only)	Yes
PA 73 P.S. § 2301 et seq.	AC + AQ + RH	NH	I, O, CRA	No
RI R.I. Gen. Laws § 11-49.3-1 et seq.	AQ, SRID	NH	I, O, AG*, CRA (500+ only)	Yes
SC S.C. Code § 39-1-90	AQ + RH or RM	NH	I, O, OA (1000+ only), CRA	Yes

TN Tenn. Code § 47-18-2107	AQ		I, O, CRA	Yes
TX Tex. Bus. & Com. Code §§ 521.002, 521.053	AQ	AN	I, O, CRA (10,000+ persons)	No
UT Utah Code § 13-44-101 et seq.	AQ + M	NM	I, O	No
VT Vt. Stat. tit. 9, §§ 2430, 2435	AQ	NM+ informs state AGorother stateagency	I, O, CRA, AG or OA	No
VA Va. Code §§ 18.2-186.6, 32.1 127.1:05	AC + AQ + RID		I, O, AG, CRA	Yes
WA Wash. Rev. Code §§ 19.255.010, 42.56.590	AQ	NH	I, O, AG*	Yes
WV W. Va. Code § 46A-2A-101 et seq.	AC + AQ + RID		I, O, CRA	No
WI Wis. Stat. § 134.98	AQ + RID	NH	I, O, CRA	No. (But breach of law is evidence of negligence or breach of duty)
WY Wyo. Stat. § 40-12-501 et seq.	AQ + RM	NH, NM	I, O	No

* If more than 500 people affected, must make records available to AG for investigations

Some examples of leading state breach notification laws:

California, Cal. Civ. Code §§ 1798.29, 1798.82, 1798.84

The law's trigger for notification is a reasonable belief of the acquisition of personal information. This statute does not provide for exceptions to such notice. It requires that the affected individual and the owner or licensee of the data be informed. Finally, the statute provides for a private right of action to "any customer injured by a violation of this title." It also provides an additional penalty for willful, intentional, and reckless violations of the statute's requirement of reasonable security procedures and practices. A 2013 amendment to the breach notification law expanded the definition of "personal information" to include "a user name or email address, in combination with a password or security question and answer that would permit access to an online account.

Iowa, Iowa Code § 715C.1

This state provides an acquisition trigger for notification. It exempts from disclosure obligations a breach when "no reasonable likelihood of financial harm to consumers" exists, and there has been either "an appropriate investigation" or "consultation with the relevant federal, state or local agencies responsible for law enforcement." When

10

DATA SECURITY

a breach notification is required, the notice is to be provided to affected individuals and the "owner or licensor." There is no private right of action under the act; only the attorney general may enforce it.

Massachusetts, Mass. Gen. Laws ch. 93H, § 1, 201 Mass. Code Regs. 17.03, 17.04
This statute requires notification when there is an acquisition of breached data plus "a substantial risk of identity theft or fraud against a resident of the commonwealth." The Massachusetts statute does not provide for exceptions to such notice. It requires notification of affected state residents, the attorney general, director of consumer affairs and business regulations, other state agencies, and consumer reporting agencies. There is no private right of action provided by the statute; only the attorney general may bring an action under it for a failure to "maintain a comprehensive information security program."

New York, N.Y. State Tech. Law § 57-A:208, N.Y. Gen. Bus. §§ 399-h, 899-aa
This state requires notification upon the acquisition of breached data. It does not provide for exceptions to such notice. This notification is to be provided to affected individuals, the owner or licensee of the information, the attorney general, Consumer Protection Board, State Office of Cyber Security and Critical Infrastructure Coordination, and consumer reporting agencies if more than 5,000 persons must be notified of the breach.

PII DEFINITIONS IN STATE DATA SECURITY BREACH NOTIFICATION LAWS (OVERVIEW)	
ELEMENT OF PII (WHEN ASSOCIATED WITH FIRST NAME/INITIAL AND LAST NAME)	**STATES INCORPORATING THE ELEMENT**
Social Security number (SSN)	47 States and DC
Driver's license number or state identification card number (DL)	47 States and DC
Financial account number, credit card number, debit card number in combination with any required security code, access code, or password (FIN)	47 States and DC
Medical information (MED)	AR, CA, MO, TX
Health insurance information (HEALTH)	CA, CT, FL, MO, MT, TX
Passport number (PPN)	CT, MT, NC, OR
Alien registration number (ALIEN)	CT
Password, access code, PIN (PW)	AK, DC, GA, ME, MT, NY, NC, SC, VT
Unique electronic identification number (UEIN)	IA, MO, NE, NC, TX
Individual taxpayer identification number (TAX)	MD, MT, NC, ND
Tribal identification number (TRIBAL)	MT, WY
Mother's maiden name (MAIDEN)	NY, NC, ND, TX
Date of birth (DOB)	ND, TX
Digital or electronic signature (SIG)	NC, ND

Privacy Law Fundamentals

PII DEFINITIONS IN STATE DATA SECURITY BREACH NOTIFICATION LAWS (OVERVIEW)

Telecommunication access device (TELE)	TX
Biometric data (BIOMETRIC)	IA, NE, NC, TX, WI
DNA profile (DNA)	WI
OTHER PROVISIONS: Extends protection to elements even if not connected to a person's name if the information would still be sufficient for identity theft	GA, ME, OR
Social Security number is PII absent connection to name	IN, MT
Exemption for last 4 digits of SSN, driver's license number, or state/federal identification number as non-PII	NV
Includes signature, home address and telephone number along with name as first identifying element	MT
No mention of name as necessary element for PII	NY, CT, TX (lists names as an identifying element)

PII DEFINITIONS IN STATE DATA SECURITY BREACH NOTIFICATION LAWS (STATE BY STATE)

STATE STATUTE	PII ELEMENTS
AK Alaska Stat. § 45.48.010 et seq.	SSN, DL, FIN, PW
AZ Arz. Rev. Stat. § 44-7501	SSN, DL, FIN
AR Ark. Code § 4-110-101 et seq.	SSN, DL, FIN, MED
CA Cal. Civ. Code §§ 1798.29, 1798.80 et seq.	SSN, DL, FIN, MED, HEALTH, PW
CO Colo. Rev. Stat. § 6-1-716	SSN, DL, FIN
CT Conn. Gen. Stat. § 36a-701b	SSN, DL, FIN, HEALTH, TAX, PPN, ALIEN, BIOMETRIC
DE Del. Code tit. 6, § 12B-101 et. seq.	SSN, DL, FIN
DC D.C. Code § 28-3851 et seq.	SSN, DL, FIN, PW
FL Fla. Stat. § 817.5681	SSN, DL, FIN, PW, HEALTH
GA Ga. Code § 10-1-910, -911, -912; § 46-5-214	SSN, DL, FIN, PW, Extends protection to elements even if not connected to a person's name if the information would still be sufficient for identity theft
HI Haw. Rev. Stat. § 487N-1 et seq	SSN, DL, FIN
ID I.C. § 28-51-104 to 107	SSN, DL, FIN
IL 815 Ill. Comp. Stat. 530/1 et seq.	SSN, DL, FIN, MED, HEALTH, BIOMETRIC, PW
IN Ind. Code § 4-1-11-1 et seq., § 24-4.9 et seq.	SSN, DL, FIN, Social Security number is PII absent connection to name
IA Iowa Code §§ 715C.1, 715C.2	SSN, DL, FIN, UEIN, BIOMETRIC

KS	Kan Stat. § 50-7a01 et seq.	SSN, DL, FIN
KY	KRS § 365.732	SSN, DL, FIN
LA	La. Rev. Stat. Ann. §§ 51:3071 et seq. La. Admin. Code tit. 16, pt. III, § 701	SSN, DL, FIN
ME	Me. Rev. Stat. tit. 10, § 1347 et seq.	SSN, DL, FIN, PW, Extends protection to elements even if not connected to a person's name if the information would still be sufficient for identity theft
MD	Md. Code Com. Law § 14-3501 et seq.	SSN, DL, FIN, TAX
MA	Mass. Gen. Laws ch. 93H, § 1 et seq. Mass. Code Regs. § 17.01 et seq.	SSN, DL, FIN (including financial information with or without required security code, access code, or password)
MI	Mich. Comp. Laws §§ 445.63, 445.72	SSN, DL, FIN
MN	Minn. Stat. §§ 325E.61, 325E.64	SSN, DL, FIN
MS	Miss. Code § 75-24-29	SSN, DL, FIN
MO	Mo. Rev. Stat. § 407.1500	SSN, DL, FIN, MED, HEALTH
MT	Mont. Code § 30-14-1701 et seq.	SSN, DL, FIN, HEALTH, MED, PPN, PW, TAX, TRIBAL, Social Security number is PII absent connection to name; includes signature, home address, and telephone number along with name as first identifying element
NE	Neb. Rev. Stat. § 87-801 et seq.	SSN, DL, FIN, UEIN, BIOMETRIC, PW
NV	Nev. Rev. Stat. §§ 603A.010-603A.920	SSN, DL, FIN, MED, HEALTH Exemption for last 4 digits of SSN, driver's license number, or state/federal identification number as non-LP
NH	N.H Rev. Stat. § 359-C:19 et seq.	SSN, DL, FIN
NJ	N.J. Stat. § 56:8-161	SSN, DL, FIN, Includes otherwise dissociated PII data if the means to link the dissociated data were also accessed.
NY	N.Y. State Tech. Law § 57-A:208 N.Y. Gen. Bus. § 899aa	SSN, DL, FIN
NC	N.C. Gen. Stat. § 75-60 et seq.	SSN, DL, FIN, PPN, PW, UEIN, TAX, MAIDEN, SIG, BIOMETRIC
ND	N.D. Cent. Code § 51-30-01 et seq.	SSN, DL, FIN, MAIDEN, DOB, SIG, MED, HEALTH
OH	Ohio Rev. Code §§ 1347.12, 1349.19, 1349. 191, 1349.192	SSN, DL, FIN
OK	Okla. Stat. tit. 24, § 161 Okla. Stat. tit. 74, § 3113.1	SSN, DL, FIN
OR	Or. Rev. Stat. § 646A.600 et seq.	SSN, DL, FIN, PPN, BIOMETRIC, HEALTH, MED, Extends protection to elements even if not connected to a person's name if the information would still be sufficient for identity theft

PA 73 P.S. § 2301 et seq.	SSN, DL, FIN
RI R.I. Gen. Laws § 11-49.3-1 et seq.	SSN, DL, FIN, MED, HEALTH, PW
SC S.C. Code § 39-1-90	SSN, DL, FIN, PW
TN Tenn. Code § 47-18-2107	SSN, DL, FIN
TX Tex. Bus. & Com. Code Ann. §§ 521.002, 521.053	SSN, DL, FIN, MED, HEALTH, UEIN, MAIDEN, DOB, TELE, BIOMETRIC, No mention of name as necessary element for PII (lists name as an identifying element)
UT Utah Code § 13-44-101 et seq.	SSN, DL, FIN
VT Vt. Stat. tit. 9, §§ 2430, 2435	SSN, DL, FIN, PW
VA Va. Code §§ 18.2-186.6, 32.1, 127.1:05	SSN, DL, FIN
WA Wash. Rev. Code §§ 19.255.010, 42.56.590	SSN, DL, FIN
WV W. Va. Code § 46A-2A-101 et seq.	SSN, DL, FIN
WI Wis. Stat. § 134.98	SSN, DL, FIN, BIOMETRIC, DNA
WY Wyo. Stat. Ann. § 40-12-501 et seq.	SSN, DL, FIN, TRIBAL, MED, HEALTH, PPN, TAX, BIOMETRIC, PW

State Credit Freeze Statutes

Numerous states have security freeze statutes. These laws require consumer credit reporting agencies to place a security freeze on the consumer's credit report upon request by the consumer. Once such a freeze is placed on a credit report, credit reporting agencies cannot generally release the frozen report to a third party in the absence of the consumer's express authorization. States with such laws include Arizona, California, Connecticut, Florida, Indiana, Iowa, New York, Oregon, Texas, Washington, and Wisconsin.

FTC ENFORCEMENT UNDER SECTION 5 OF THE FTC ACT

In a number of cases, the FTC has brought actions against companies that failed to adequately protect the security of personal information. Many of these cases involved data security breaches or improper disclosures and leaks, but some cases involved the mere failure to provide adequate security without any breach or leak occurring.

Leading Cases

FTC v. Wyndham Worldwide Corp., 799 F.3d 236 (3d Cir. 2015)

Affirming FTC's authority to bring cases against companies with inadequate data protection practices. A company's failure to maintain reasonable and appropriate data security could constitute unfair competition under the FTC's Section 5 authority. FTC Act and prior FTC guidelines and actions were sufficient notice that Wyndham's conduct fell within statutory authority.

Resnick v. AvMed, Inc., 693 F.3d 1317 (11th Cir. 2012)

Class action against healthcare company that had two unencrypted laptops stolen with customers' personal information on them. The 11th Circuit granted standing where named plaintiffs alleged sufficient injury-in-fact by demonstrating they had their identities stolen after the data breach, paid for identity-theft protection services, and had never had their identities stolen prior to the breach.

PATCO Constr. Co. v. People's United Bank, 684 F.3d 197 (1st Cir. 2012)

Under Article 4A of the Uniform Commercial Code, a bank is generally held not liable for losses if it followed commercially responsible security procedures to verify the transaction. The defendant bank had not used commercially reasonable security procedures in light of its "collective failures, taken as a whole" measured against security knowledge at the time of the transaction. As an example, it failed to implement additional procedures despite its knowledge of ongoing fraud involving keylogging malware.

Leading FTC Data Security Enforcement Actions

In re Eli Lilly & Co., FTC No. C-4047 (May 8, 2002)

Eli Lilly, a pharmaceutical company, sent e-mail reminders to Prozac users with all subscribers listed in the "to" line of the message. The FTC alleged that the company's privacy policy promising confidentiality was deceptive because the company failed to establish adequate security protections for its consumers' data. The January 2002 settlement between Eli Lilly and the FTC required the company to establish a new security program.

In re Microsoft Corp., FTC No. C-4049 (Dec. 20, 2002)

The FTC charged that Microsoft had made unfair and deceptive representations that NET Passport, an online authentication service, was "protected by powerful online security technology and a strict privacy policy." Microsoft settled with the FTC and agreed to create a comprehensive information security program and to conduct an annual audit to assess its security practices for a period of 20 years.

In re Guess?, Inc., FTC No. C-4091 (July 30, 2003)

Guess, a clothing company, had promised that all personal information "including … credit card information and sign-in password, are stored in an unreadable, encrypted format at all times." This assertion of company policy was false, and the FTC initiated an action even before data was leaked or improperly accessed. The case was eventually settled.

United States v. ChoicePoint, Inc., No. 1:06-cv-00198-JTC (N.D. Ga. Feb. 15, 2006)

The FTC found that ChoicePoint violated the FCRA by furnishing credit histories to subscribers without a permissible purpose and violated the FTC Act by making false and misleading statements about its privacy practices. ChoicePoint agreed to pay $10 million in civil penalties and $5 million into a consumer redress fund. ChoicePoint also promised changes to its business and improvements to its security practices. One requirement that the FTC settlement placed on Choice-

Point was to verify the identity of businesses that apply to receive consumer reports by auditing subscribers' use of consumer reports and by making site visits to certain customers.

In re Reed Elsevier Inc., FTC No. C-4226 (July, 29, 2008)

The FTC alleged that Seisint, a wholly owned subsidy of Reed Elsevier, failed to provide "reasonable and appropriate security to prevent authorized access" to sensitive consumer information. The allegations included a failure by Seisint to establish reasonable policies and procedures to govern the creation and authentication of user credentials for authorized customers. Seisint settled with the FTC, agreeing to establish a comprehensive information security program and permit audits of its program for a period of 20 years.

In re Twitter, Inc., FTC No. C-4316 (Mar. 2, 2011)

The FTC charged that Twitter was deceptive in promising to protect the security of users' private tweets to approved followers. Hackers broke in (1) by gaining administrative control to Twitter because the password was weak (all lowercase) and (2) by obtaining access to passwords stored in an employee's personal e-mail account. The FTC charged Twitter with failing to require employees to use hard-to-guess passwords, to disable administrative passwords after several unsuccessful login attempts, to force periodic changes to administrative passwords, and to implement other security controls.

In re Ceridian Corp., FTC No. C-4325 (June 8, 2011)

FTC entered into 20-year consent decree with provider of online payroll software for small businesses following complaint under FTC Act for inadequate data security practices. FTC complaint followed successful SQL injection attack by hackers that yielded personal information associated with more than 27,000 customers of Ceridian's Powerpay software. Ceridian had indefinitely stored customers' personal information as unencrypted plaintext and failed to implement low-cost defenses against SQL injection attacks.

In re EPN, Inc., FTC No. C-4370 (Oct. 3, 2012)

The debt collection company's chief operating officer installed P2P file-sharing software on the system, exposing sensitive personal data to any computer connected to the P2P network. The FTC charged that the company engaged in an "unfair act or practice" because it failed to have an appropriate security plan, to adequately train employees, or to scan its networks to identify P2P applications.

In re Snapchat, Inc., FTC No. C-4501 (Dec. 23, 2014)

Failure to secure "Find Friends" feature resulted in a breach permitting attackers to compile a database of 4.6 million Snapchat usernames and phone numbers. Snapchat failed to verify user phone numbers during registration, resulting in users sending "snaps" to strangers who registered phone numbers belonging to them.

In the Matter of TRENDnet, Inc., FTC No. C-4426 (Jan. 16, 2014)

FTC entered into 20-year consent decree with manufacturer of webcams marketed as secure, but the feed from which could be accessed over the Internet without properly secured login credentials. TRENDnet allegedly ignored numerous notifications from third parties that its devices were not secure, stored user login credentials as unsecured text, and generally did not implement adequate security practices. This case is notable as the first FTC enforcement action related to the "Internet of Things."

In re Credit Karma, Inc., FTC No. C-4480 (Aug. 13, 2014)
In re Fandango, LLC, FTC No. C-4481 (Aug. 13, 2014)

Credit Karma provided a website and mobile app that allowed consumers to monitor and evaluate their credit and financial status. Its mobile app was alleged to have failed to validate SSL certificates, which left it vulnerable to "man-in-the-middle attacks." This spoofing technique took place on a public Wi-Fi network in which an attacker presented an invalid certificate to the app. Moreover, until the staff of the FTC contacted Credit Kara, it did not perform an adequate security review of the Credit Karma mobile app and did not provide adequate oversight of its service providers' security practices. Fandango provided a website and mobile app that allowed consumers to purchase movie tickets and view showtimes. Like Credit Karma, it allegedly failed to validate SSL certificates, which also left it vulnerable to "man-in-the-middle attacks." Moreover, Fandago failed to have a "clearly publicized and effective channel for receiving security vulnerability reports" and misrepresented the security that it provided to consumers. Under the terms of the respective settlements with the two companies, the FTC required the companies to establish and maintain comprehensive security programs designed to address security risks and to cease misrepresenting their privacy or security.

In re Snapchat, Inc., FTC No. C-4501 (Dec. 23, 2014)

Alleging misrepresentations regarding irretrievability of messages sent via mobile app. Complaint alleges that Snapchat privacy promises were deceptive because of behavior of third-party develops using Snapchat's own API. Snapchat also made deceptive promises regarding analytics tracking.

In re Oracle Corp., FTC No. C-4571 (Mar. 28, 2016)

Complaint alleged that Oracle knew of security vulnerabilities in older Java versions, but in update removed only the most recent version of the software. Oracle agreed to refrain from misrepresenting the security of its software. Oracle further agreed to notify consumers of risks associated with older Java versions present on computers and to provide notice of the settlement on its website.

In re ASUSTeK Comput., Inc., FTC No. C-4587 (July 18, 2016)

Pioneering Internet of Things enforcement action by the FTC. Company alleged to misrepresent its router security features. Among other things, the complaint alleged that ASUSTeK encouraged customers to set up accounts on its private cloud network with weak security presets and authentication bypass vulnerabilities. Company also allegedly failed to provide consumers timely notification of vulnerabilities after receiving customer complaints.

CFPB ENFORCEMENT

In re Dwolla, Inc., **CFPB No. 2016-CFPB-0007 (Mar. 2, 2016)**
CFPB's first data security action. Misrepresentation alleged of security of online payment system. Dwolla claimed that customer transactions would be "safe" and "secure" in compliance with standards set by the trade group Payment Card Industry Security Standards Counsel, but its practices fell below those standards. Inadequate or unreasonable practices alleged related to adopting and implementing data-security policies, assessing foreseeable security risks, ensuring employee security training, using encryption technology, and practicing secure software development. Pursuant to deceptive acts and practices authority, the CFPB ordered Dwolla to refrain from misrepresenting the security of its online payment system, enact data security measures and policies to correct the above deficiencies, and pay $100,000 civil money penalty.

FCC ENFORCEMENT

In re AT&T Servs., Inc., **FCC No. EB-TCD-00016243 (Apr. 8, 2015)**
In its largest data security action, the FTC entered a $25 million settlement with AT&T to resolve investigation into data breaches at AT&T's call centers in Mexico, Colombia, and the Philippines. These breaches resulted from employees' unauthorized use of customers' information, jeopardizing the confidentiality of almost 280,000 customers' personal information. In addition to the money penalty, FCC ordered AT&T to appoint a compliance officer, develop and implement a compliance plan that included risk assessment, review and training, and provide notice to affected customers.

In re Cox Comm'ns, Inc., **FCC No. EB-IHD-14-00017829 (Nov. 5, 2015)**
Cox entered into a consent decree following a 2014 data breach and subsequent FCC allegations of unreasonable data security practices. Unlike enforcement practices typically mandated by the FTC, the FCC consent order required specific security practices rather than general "reasonable" security maintenance. $595,000 civil penalty assessed. FCC's first data security action against a cable provider and first action regarding a hacking incident.

In re TerraCom, Inc., **FCC No. EB-TCD-13-00009175 (July 9, 2015)**
TerraCom and YourTel entered into a consent decree following FCC allegations that they failed to protect the sensitive information of customers applying for their Lifeline phone services. Specifically, they allegedly stored customer data on online servers without password protection or encryption, leading to a data breach. The companies jointly agreed to pay a $3.5 million civil penalty, appoint a compliance officer and develop a compliance plan, implement an information security program, and other measures.

TORT

Tort cases for data security breaches have thus far not been very successful. Most cases have been dismissed for failing to state a cognizable injury.

WHAT CONSTITUTES A PRIVACY HARM?		
THEORY OF HARM	INJURY IN FACT (STANDING)	COGNIZABLE HARM
Increased risk of identity theft	Most courts reject. See, e.g., *Amburgy v. Express Scripts, Inc.*, 671 F. Supp. 2d 1046 (E.D. Mo. 2009); *Key v. DSW, Inc.*, 454 F. Supp. 2d 684 (S.D. Ohio 2006). But at least one court recognized this theory. *Kottner v. Starbucks Corp.*, 683 F.3d 1139 (9th Cir. 2010)	No court has yet recognized as a cognizable harm.
Credit monitoring expenses	Most courts reject.	Most courts reject, except for one case by the First Circuit. *Anderson v. Hannaford Bros. Co.*, 659 F.3d 151 (1st Cir. 2011).
Emotional distress	Most courts reject emotional distress alone without an accompanying physical or financial injury.	Most courts reject emotional distress alone without an accompanying physical or financial injury.
Lost benefit of the bargain (overpayment for services)	Courts have rejected the theory when plaintiffs have failed to establish adequate evidence. See, e.g., *McLoughlin v. People's United Bank, Inc.*, 2009 WL 2843269 But cases can be successful where plaintiffs can establish this injury. See, e.g., *Doe 1 v. AOL, LLC*, 719 F.Supp. 2d 1102 (N.D. Cal. 2010)	At least one court has held that if plaintiffs can provide evidence of signing up for services and paying fees based upon promises of security, then they can establish a legally cognizable harm. See *Doe 1 v. AOL, LLC*, 719 F.Supp. 2d 1102 (N.D. Cal. 2010)

Loss of intrinsic value of data property	Most courts reject, but some courts have expressed vague receptivity to this theory. See, e.g., *Claridge v. RockYou, Inc.*, 785 F. Supp. 2d 855 (N.D. Cal. 2011) (noting that PII can constitute "valuable property" exchanged for defendant's promise to employ reasonable security).	Some courts have been receptive to this theory. See, e.g., *Claridge v. RockYou, Inc.*, 785 F. Supp. 2d 855 (N.D. Cal. 2011); *Rowe v. UniCare Life & Health Ins. Co.*, 2010 WL 86381 (N.D. Ill 2010) (rejecting motion to dismiss but noting that plaintiff's proof of this claim was quite dubious).
Increased risk of junk mail	All courts have rejected thus far. See, e.g., *Bell v. Acxiom XCorp.*, 2006 WL 2850042 (E.D. Ark. 2006).	All courts have rejected thus far. See, e.g., *Bell v. Acxiom XCorp.*, 2006 WL 2850042. But in a spyware case, one court held that burdening of resources and loss of functionality could constitute a cognizable injury. *Sotelo v. Direct Revenue, LLC*, 384 F.Supp. 2d 1219 (N.D. Ill. 2005).
Time and effort expended to deal with the breach	All courts have rejected thus far. See, e.g., *Holmes v. Countrywide Fin. Corp.*, 2012 WL 2873892 (W.D. Ky. 2012).	All courts have rejected thus far. See, e.g., *In re Hannaford Bros. Co. Customer Data Security Breach litigation*, 4 A.3d 492 (Me. 2010)

DATA DISPOSAL

Numerous states have laws that require a business to destroy personal information in a safe and effective fashion once it will no longer retain it.

STATE DATA DISPOSAL STATUTES	
AK	Alaska Stat. § 45.48.500
AZ	Ariz. Rev. Stat. Ann. § 44-7601
AR	Ark. Code Ann. § 4-110-104
CA	Cal. Civ. Code § 1798.81
CO	Colo. Rev. Stat. § 6-1-713
CT	Conn. Gen. Stat. § 42-471
GA	Ga. Code Ann. § 10-15-2
HI	Haw. Rev. Stat. § 487R-2
IL	20 Ill. Comp. Stat. 450/20
IN	Ind. Code §§ 24-4-14-8, 24-4.9-3-3.5(c)
KS	Kan. Stat. Ann. § 50-7a03
KY	Ky. Rev. Stat. Ann. § 365.725
MA	Mass. Gen. Laws ch. 93I, § 2
MD	Md. Code Ann., Comm. Law § 14-3507
MI	Mich. Comp. Laws § 445.72a
MO	Mo. Rev. Stat. § 288.360
MT	Mont. Code Ann. § 30-14-1703
NV	Nev. Rev. Stat. § 603A.200
NJ	N.J. Stat. Ann. § 56:8-162
NY	N.Y. Gen. Bus. Law § 399-H
NC	N.C. Gen. Stat. § 75-64
OR	Or. Rev. Stat. § 646A.622
RI	R.I. Gen. Laws § 6-52-2
SC	S.C. Code Ann. § 37-20-190
TX	Tex. Bus. & Com. Code. Ann. § 72.004
UT	Utah Code Ann. § 13-44-201
VT	9 Vt. Stat. Ann. § 2445
WA	Wash. Rev. Code § 19.215.020
WI	Wis. Stat. § 134.97

Illustrative statutes include:

California, Cal. Civ. Code § 1798.81
Requires a business to take all reasonable steps to destroy or arrange for the destruction of a customer's records within its custody or control that contain personal information and that are no longer to be retained by the business. Destruction is by (1) shredding, (2) erasing or (3) otherwise modifying the personal information in those records to make it unreadable or undecipherable through any means.

Illinois, 20 Ill. Comp. Stat. 450/20
Covers the public sector alone. Requires the Department of Central Management Services or any other authorized agency that disposes of surplus electronic data processing equipment by sale, donation, or transfer to implement a policy mandating that computer hardware be cleared of all data and software before disposal by sale, donation, or transfer.

New York, N.Y. Gen. Bus. Law § 399-H
Prohibits a business, firm, partnership, association, corporation, or business person from disposing of a record containing personal identifying information unless it does any of the following: "a. shreds the record before the disposal of the record; or b. destroys the personal identifying information contained in the record; or c. modifies the record to make the personal identifying information unreadable; or d. takes actions consistent with commonly accepted industry practices that it reasonably believes will ensure that no unauthorized person will have access to the personal identifying information contained in the record."

Texas, Tex. Bus. & Com. Code Ann. § 72.004
Requires a business disposing of a business record that contains personal identifying information of a customer of the business to "modify, by shredding, erasing, or other means, the personal identifying information so as to make the information unreadable or undecipherable." Provides that a business is considered to comply with this law if it contracts with a person engaged in the business of disposing of records in accordance with these statutory requirements.

Washington, Wash. Rev. Code § 19.215.020
Requires an "entity" to "take all reasonable steps to destroy or arrange for the destruction of personal financial and health information and personal identification numbers issued by government entities in an individual's records within its custody or control when the entity is disposing of records that it will no longer retain."

FOR FURTHER REFERENCE

Treatises

Chris Hadnagy, *Social Engineering: The Art of Human Hacking* (**2011**)
A thorough overview of the techniques fraudsters use to trick people.

Cybersecurity: A Practical Guide to the Law of Cyber Risk (**Edward R. McNicholas & Vivek K. Mohan eds., 2016**)
Succinct yet thorough treatise on cybersecurity law.

Ronald N. Weikers, *Data Security and Privacy Law* (**2016**)
2400-page treatise on data security and privacy law.

Books

Securing Privacy in the Internet Age (**Anupam Chander et al., eds., 2008**)
An insightful set of essays focusing on a variety of proposals to heighten privacy and data security, whether through the common law, statutory reforms, or the market.

Kevin Mitnick, *Ghost in the Wires: My Adventures as the World's Most Wanted Hacker* (**2012**)
Engaging stories about how hackers can con people into providing access to computer networks.

Bruce Schneier, *Liars and Outliers: Enabling the Trust that Society Needs to Thrive* (**2012**)
A sociological examination of trust and security.

Bruce Schneier, *Schneier on Security* (**2008**)
Sage wisdom from a leading security expert on security technology and policy.

Bruce Schneier, *Secrets and Lies: Digital Security in a Networked World* (**2004**)
A practical—yet also philosophical—guide to data security that focuses on the big picture as well as the key details.

P.W. Singer & Allan Friedman, *Cybersecurity and Cyberwar: What Everyone Needs to Know* (**2014**)
In an FAQ format, this book discusses cybersecurity with many stories and anecdotes.

Privacy Law Fundamentals

Articles and Other Sources

Harboring Data: Information Security, Law, and the Corporation (Andrea M. Matwyshyn ed., 2009)
Offering a range of multidisciplinary and international perspectives on the evolving landscape of data security.

Privacy Rights Clearinghouse, *Chronology of Data Breaches*, www.privacyrights. org/data-breach
A comprehensive searchable database of data security breach incidents from 2005 to the present.

Sasha Romanosky, David Hoffman & Alessandro Acquisti, *Empirical Analysis of Data Breach Litigation*, 11 J. Empirical Legal Stud. 74 (2014)
The article empirically explores data breach litigation. Despite the fact that the law is strongly against plaintiffs in data breach class actions, about 50% of cases settle. A firm is 3.5 times more likely to be sued when a data breach causes individuals financial harm, but six times lower when the firm provides free credit monitoring. There were 86 different types of causes of action in the cases they studied, the most common being State Unfair Business Practice statutes, the federal Fair Credit Reporting Act, breach of contract, negligence, the federal Privacy Act, and the privacy torts.

Paul M. Schwartz & Edward J. Janger, *Notification of Data Security Breaches*, 105 Mich. L. Rev. 913 (2007)
Advocating greater automatic protection for consumers, clearer consumer notification, coordinated sharing of information about data incidents among affected organizations and heightened oversight of the decision by breached entities whether to inform consumers or other entities.

Andrew B. Serwin, *Poised on the Precipice: A Critical Examination of Privacy Litigation*, 25 Santa Clara Computer & High Tech. L.J. 883 (2009)
An examination of trends in privacy litigation involving data security breaches.

Daniel J. Solove & Woodrow Hartzog, *The FTC and the New Common Law of Privacy*, 114 Colum. L. Rev. 583 (2014)
Argues that "the FTC's privacy jurisprudence is functionally equivalent to a body of common law." Companies look to these agreements as a quasi-common law for determining best practices, and the structures of these FTC agreements amount to a common law equivalent—and one that is amenable to study.

CHAPTER 11

Education Privacy

ESSENTIAL POINTS

- Student education records are protected by the Family Educational Rights and Privacy Act (FERPA), but this statute lacks a private cause of action, decreasing the effectiveness of enforcement.

- Although FERPA is the primary federal statute protecting education records, other federal statutes also are applicable such as the Protection of Pupil Rights Act (PRPA), the Individuals with Disabilities Education Act (IDEA), and the National School Lunches Act (NSLA), among others.

- Students have Fourth Amendment privacy rights on public school campuses against unreasonable search or seizure. But courts tend to be deferential to school officials, so student rights are limited.

- Numerous states are enacting statutes forbidding educational institutions from requesting social media account information from students or prospective students.

STUDENT RECORDS

Family Educational Rights and Privacy Act of 1974 (FERPA)
20 U.S.C. § 1232g

Primary Function: To protect the privacy of student education records.

Applies to: "Education records," which are "those records, files, documents, and other materials which (i) contain information directly related to a student; and (ii) are maintained by an educational agency or institution." 20 U.S.C. §1232g(a)(4)(A). FERPA covers only records and information from records, not information generally. The personal knowledge and observations of educators that are not part of an education record are not covered by FERPA.

Ownership of Rights: FERPA rights initially belong to the parents/guardians of a student. When a student *either* turns 18 *or* attends an institution of postsecondary education (an "eligible student"), FERPA rights transfer from the parents to the student. At the college level, FERPA rights always belong to the student, regardless of age.

Rights: FERPA provides parents/guardians or eligible students with the following rights:

1. To review the student's education records

2. To correct any inaccuracies or misleading information in those records

3. To control certain disclosures of the information in those records

4. To file a complaint with the U.S. Department of Education in the event of a violation of the above rights

Notice: Each year, schools must inform parents or eligible students of their rights under FERPA.

Opt-Out: Unless a parent or eligible student opts out, a school may release to the public "directory information" designated by the school, such as the student's name, address, telephone numbers, birth date, major, activities and sports, dates of attendance, degrees and awards received, and certain other data. 20 U.S.C. § 1232g(b)(5).

Opt-In: Schools generally cannot disclose other information from a student's education records without the written consent of a parent or "eligible student."

Exceptions: Schools may (but are not required to) disclose information without consent in a number of cases, such as to school officials with legitimate educational interests; to the parents of a student who is their dependent for federal tax purposes; to "appropriate parties" in the event of a threat to health or safety; to other schools to which a student is transferring or has transferred; in connection with financial aid; to comply with a judicial order or subpoena; to organizations conducting studies on behalf of the school; and in several other circumstances. 34 C.F.R. § 99.31.

Law Enforcement Records: Records that are both created and maintained by a separate law enforcement unit of a school (either commissioned police or public safety) at least in part for law enforcement purposes are not considered "education records" and are not subject to FERPA protections.

Treatment Records: These records are the medical or psychological records of a student 18 years or older who is being treated by a physician, psychiatrist, psychologist, or other related professional or paraprofessional. 34 C.F.R. § 99.3. They are not considered "education records" as long as they are not shared with others not involved in the student's treatment.

Enforcement: FERPA authorizes the secretary of education to take any "appropriate actions to enforce" FERPA, potentially including the termination of all education-related federal funding, if a school fails to comply with the statute. 20 U.S.C. § 1232g(f). The Department of Education's Family Policy Compliance Office (FPCO) oversees the enforcement of FERPA. *See* 34 C.F.R. § 99.60(b). Before the FPCO takes action, an individual must file a complaint against a school. The FPCO then investigates and if the school is found in violation of FERPA, the FPCO recommends specific steps that the institution must take to comply. If the school fails to comply, then enforcement actions may be taken.

FERPA Regulations (2011), 34 C.F.R. § 99.3: The regulations define two previously undefined terms in FERPA in order to expand the sharing of student personal data. FERPA permits access to student personal data—without consent—to "authorized representatives" of state or federal "education programs." The new regulations expand both definitions to allow a myriad of types of third parties to access student data.

Leading Cases

Owasso Indep. Sch. Dist. No. I-011 v. Falvo, 534 U.S. 426 (2002)
"Education records" under FERPA does not include student homework or classroom work while in the hands of students. Teachers can have students in the class grade each other's papers or exams or see each other's homework.

Gonzaga Univ. v. Doe, 536 U.S. 273 (2002)
A university contacted the state agency for teacher certification to inform the agency about allegations of sexual misconduct on the part of a university student applying to become an elementary school teacher. The allegations of misconduct were later recanted. The student sued the school under 42 U.S.C. § 1983, alleging a violation of FERPA. The Court held that FERPA could not be enforced by a private right of action under § 1983. However, state common law and some other privacy rights continue to be enforceable by private action.

United States v. Miami Univ., 294 F.3d 797 (6th Cir. 2002)
A student newspaper sought disciplinary records from a university. The Ohio Supreme Court held that the records fell within the Ohio Public Records Act, which mandated disclosure. Upon learning the school planned to disclose the records, the U.S. Department of Education intervened and filed a complaint in federal court. Ultimately, the Sixth Circuit concluded that disciplinary records are "education records" under FERPA and the statute bars their disclosure.

Protection of Pupil Rights Amendment of 1978 (PPRA)
20 U.S.C. § 1232h

Primary Function: To protect the privacy of students in surveys, medical exams, and marketing programs.

11

Surveys: Provides an opt-in and opt-out right depending upon the kind of information involved:

1. *Opt-in*—written parental consent required when conducting a survey involving information about politics, mental health, sex, illegal activity, income, and other sensitive information.

2. *Opt-out*—required for any surveys involving other kinds of information. 34 C.F.R. § 98.

Medical Examinations: Provides an opt-out right for any medical exam that involves exposure of private body parts or incision, insertion, or injection into the body. No right to opt out if the exam is necessary to protect the immediate health or safety of a student; for hearing, vision, or scoliosis; or is required by law. 34 C.F.R. § 98.

Marketing: If the school (or a contractor) collects, discloses, or uses personal data from students for marketing purposes, parents or eligible students must be given the right to opt out. 34 C.F.R. § 98.

Every Student Succeeds Act (ESSA)
Pub. L No. 114-95, 129 Stat. 1802 codified as amended in scattered sections of 20 U.S.C.) (2015)

Primary Function: Governs law for K-12 public education policy and replaces No Child Left Behind Act. The law requires grantees to possess knowledge of FERPA's responsibilities.

Homeless Students: ESSA mandates that homeless students' living situations not be listed in directories; instead, this information is considered a part of the student's educational record and thus protected by FERPA.

Congressional Findings: Congress included a section on the importance of protecting student privacy, calling for recipients of funding to ensure PII is held in strict confidence.

Individuals with Disabilities Education Act (IDEA)
20 U.S.C. § 1400 (1975)

Primary Function: In addition to many other provisions, IDEA has privacy protections for students involved in special education. Many of these protections are identical to those in FERPA, but there are some differences, explained below.

Destruction of Data: When information about children with disabilities is no longer needed, agencies maintaining it must inform their parents. The parents can request that it be destroyed. 34 C.F.R. § 300.573.

Public Notice: State educational agencies must provide public notice about the collection of personally identifiable information and a summary of their privacy policies. 34 C.F.R. § 300.561.

Privacy Official: State educational agencies must have an official responsible for ensuring that the privacy of personally identifiable information is properly maintained and officials handling such information are properly trained. 34 C.F.R. § 300.572.

National School Lunch Act (NSLA)
42 U.S.C. § 1758(6) (1946)

Primary Function: In addition to many other provisions, the NSLA mandates that the names of children participating in the National School Lunch Program must remain confidential.

Applies to: Any person "directly connected with the administration or enforcement" of a school lunch program or federal education program, or state health or education program. 42 U.S.C. § 1758(6)(A)(i).

Enforcement: A person "who publishes, divulges, discloses, or makes known in any manner, or to any extent not authorized by Federal law (including a regulation), any information obtained under this subsection shall be fined not more than $1,000 or imprisoned not more than 1 year, or both." 42 U.S.C. § 1758(6)(C); 7 C.F.R. § 245.8.

Jeanne Clery Disclosure of Campus Security Policy and Campus Crime Statistics Act (Clery Act)
20 U.S.C. § 1092(f) (1990)

Primary Purpose: Mandates disclosure of college and university campus crime statistics and security policies.

Disclosures of Sex Offenses: "Both the accuser and the accused must be informed of the outcome of any institutional disciplinary proceeding brought alleging a sex offense." 34 C.F.R. § 668.46(b)(11)(vi)(B). (Such disclosures are also expressly permitted by FERPA.)

Other Regulations

Gainful Employment Rule (2011)
20 U.S.C. § 1002
This rule, which seeks to determine whether education at postsecondary schools leads to gainful employment, will use income data from the Social Security Administration.

Other Statutes

Beyond the statutes listed above, many schools might be subject to other federal statutes:

Children's Online Privacy Protection Act (COPPA): Applies if a school has a website "directed to children" or with "actual knowledge that it is collecting personal information from a child." 15 U.S.C. § 6502(a)(1).

Electronic Communications Privacy Act (ECPA): Applies if a school engages in certain kinds of electronic surveillance (e.g., audio surveillance and surveillance of electronic communications). 18 U.S.C. §§ 2510-2522.

Computer Fraud and Abuse Act (CFAA): The CFAA criminalizes all "unauthorized access" to any kind of computer with Internet access. Because there is no exception for school officials, anytime a school official searches a student-owned computer without consent, it could constitute a CFAA violation. 18 U.S.C. § 1030.

Health Insurance Portability and Accountability Act (HIPAA): In some limited circumstances, some school records might be regulated under the HIPAA Privacy Rule. But any records that are either "education records" or "treatment records" under FERPA—which is to say virtually all health-related records that a school may have about its students—are exempt from HIPAA. 45 C.F.R. § 160.103.

STATE LAWS

Student Data Collection, Use, and Disclosure

Alabama, State Board of Education Policy (2013)
In October 2013, the Alabama State Board of Education adopted a new policy on student data that allows the state to share student data with the federal government only in aggregate form. The policy also calls on school districts to adopt their own policies on the collection and sharing of student data.

California, Student Online Personal Information Protection Act (2014)
New law restricting companies from selling or disclosing personal information about students from kindergarten through high school. The statute specifically targets operators of Internet web sites, online services, online applications, or mobile applications. These companies are prohibited from knowingly engaging in targeted advertising to students or their parents, from using covered information to amass student profiles, from selling students' information, or from disclosing covered information. The law also requires an operator to implement and maintain reasonable security procedures and practices appropriate to the nature of the covered information.

Georgia, Executive Order (May 15, 2013)
Executive Order prohibiting the state from collecting or sharing personally identifiable data on students and prohibiting student data from being collected for the
development of commercial products or services.

Iowa, Executive Order No. 83 (2013)
Student data in Iowa should be collected in accordance with state and federal privacy
laws and only aggregate student data is to be provided to the federal government.

Texas, H.B. 2268 (2013)
Texas law enforcement officials must obtain a warrant before accessing email and
other communications content.

Social Media Account Access
Numerous states are enacting statutes forbidding educational institutions from
requesting social media account information from students or prospective students.
Some examples are below.

Louisiana, Personal Online Account Privacy Protection Act (2014)
This law prohibits educational institutions, such as primary and secondary schools
and universities, from requiring students or prospective students from disclosing
authorizing information to personal online accounts. The educational institution may
place conditions, however, on the use of the school's equipment or online services.

Illinois, Right to Privacy in the School Setting Act (2013)
This law prohibits post-secondary educational institutions from requiring students
or their parents or guardians to provide passwords or other account information in
order to gain access to a student's account or profile on social networking websites.
The law does not prohibit a covered school from monitoring use of the school's
equipment or services and does not include email within the meaning of "social
networking website." An elementary or secondary school may request or require
account information when there is reasonable cause to believe the account contains
evidence that the student violated a school rule or policy, but the school must notify
the student and his or her parents or guardians.

New Mexico, S.B. 422 (2013)
This law prohibits post-secondary educational institutions from requesting or requiring students or potential students to provide passwords in order to gain access to a
social networking website account or profile. Post-secondary educational institutions
are further prohibited from taking adverse action against a student or potential student for refusing to grant access to a social networking website account or profile.

Oregon, S.B. 344 (2013)
This bill prohibits a public or private educational institution from requiring, requesting, or otherwise compelling a student or prospective student to disclose or to provide access to a personal social media account.

STUDENT SPEECH AND EXPRESSION

Student speech and expression can be invasive of privacy or constitute harassment or cyberbullying. In certain circumstances, the First Amendment limits the ability of schools to discipline students for such speech.

First Amendment and On-Campus Speech: Students have First Amendment rights on campus. *Tinker v. Des Moines Indep. Cmty. Sch. Dist.,* 393 U.S. 503 (1969). These rights, however, are limited, as school officials have discretion to discipline students for the "use of vulgar and offensive terms." *Bethel Sch. Dist. No. 403 v. Fraser,* 478 U.S. 675 (1986). Speech that is "reasonably viewed as promoting illegal drug use" can be punished when at a school event. *Morse v. Frederick,* 551 U.S. 393 (2007). "Educators do not offend the First Amendment by exercising editorial control over the style and content of student speech in school-sponsored expressive activities." *Hazelwood Sch. Dist. v. Kuhlmeier,* 484 U.S. 260 (1988).

The First Amendment and Off-Campus Speech: Schools have much less ability to respond to off-campus speech. Only when the speech causes a "substantial disruption of or a material interference with school activities" does the school have the power to sanction a student under the First Amendment. The "substantial disruption" test comes from *Tinker. Morse v. Frederick,* 551 U.S. 393 (2007), recognizes school officials' authority to restrict speech at off-campus school events when "reasonably viewed as promoting drug use."

Anti-Bullying Laws: Many states have passed anti-bullying laws that address cyberbullying—the use of the Internet or electronic devices to attack another student with insults, harassment, or invasion of privacy.

State Anti-Bullying Laws	
AR	Ark. Code Ann. § 6-18-514
CA	Cal. Educ. Code §§ 32260
DE	Del. Code Ann. tit. 14, § 4112D
FL	Fla. Stat. § 1006.147
ID	Idaho Code Ann. § 18-917A
IL	720 Ill. Comp. Stat. 5/12-7.5
IN	Ind. Code § 20-30-5.5-3
IA	Iowa Code § 280.28

State Anti-Bullying Laws	
KS	Kan. Stat. Ann. § 72-8256
MD	Md. Code Ann., Educ. § 7-424.1
ME	Me. Rev. Stat. Ann. tit. 20-A, § 6554
MN	Minn. Stat. § 121A.0695
MO	Mo. Rev. Stat. § 160.775
NE	Neb. Rev. Stat. § 79-2,137
NJ	N.J. Stat. Ann. § 18A:37-15
NM	N.M. Stat. Ann. § 22-2-21
OK	Okla. Stat. tit. 70, § 24-100.3
OR	Or. Admin R. 581-022-1140
PA	24 Pa. Cons. Stat. § 13-1303.1-A
RI	R.I. Gen. Laws § 16-21-26
SC	S.C. Code Ann. § 59-63-120
TN	Tenn. Code Ann. § 49-6-4501
UT	Utah Code Ann. § 53-A-11a-102
WA	Wash. Rev. Code § 28A.300.285

SEARCHES AND SURVEILLANCE

Fourth Amendment
The Fourth Amendment protects student privacy at public schools, but warrants and probable cause are not required for school officials to engage in searches. Searches are justified when there are "reasonable grounds" that they will reveal evidence of a crime or a violation of school policy. At private schools, searches are governed primarily by contract and state common law privacy principles.

Leading Cases

New Jersey v. T.L.O., 469 U.S. 325 (1985)
Students have Fourth Amendment rights at school. Warrants and probable cause are not required. A search is justified "when there are reasonable grounds for suspecting that the search will turn up evidence that the student has violated or is violating either the law or the rules of the school."

Vernonia Sch. Dist. 47J v. Acton, **515 U.S. 646 (1995)**
Mandatory drug testing of student athletes is constitutional under the Fourth Amendment. Athletes have a "reduced expectation of privacy," and the search was relatively unobtrusive. The school has a compelling interest in combating illegal drug use.

Bd. of Educ. v. Earls, **536 U.S. 822 (2002)**
Mandatory drug testing of all students participating in any extracurricular activity is constitutional under the Fourth Amendment. Students in extracurricular activities have a reduced expectation of privacy. The school demonstrated that it had reason to address illegal drug use.

Safford Unified Sch. Dist. No. 1 v. Redding, **557 U.S. 364 (2009)**
Although school officials had reasonable suspicion to search a student's backpack and outer clothing for illegal drugs, requiring a student to expose private parts beneath underwear and bras went beyond the permissible scope of the search. There was no "indication of danger" from the drugs or reason to suspect the student was hiding them in her underwear.

SELF-REGULATORY MEASURES

Future of Privacy Forum, *Student Data Privacy Pledge* **(2014)**
Drafted by the Future of Privacy Forum, this pledge involves companies declaring that they will refrain from selling information on K-12 students; refrain from using students' data to target them with advertisements; and refrain from compiling personal profiles of students unless authorized by schools or parents. Although not contractually binding, this pledge creates a public commitment for the companies of the kind that could lead to enforcement actions by the FTC should these privacy promises be violated. Two hundred school service providers have signed the pledge, which has Presidential endorsement.

FOR FURTHER REFERENCE

Treatises

Mary A. Lentz, *Campus Security for Public and Private Colleges and Universities* **(2016)**
Detailed discussion of FERPA and related statutes.

Mary A. Lentz, *Lentz School Security* **(2016)**

The Family Educational Rights and Privacy Act: A Legal Compendium **(Steven McDonald ed., 2d ed. 2002)**
Useful collection of background material, articles, interpretative material, and sample policies and forms. Includes a detailed annotated bibliography.

James A. Rapp, *Education Law* **(2016)**
Comprehensive treatment of the law of educational records and related legal issues. Available online through LexisNexis.

LeRoy Rooker, *American Association of Collegiate Registrars and Admissions Officers (AACRAO) 2012 FERPA Guide* **(2012)**
Comprehensive overview of FERPA with quiz questions, sample forms, and FPCO letters.

Articles and Other Sources

Darryn Cathryn Beckstrom, *State Legislation Mandating School Cyberbullying Policies and the Potential Threat to Students' Free Speech Rights,* **33 Vermont L. Rev. 283 (2008)**
Examines state cyberbullying laws and their free speech implications.

Lynn M. Daggett, *FERPA in the Twenty-First Century: Failure to Effectively Regulate Privacy for All Students,* **58 Cath. U. L. Rev. 59 (2008)**
A detailed overview and critique of FERPA.

Family Policy Compliance Office (FPCO) Website, http://www2.ed.gov/policy/gen/guid/fpco/index.html Contains guidance about FERPA and PRPA.

Joel Reidenberg et al., *Privacy and Cloud Computing in Public Schools,* **Fordham Ctr. on Law & Info. Policy (2013)**
This study examines how school districts address privacy when they transfer student information to cloud computing service providers. To conduct this study, Fordham's Center on Law and Information Policy selected a national sample of school districts from every geographic region of the country and requested from each selected district all of the district's cloud service agreements, notices to parents, and computer use policies for teachers.

Richard Salgado, Comment, *Protecting Student Speech Rights While Increasing School Safety: School Jurisdiction and the Search for Warning Signs in a Post-Columbine/Red Lake Environment,* **2005 B.Y.U. L. Rev. 1371 (2005)**
Addresses the issue of how schools can combat off-campus threats and online bullying.

CHAPTER 12

Employment Privacy

ESSENTIAL POINTS

- The Fourth Amendment applies to searches by the government that affect public- or private-sector employees. The "special needs" doctrine applies only when the government is the employer; that is, to public-sector employees.

- The constitutional right of informational privacy, as articulated in *Whalen v. Roe*, applies to government searches but not those by private-sector employers.

- Many kinds of searches and surveillance by private-sector employers will not run afoul of privacy laws if the employers obtain employee consent beforehand. Even where employers have threatened to terminate employees if they do not consent, the consent has been deemed valid.

- The Electronic Communications Privacy Act (ECPA) applies not only to government and law enforcement officials, but to private parties as well. Its jurisdiction extends to employers that monitor employee telephone and e-mail communications and Internet use. Obtaining employee consent beforehand typically exempts most instances of electronic surveillance of employees from ECPA's restrictions.

- The National Labor Relations Act (NLRA) ensures that employees (whether unionized or not) can engage in "concerted activity" to discuss workplace conditions and terms and conditions of employment. According to the National Labor Relations Board (NLRB), which enforces the NLRA, overly broad social media policies that restrict employee expression on social media can chill protected activity under the NLRA.

SEARCHES

Government Employees: Fourth Amendment
When government employers engage in searches of government employees for non–law enforcement purposes, the Fourth Amendment "special needs" doctrine merely requires the search to be "reasonable." No warrant or probable cause is needed.

O'Connor v. Ortega, 480 U.S. 709 (1987)
Government employees have a reasonable expectation of privacy at the workplace. They can expect privacy as to items they bring to work. They have limited expectations of privacy in their office depending upon the context. Based on the "special needs" doctrine, the Fourth Amendment does not require government employers to obtain a warrant or have probable cause to carry out a search. The search only needs to be "reasonable … under all the circumstances."

Nat'l Treasury Emps. Union v. Von Raab, 489 U.S. 656 (1989)
Drug testing at the workplace for noncriminal purposes falls under the "special needs" doctrine. The constitutionality of workplace drug tests is evaluated by balancing the interference with privacy against the government interest in testing.

Skinner v. Railway Labor Executives' Ass'n, 489 U.S. 602 (1989)
Mandatory drug testing for railroad employees involved in railroad accidents is reasonable under the Fourth Amendment. Because railroads are a highly regulated industry, employees have minimal privacy expectations. The government has a compelling interest in preventing accidents from drug impairment.

Chandler v. Miller, 520 U.S. 305 (1997)
A drug-testing requirement for candidates for public office violates the Fourth Amendment. Ordinary law enforcement methods are sufficient to prevent drug use, and candidates are subject to relentless scrutiny.

Private Sector Employees: Fourth Amendment
In the private-sector employer context, employees are protected by the Fourth Amendment if they have a reasonable expectation of privacy in their offices, desk drawers, or computers. If it is the government alone doing the searching, employees have full Fourth Amendment protection. The government needs a warrant and probable cause to search when the employee has a reasonable expectation of privacy. The "special needs" doctrine does not apply because the government is not the employer.

Since the employer owns (and often exercises common authority over) employee offices and computers, the employer can consent to the search. If the employer cooperates, the search is valid under the consent exception to the Fourth Amendment. The consent exception does not apply in the case of searches by government employers, since the government cannot consent to its own search.

Leading Cases

Mancusi v. DeForte, 392 U.S. 364 (1968)
A person can have a reasonable expectation of privacy in an office at a private-sector workplace. "[C]apacity to claim the protection of the Amendment depends not upon a property right in the invaded place but upon whether the area was one in which there was a reasonable expectation of freedom from governmental intrusion."

United States v. Ziegler, 474 F.3d 1184 (9th Cir. 2007)
The FBI directed a search of the computer of an employee at a private-sector company. "[I]n the private employer context, employees retain at least some expectation of privacy in their offices." But the employer had common authority over the employee's computer and could give valid consent to search it as well as the employee's office.

Leventhal v. Knapek, 266 F.3d 64 (2d Cir. 2001)
An employee has a reasonable expectation of privacy as to his office computer when he doesn't share it with others, nobody else has regular access to it, and his employer does not engage in the practice of routine computer searches.

United States v. Simons, 206 F.3d 392 (4th Cir. 2000)
An employee lacks a reasonable expectation of privacy as to his workplace computer when the employer's Internet use policy states that the company will monitor employees' Internet use.

Searches and Surveillance by Private-Sector Employers

Employee Consent: Many searches and types of surveillance by private-sector employers will not run afoul of privacy laws. At-will employees can consent to very invasive searches and surveillance as a condition of employment. *Jennings v. Minco Tech. Labs, Inc.*, 765 S.W.2d 497 (Tex. Ct. App. 1989).

Public Policy: Some limits exist on the kind of searches that the law permits employers to carry out. In some states, terminating an at-will employee for not submitting to invasive searches or surveillance will be in violation of public policy. *Borse v. Piece Goods Shop, Inc.*, 963 F.2d 611 (3d Cir. 1992) (holding that "dismissing an employee who refused to consent to urinalysis testing and to personal property searches would violate public policy if the testing tortiously invaded the employee's privacy").

In some states, not only is tort law a source of public policy, but constitutional law is as well—even though it does not ordinarily apply to the private sector. *Hennessey v. Coastal Eagle Point Oil Co.*, 609 A.2d 11 (N.J. 1992).

State Constitutional Protections: Some state constitutions do not require "state action" for their privacy protections to be applicable. As a consequence, their privacy provisions can apply to the actions of private parties and not just to the government. The California Supreme Court has held that the right to privacy in the California

Constitution "creates a right of action against private as well as government entities." *Hill v. NCAA*, 865 P.2d 633 (Cal. 1994). To assert a claim for invasion of one's constitutional right to privacy, a plaintiff in California must establish: (1) a legally protected privacy interest, (2) a reasonable expectation of privacy under the circumstances and (3) conduct by the defendant that constitutes a serious invasion of privacy. Once a plaintiff establishes these three elements, the defendant may prove that the invasion of privacy is justified because it furthers "legitimate and important competing interests." *Id.; see also Hernandez v. Hillsides, Inc.*, 211 P.3d 1063 (Cal. 2009).

State Statutes: Some states have enacted laws prohibiting certain kinds of searches and surveillance in the workplace. For example, Conn. Gen. Stat. § 31-48b(b) prohibits an employer from "recording or monitoring the activities of his employees in areas designed for the health or personal comfort of the employees or for safeguarding of their possessions, such as rest rooms, locker rooms or lounges." Such laws cannot be contracted around, even by unions. *Cramer v. Consol. Freightways, Inc.*, 255 F.3d 683 (9th Cir. 2001) (en banc) (union cannot agree in collective bargaining agreement to allow employer to engage in surveillance prohibited by criminal law).

QUESTIONING AND TESTING

Fourth Amendment
The Fourth Amendment will generally not limit "mere questioning" by government employers even when questions demand "highly personal private information." *Greenawalt v. Ind. Dep't of Corr.*, 397 F.3d 587 (7th Cir. 2005).

Constitutional Right to Information Privacy
The constitutional right to information privacy was first identified in *Whalen v. Roe*, 429 U.S. 589 (1977). *See* Chapter 6. Courts have held that it protects against government employers making unwarranted disclosures of employee information. *See, e.g., Am. Fed'n of Gov't Emps., AFL-CIO v. HUD*, 118 F.3d 786 (D.C. Cir. 1997) ("[T]he employees could cite no case in which a court has found a violation of the constitutional right to privacy where the government has collected, but not disseminated, the information."). The constitutional right to information privacy does not restrict public employers from asking background check questions involving private matters. *NASA v. Nelson*, 562 U.S. 134 (2011).

The government must provide appropriate safeguards for the information it collects from employees or else it will violate the constitutional right to information privacy. "Safeguards against disclosure of private material have been held to be adequate when there exists a statutory penalty for unauthorized disclosures; when there exist security provisions to prevent mishandling of files coupled with an express regulatory policy prohibiting disclosure, and in a unique situation when, even absent an explicit statutory or regulatory policy, the record supported the conclusion that those officials with private information would not disclose it." *Fraternal Order of Police, Lodge No. 5 v. City of Phila.*, 812 F.2d 105 (3d Cir. 1987).

Employee Polygraph Protection Act of 1988 (EPPA)
29 U.S.C. §§ 2001–2009

Primary Function: To regulate the use of polygraphs by private-sector employers.

Applies to: Private-sector employers. Specifically exempts government employers.

Limitations on Polygraph Testing: Private-sector employers cannot require employees to submit to polygraph examinations. 29 U.S.C. § 2002.

Exception—Investigations: Employers can require employees to submit to polygraphs when "the test is administered in connection with an ongoing investigation involving economic loss or injury to the employer's business, such as theft, embezzlement, misappropriation or an act of unlawful industrial espionage or sabotage" and the employer "has a reasonable suspicion that the employee was involved in the incident or activity under investigation." 29 U.S.C. § 2006(d)(3).

Exception—Security Services: Employers who engage in security services are exempt if they protect government interests or "currency, negotiable securities, precious commodities or instruments, or proprietary information." 29 U.S.C. § 2006(e)(1) (B). When polygraphs are used under these exceptions, the test or the refusal to take the test cannot be the sole basis of any adverse employment action. 29 U.S.C. § 2007(a). Polygraph examiners cannot ask questions concerning beliefs regarding religion, racial matters, politics, sexual behavior or union activities. 29 U.S.C. § 2007(b). Disclosure of polygraph information to people authorized by the examinee or the employer, or pursuant to a court order. 29 U.S.C. § 2008.

Enforcement: Violations will result in a civil penalty of up to $10,000. The secretary of labor may bring an action to obtain restraining orders and injunctions to require compliance with the EPPA. Employers who violate the EPPA are liable to employees or prospective employees for legal and equitable relief including reinstatement, promotion, and payment of lost wages and benefits. 29 U.S.C. § 2005.

Preemption: The EPPA does not preempt state law. About half of the states regulate the use of polygraphs by statute.

Americans with Disabilities Act of 1990 (ADA)
42 U.S.C. § 12101 *et seq.*

Primary Function: To protect the rights of people with disabilities, and in doing so, regulate how employers can conduct medical examinations.

Applies to: Government and private-sector employers. A "disability" is defined as "a physical or mental impairment that substantially limits one or more major life activities of such individual." 42 U.S.C. § 12102(1)(A).

Pre-Employment: The ADA treats pre-employment and post-employment examinations and inquiries differently. Employers are prohibited in conducting medical examinations or inquiries to determine if the individual has a disability or the "nature and severity of such disability." But the employer "may make pre-employment inquiries into the ability of an applicant to perform job-related functions." 42 U.S.C. § 12112(d)(2)(B).

Post-Hiring: Employers are prohibited from conducting medical examinations or inquiries to determine if the individual has a disability or the "nature and severity of such disability" unless there is a job-related reason "consistent with business necessity." 42 U.S.C. § 12112(d)(4)(A). Drug testing is not considered a "medical examination" under the ADA. 42 U.S.C. § 12114(d).

Confidentiality of HIV: The EEOC issued a document called *Living with HIV Infection: Your Legal Rights in the Workplace Under the ADA* (2015) to address the protections required under the ADA for applicants and employees with HIV infection. Generally, persons with HIV infection are allowed to keep their condition private. If persons disclose their condition, employers have an obligation to keep the medical information confidential, "even from co-workers."

Occupational Safety and Health Act (OSHA)
29 U.S.C. § 654 *et seq.* (1970)

OSHA provides a right of employees to access their medical records maintained by their employers. This includes questionnaires and results of examinations. 29 C.F.R. § 1910.1020(e)(2)(ii)(A). Employers must avoid disclosing the names of employees suffering an injury to an "intimate body part," "resulting from a sexual assault," relating to mental illness, or involving "HIV infection, hepatitis, or tuberculosis," among other things. 29 C.F.R. § 1904.29(b)(7).

Genetic Information Nondiscrimination Act of 2008 (GINA)
42 U.S.C. § 2000ff *et seq.*

GINA prohibits employers from discriminating on the basis of genetic information. It also prohibits employers from demanding or buying an employee's genetic information. 42 U.S.C. § 2000ff-1(b). There are a few very limited exceptions. The law also has a provision requiring confidentiality of any genetic information maintained by the employer. 42 U.S.C. § 2000ff-5.

State Employment Testing and Inquiry Laws
Many states restrict certain forms of employment testing and questionnaires. For example, Wisconsin prohibits employers from requiring employees or applicants to undergo HIV testing. Wisc. Stat. § 103.15(2). Massachusetts prohibits employers from asking prospective employees about arrests not leading to conviction, misdemeanor convictions, or any prior commitment to medical treatment facilities. Mass. Gen.

Laws ch. 151B, § 4(9). A number of states restrict genetic testing. Cal. Gov't Code § 12940(o); Conn. Gen. Stat. § 46a-60(11)(A); Del. Code Ann. tit. 19, § 711(e); N.Y. Exec. Law § 296.19(a)(1).

State Criminal Background Check "Ban the Box" Laws

Nine states—Connecticut, Hawaii, Illinois, Massachusetts, Minnesota, New Jersey, Oregon, Rhode Island, and Vermont—the District of Columbia, and many localities have passed "Ban the Box" laws and ordinances. The term "Ban the Box" originated in a campaign by various advocacy groups to stop the check box on hiring applications asking applicants about whether they have a criminal record. Examples of recent laws include:

D.C., Fair Criminal Record Screening Amendment Act (2014)

Restricts employers from using criminal background checks during the application process. Once employers make a conditional employment offer, they are then permitted to consult criminal background check information. Employers "cannot make any inquiry or require an applicant to disclose or reveal any criminal conviction until after making a conditional offer of employment." Conditional offers may be withdrawn for a "legitimate business reason" and must be reasonable. When such an offer is withdrawn, applicants can request all records considered by the employer. There is no private right of action, but people can file complaints with the DC Office of Human Rights. Penalties range between $1,000 and $5,000, with half going to the complaining individual. Exemptions include courts; the federal government; when any law requires consideration of criminal history; or when the position involves "direct care to minors or vulnerable adults."

Illinois, Job Opportunities for Qualified Applicants Act (2015)

Employers with 15 or more employees may not inquire about the criminal history of an applicant until the applicant has been selected for an interview and notified about such selection. For hiring without interviews, inquiries into criminal history cannot occur until after a conditional employment offer is made. Exemptions include public-sector employers as well as when laws exclude employees with criminal convictions from certain jobs. No private right of action, and first offenses receive a warning. Subsequent violations are punished with fines.

San Francisco, Police Code Article 49 and Administrative Code Article 12 (2014)

Employers with 20 or more employees within the City are prohibited from inquiring into or considering arrests that did not lead to conviction; expunged or voided convictions; juvenile justice system convictions; and convictions older than seven years, among other things. "Inquiry" is defined as "any direct or indirect conduct intended to gather information from or about an applicant." Convictions older than seven years or unresolved arrests can be considered if they have "a direct and specific negative bearing on that person's ability to perform the duties or responsibilities necessarily related to the employment position." Notice must be provided to an applicant or employee before the employer takes adverse action based upon conviction history.

Rhode Island, Fair Employment Practices Law (2014)
Employers of four or more people are restricted from inquiring into the criminal backgrounds of applicants prior to the first interview. The law applies to both private sector and government employers.

EMPLOYEE ACCESS TO THE COMPUTER NETWORK

United States v. Nosal, 676 F.3d 854 (9th Cir. 2012) (en banc)
A former employee who accessed confidential information from his employer's databases did not exceed "authorized access" under the CFAA. Circuit courts remain split on this issue.

United States v. Rodriguez, 628 F.3d 1258 (11th Cir. 2010)
An employee violated the CFAA by using his employer's computer for nonbusiness purposes because his employer had clearly told him not to do so.

There is currently a major circuit split on the issue in the cases above.

SURVEILLANCE AND MONITORING

Electronic Communications Privacy Act (ECPA)
ECPA applies not only to government and law enforcement officials, but also to private parties. Thus, employers are subject to the restrictions of federal electronic surveillance law. However, three notable exceptions to electronic surveillance law are relevant to the employment context:

- The Wiretap Act and SCA do not apply when one party to a communication consents to the interception or access.

- When employers are the providers of the communications service, they are exempt from the Wiretap Act or SCA if they are acting in a way necessary to render the service or protect the rights or property of the service.

- The Wiretap Act does not apply when an employer uses certain intercepting devices "in the ordinary course of [the employer's] business." The device must be furnished to the employer by the provider of the communication service.

Employers must be careful to monitor employees as they have set forth in their policies. For example, in *Watkins v. L.M. Berry & Co.*, 704 F.2d 577 (11th Cir. 1983), an employer promised employees that it would not monitor personal calls, but it ultimately ended up listening in on an employee's call about a new job. The court held that the employer exceeded the scope of what was told to the employee.

City of Ontario v. Quon, 560 U.S. 746 (2010)

Despite the police department's official general Internet use policy, which prohibited use for personal benefit, the department had an informal policy of allowing personal uses of department-supplied pagers so long as employees paid for the extra usage. The department monitored an employee's personal use of the pager, and the employee alleged a violation of the Fourth Amendment. The court assumed for the purposes of argument that the employee had a reasonable expectation of privacy and held that the search was reasonable because it was "motivated by a legitimate work-related purpose" and was "not excessive in scope."

What Every Employer Must Know to Comply with ECPA

1. Clearly notify employees of the monitoring policy.

2. Putting employees on notice of the policy is typically sufficient to establish consent under ECPA.

3. We recommend using computer login screens where users need to accept the terms of the monitoring. This creates the most unambiguous consent.

EMPLOYMENT PRIVACY LAW: PUBLIC VS. PRIVATE SECTOR

TYPE OF PROTECTION	PUBLIC SECTOR	PRIVATE SECTOR
Fourth Amendment	Searches must be reasonable under the circumstances. *O'Connor v. Ortega*, 480 U.S. 709 (1987). This is determined by balancing the invasion of privacy against the government's interest.	No Fourth Amendment restrictions on employer searching. The Fourth Amendment protects employees from government searches of their offices, but not if the employer permits the government to engage in the search.
Constitutional Right to Informational Privacy	Government employers must avoid unwarranted disclosures of employee personal data and provide appropriate safeguards to the information it collects from employees.	When private employer collects information from employees, it does not implicate this constitutional right due to lack of state action.

EMPLOYMENT PRIVACY

12

State Constitutional Law	State constitutions will also regulate the government employers of that state.	Most state constitutions do not apply to the private sector. There are some exceptions (*e.g.*, California).
Breach of Contract	If privacy is promised by employers in a contract, then an employee would have a cause of action for a breach.	
Privacy Torts	Employers can violate the privacy torts, but the employer can make consenting to certain kinds of searches and surveillance conditional on employment.	
Wrongful Termination in Violation of Public Policy	Employers cannot terminate an employee for refusing to consent to a privacy invasion in violation of public policy. The sources of public policy can include tort law, constitutional law, and criminal law.	Employers cannot terminate an employee for refusing to consent to a privacy invasion in violation of public policy. Since constitutional law does not apply to private sector employers, most courts hold it can't be a source of public policy. But in some states, courts have held that the constitution can serve as a source of public policy against private-sector employers. In many instances, tort law can be contracted around, but criminal law cannot.
Federal Electronic Surveillance Law	Government and private-sector employers must follow the requirements of federal electronic surveillance law.	
State Electronic Surveillance Law	Government and private-sector employers must follow the requirements of federal electronic surveillance law.	

EMPLOYER SOCIAL MEDIA POLICIES AND PRACTICES

National Labor Relations Act (NLRA)

In a series of three memos issued in 2011 and 2012, the National Labor Relations Board (NLRB) acting general counsel describes many NLRB investigations and cases involving social media issues. These materials reveal that employer social media policies will run afoul of the NLRA, 29 U.S.C. §§ 151–169, when they are overbroad and could be construed as chilling employee discussion about the terms and conditions of employment with other employees via social media. The third memo in this series provides specific examples of different employer policies and rules, both acceptable and unacceptable.

- First Report: Office of the Gen. Counsel, NLRB, *Report of the Acting General Counsel Concerning Social Media Cases* (August 18, 2011).

- Second Report: Office of the Gen. Counsel, NLRB, *Report of the Acting General Counsel Concerning Social Media Cases* (January 24, 2012).

- Third Report: Office of the Gen. Counsel, NLRB, *Report of the Acting General Counsel Concerning Social Media Cases* (May 30, 2012).

The NLRA and Social Media Policies

The NLRA ensures that employees (whether unionized or not) can engage in "concerted activity" under the NLRA § 7 to complain about workplace conditions and other issues pertaining to the terms and conditions of employment. Broad social media policies that restrict disparaging or vulgar comments run afoul of § 7 if they can be construed as potentially extending to concerted activity. According to the NLRB memoranda and actions, such policies are overbroad and can chill concerted activity.

The NLRA does not prohibit:

- Restricting individual outbursts by employees that are not part of concerted activity with other employees

- Insulting people or the company, or revealing confidential information that does not pertain to the terms and conditions of employment

Leading Cases

Costco Wholesale Corp., 358 N.L.R.B. No. 106 (2012)

The NLRB concluded that Costco violated Section 8 of the NLRA by maintaining a social media policy that prohibited employees from electronically posting statements that "damage the Company ... or damage any person's reputation." This language would tend to chill employees' exercise of their Section 7 rights, which protect a range of collective activities.

Karl Knauz Motors, Inc., 358 N.L.R.B. No. 164 (2012)

Salesperson at a car dealership allowed the 13-year-old son of a customer to sit in the driver's seat of a car. An accident occurred where the car ran over the customer's foot and ended up in a pond. Another sales person took photos and posted them to Facebook and said: "This is your car. This is your car on drugs." The employee who posted on Facebook was fired. The NLRB concluded that this post did not relate to protected activity, and the firing did not violate the NLRA. However, the employer's social media policy which prohibited being "disrespectful" or "using profanity or other language which injures the image or reputation of the Dealership" was overbroad. The policy was missing a disclaimer that NLRA-protected speech was not prohibited by the policy.

Hispanics United of Buffalo, Inc., 359 N.L.R.B. No. 37 (2012)
Five employees were fired for making comments on Facebook responding to a co-worker's criticisms about their job performance. The NLRB concluded that the speech involved protected activity under the NLRA and that the employees were improperly fired.

Three D, LLC (Triple Play), 361 N.L.R.B. No. 31 (2014)
Several employees at a non-union employer—a bar and restaurant—posted comments to a Facebook post by a former employee criticizing the employer for a tax withholding issue, among other things. Some current employees and others commented on the post, including a statement that the employer believed to be defamatory. One employee called the employer an "asshole." One employee hit the Like button. The employee who called the employer an "asshole" and the employee who "Liked" the post were fired. The NLRB concluded that the comment and Like were related to the post about the tax issue, which involved workplace terms and conditions. Just because there is a comment or a Like does not mean that these employees endorse everything in a discussion thread. The employer's social media policy prohibiting "engaging in inappropriate discussions about the company, management, and/or co-workers" was too vague and chilled employee NLRA rights.

Hoot Winc, LLC, NLRB No. 31-CA-104872 (2014)
NLRB deemed employer confidential information policy overbroad and chilling of Section 7 activity. Employer policy prohibited unauthorized disclosure of "sensitive Company operating materials or information" that "includes but is not limited to, recipes, policies, procedures, financial information, manuals or any other information in part or in whole as contained in any Company records." Some of this information could involve employment terms and conditions, and there was no exemption in the policy for protected activities.

Lily Transp. Corp., 362 N.L.R.B. No. 54 (2015)
Confidentiality policy that prohibited the disclosure of "confidential information, including Company, customer information and employee information maintained in confidential personnel files," was overbroad because information about wages and other matters involving terms and conditions of employees could be included. Social media policy that employees refrain from "disparaging, negative, false or misleading" information about the company failed to make clear the zone of NLRA-protected speech.

Durham School Services, L.P., 360 N.L.R.B. No. 85 (2014)
Employer, a company operating school busses, had a social media policy requiring employees to keep "communication with coworkers … professional and respectful, even outside of work hours" and threatened to punish employees who share with the public "unfavorable" information about the company, its employees, or customers. This policy was overbroad and failed to define what "respectful" or "unfavorable" information was, and risked chilling NLRA-protected speech.

Laurus Tech. Inst., 360 N.L.R.B. No. 133 (2014)
Employer policy prohibited "gossip about the company, an employee, or customer." The policy defined gossip as "[n]egative or untrue or disparaging comments" about others or "repeating" a "rumor" or "information that can injure a person." The NLRB deemed the policy overbroad and ambiguous.

Prof'l Elec. Contractors of Conn., Inc., NLRB No. 34-CA-071532 (2014)
Employer policy prohibiting "using personal computers in any manner that may adversely affect company business interests or reputation" was overbroad because it failed to exclude NLRA-protected activities.

Landry's Inc., 362 N.L.R.B. No. 69 (2015)
NLRB held that a policy was lawful, where it urged employees not to post anything that could result in morale problems, but did not explicitly prohibit employees from posting information related to the job or co-workers.

Boch Imports, Inc., 362 N.L.R.B. No. 83 (2015), *aff'd, Boch Imports, Inc. v. NLRB*, 2016 WL 3361733 (1st Cir. June 17, 2016)
NLRB found a social media policy violative of Section 8 of the NLRA, which required employees to self-identify when posting comments about the employer, the employer's business, or policy issues.

Chipotle Services LLC, NLRB No. 04-CA-147314 (2016)
In this NLRB action, an administrative law judge concluded that some aspects but not all of Chipotle's social media policy violated Section 8 of the NLRA. A provision prohibiting the disclosure of "confidential information" was violative because the policy did not define "confidential"—a term the NLRB found "vague and subject to interpretation." A provision prohibiting "disparaging" statements was violative because it was overbroad. But the ALJ upheld a provision against "harassing or discriminatory" statements.

Employer Access to Employee Social Media Accounts
Numerous states are enacting statutes forbidding workplace institutions from requesting social media account information from employees or prospective employees. Some examples are below.

Illinois, Right to Privacy in the Workplace Act (H.B. 3782) (2012)
Prohibits employers from requiring employees or applicants to provide access to their social media website accounts.

Louisiana, Personal Online Account Privacy Protection Act (2014)
Prohibits employer from requesting or requiring employees or applicants to give information such as account names or passwords giving access to a personal online account. This statute explicitly does not extend to information necessary to operate devices or online services provided by the employer, or prohibit an employer from searching public information on an employee's or applicant's online account. Inadvertently obtaining account information does not create liability, but an employer may not act upon, keep, or in any way distribute such information. The law extends a similar framework to the university-student relationship.

Maryland, User Name and Password Privacy Protection and Exclusions (S.B. 433) (2012)
Restricts employers from demanding that employees or applicants provide information to allow an employer access to a "personal account or service."

New Hampshire, Use of Social Media and Electronic Mail (2014)
Barring employers from requesting or requiring employee or applicant login information, requesting that an employer add contacts or change settings to a personal account, or disciplining employees accordingly. Inadvertently obtaining account information does not create liability, but an employer may not act upon, keep or in any way distribute such information. The act does not explicitly restrict employers from monitoring provided services and equipment, or conducting investigations under requirements of state and federal statutes.

Utah, Internet Employment Privacy Act (H.B. 100) (2013)
Enacting protections for personal Internet accounts. The Act includes provisions such as permitting or prohibiting certain actions by an employer and providing a private right of action.

Virginia (H.B. 2081) (2015)
Prohibits employers from "requiring, requesting, or causing" employees or applicants to provide usernames and passwords to social media accounts. The Act also bars employers from requiring employees to change privacy settings or add any other person to the social media account's contacts.

Wisconsin, (S.B. 223) (2013)
As a condition of employment, employers may not require employees to provide access to a personal Internet account, or discriminate against an employee refusing to give such information. Employers are also prohibited from refusing to hire an applicant because the applicant will not disclose information to gain access to a personal Internet account. Exceptions apply when the employee uses a device or service at least partially provided for by the employer. An employer may request to view a personal Internet account during an investigation following a reasonable belief that the employee transferred the employer's proprietary information. Under such circumstances, however, the employer can only request to view the account, not require the information to access the account.

FOR FURTHER REFERENCE

Treatises

Matthew W. Finkin, *Privacy in Employment Law* (4th ed. 2013)
Analysis of the law of privacy in the employment context with coverage of recent developments such as employer access to applicant and employee social media accounts.

***Workplace Data: Law and Litigation* (Robert Sprague ed., 2013)**
Analysis of legal issues relating to "electronically stored information" pertaining to employees, with a special focus on discovery issues.

Global Employee Privacy and Data Security Law
(Miriam H. Wugmeister & Christine E. Lyon eds., 2d ed. 2011)
Focusing on how global privacy and security laws create obligations within the employment context.

Articles and Other Sources

Corey A. Ciocchetti, *The Eavesdropping Employer: A Twenty-First Century Framework for Employee Monitoring*, 48 Am. Bus. L.J. 285 (2011)
Surveys the patchwork of federal and state laws regulating employment privacy and proposes a sliding-scale framework for when and how employers should conduct monitoring of employees.

Lothar Determann & Robert Sprague, *Intrusive Monitoring: Employee Privacy Expectations Are Reasonable in Europe, Destroyed in the United States*, 26 Berkeley Tech. L.J. 979 (2011)
Comparison of EU and U.S. privacy in the workplace. Conclusion is that the U.S. offers minimal to no protection in situations where there is not a preexisting basis for an expectation for privacy. With few exceptions, U.S. employers can routinely deploy contracts and notice strategies that lead employees to waive privacy rights.

Matthew W. Finkin, *Menschenbild: The Conception of the Employee as a Person in Western Law*, 23 Comp. Lab. L. & Pol'y J. 577 (2002)
Interesting comparison between U.S. law and EU civil law systems in how they handle employee privacy rights.

Pauline T. Kim, *Privacy Rights, Public Policy, and the Employment Relationship*, 57 Ohio St. L.J. 671 (1996)
Argues that the privacy torts can serve as a source of public policy limiting an employer's ability to terminate employees who refuse to be subjected to privacy intrusions.

Paul A. Secunda, *Privatizing Workplace Privacy*, 88 Notre Dame L. Rev. 277 (2012)
Discusses the U.S. Supreme Court's Fourth Amendment decision in City of Ontario v. Quon and argues that public-sector workers should have greater privacy protections than private-sector workers.

Paul A. Secunda, *Blogging While (Publicly) Employed: Some First Amendment Implications*, 47 U. Louisville L. Rev. 679 (2009)
Examining the First Amendment free speech rights of public-sector employees who use social media.

William J. Stuntz, *Implicit Bargains, Government Power, and the Fourth Amendment*, 44 Stan. L. Rev. 553 (1992)
Provides a thoughtful defense of the Fourth Amendment special needs doctrine in the government employment context.

CHAPTER 13

International Privacy Law

ESSENTIAL POINTS

- Since the Universal Declaration of Human Rights (1948), there has been a global effort to define internationally relevant and binding privacy norms.

- The phrase "data protection law" is the favored terminology for information privacy law outside of the United States.

- A number of international organizations have joined in the effort to shape and create privacy law, both international and domestic. Leading international entities involved in this process include the Organisation for Economic Co-operation and Development (OECD), the Council of Europe, the European Court of Human Justice, numerous entities of the European Union, and the Asia-Pacific Economic Cooperation (APEC).

- The EU Data Protection Directive of 1995 established common rules for data protection among member states of the European Union. It also restricted data transfers to countries outside of the EU that lack "adequate protection" for personal data. An agreement called the Safe Harbor Arrangement was the primary way for companies to transfer data on EU citizens to the US. The Safe Harbor Arrangement was invalidated in 2015.

- In 2016, the EU finalized approval of its General Data Protection Regulation (GDPR), which replaces the Data Protection Directive and will be directly applicable in all member states starting May 2018. Like the Directive, the GDPR forbids data transfers to countries outside the EU that lack "adequate protection."

- The GDPR generally creates stricter rules than the Directive and contains a number of new elements. Its enhanced individual rights include data breach notifications and a right to erasure, and data portability. Its new institutions include the creation of a European Data Protection Board. Finally, the GDPR permits the levying of significant fines for violations.

- In 2016, the EU and the US replaced the Safe Harbor Arrangement with a new agreement, the Privacy Shield (2016). Along with binding corporate rules and model contractual clauses, the Privacy Shield now provides a means for transferring personal data from EU Member states to third countries.

Data Protection and Information Privacy: A Note on Terminology

In the United States, information privacy law is the area of law concerned with the collection, use, and disclosure of personal information. In most of the rest of the world, this same area of law is termed "data protection law." This usage is followed in many English-speaking countries, including the United Kingdom.

WORLDWIDE PRIVACY RIGHTS AND GUIDELINES

Universal Declaration of Human Rights (1948)

The United Nations General Assembly adopted the Universal Declaration of Human Rights on December 10, 1948. Article 12 explicitly protects "privacy," but a number of other parts of the declaration are relevant to information privacy.

Article 1: "All human beings are born free and equal in dignity and rights."

Article 3: "Everyone has the right to life, liberty and security of person."

Article 8: "Everyone has the right to an effective remedy by the competent national tribunals for acts violating the fundamental rights granted him by the constitution or by law."

Article 12: "No one shall be subjected to arbitrary interference with his privacy, family, home or correspondence, nor to attacks upon his honor and reputation. Everyone has the right to protection of the law against such interference or attacks."

Article 19: "Everyone has the right to freedom of opinion and expression; this right includes freedom to hold opinions without interference and to seek, receive and impart information and ideas through any media and regardless of frontiers."

OECD Privacy Guidelines (1980)

The Organisation for Economic Co-operation and Development (OECD) is a group of 34 leading industrial countries concerned with global economic and democratic development.

OECD MEMBER COUNTRIES		
Australia	Hungary	Poland
Austria	Iceland	Portugal
Belgium	Ireland	Slovak Republic
Canada	Israel	Slovenia
Chile	Italy	Spain
Czech Republic	Japan	Sweden
Denmark	Korea	Switzerland
Estonia	Luxembourg	Turkey
Finland	Mexico	United Kingdom
France	Netherlands	United States
Germany	New Zealand	
Greece	Norway	

The 1980 OECD Guidelines establish eight key principles for the protection of personal information:

1. **Collection Limitation:** Data should be collected lawfully with the individual's consent.

2. **Data Quality:** Data should be relevant to a particular purpose and be accurate.

3. **Purpose Specification:** The purpose for data collection should be stated at the time of the data collection and the use of the data should be limited to this purpose.

4. **Use Limitation:** Data should not be disclosed for different purposes without the consent of the individual.

5. **Security Safeguards:** Data should be protected by reasonable safeguards.

6. **Openness Principle:** Individuals should be informed about the practices and policies of those handling their personal information.

7. **Individual Participation:** People should be able to learn about the data that an entity possesses about them and to rectify errors or problems in that data.

8. **Accountability:** The entities that control personal information should be held accountable for carrying out these principles.

The 2013 Guidelines add additional concepts to the original eight key principles. These include:

- **National privacy strategies:** While effective laws are essential, the strategic importance of privacy today also requires a multifaceted national strategy coordinated at the highest levels of government.

- **Privacy management programs:** These serve as the core operational mechanisms through which organizations implement privacy protection.

- **Data security breach notification:** This provision covers both notice to an authority and notice to an individual affected by a security breach involving personal data.

The Influence of the OECD Guidelines

Some of the major laws and regulations influenced by the OECD Guidelines are:

- U.S. Cable Communications Policy Act of 1984
- Australia's Privacy Act of 1988
- New Zealand's Privacy Act of 1993
- South Korea's Act on the Protection of Personal Information Managed by Public Agencies of 1994
- Asia-Pacific Economic Cooperation (APEC) Privacy Guidelines of 2004

UN Guidelines for the Regulation of Computerized Personal Files (1990)

Adopted by a resolution of the General Assembly on December 1, 1990, the guidelines set up 10 principles concerning minimum guarantees of national legislations:

1. **Principle of lawfulness and fairness:** Information about persons must not be collected or processed in unfair or unlawful ways or used in ways contrary to the principles of the Charter of the United Nations.

2. **Principle of accuracy:** Files are to be kept as complete as possible and persons responsible for them are to conduct regular checks on the accuracy and relevancy of data.

3. **Principle of purpose-specification:** The purpose that a file is to serve and its use in terms of that purpose should be specified, legitimate, and, once established, receive publicity or be brought to the attention of the affected party.

4. **Principle of interested-person access:** Ensures the right of access to information and right to have corrections made in the case of unlawful, unnecessary, or inaccurate entries.

5. **Principle of nondiscrimination:** Subject to exceptions made under Principle 6, data must not be compiled if it is likely to cause unlawful or arbitrary discrimination. Information that can fall into this category includes data "on racial or ethnic origin, colour, sex life, political opinions, religious, philosophical and other beliefs as well as membership of an association or trade union."

6. **Power to make exceptions:** Departures from Principles 1 to 4 are permitted only if necessary "to protect national security, public order, public health or morality, as well as, inter alia, the rights and freedoms of others." Departures

from Principle 5 are subject to these same requirements as well as the limits prescribed by the International Bill of Human Rights and the other relevant instruments for human rights and the prevention of discrimination.

7. *Principle of security:* Appropriate measures must be taken to protect files against natural and human dangers.

8. *Supervision and sanctions:* The law in every country must designate an authority "to be responsible for supervising observance of the principles set forth above."

9. *Transborder data flows:* Information should be able to circulate freely between two countries that offer comparative legislative safeguards for the protection of privacy. In the absence of "reciprocal safeguards," a country may not restrict circulation of information "unduly" and may do so "only in so far as the protection of privacy demands."

10. *Field of application:* The principles are to apply to all public and private computerized files as well as to manual files, subject to appropriate adjustments.

EUROPE

European Convention on Human Rights (ECHR)
Article 8—The Right to Respect for Private and Family Life (1950)

The ECHR: The ECHR protects a wide range of civil and political rights. It was adopted in 1950, shortly after the Universal Declaration of Human Rights of the United Nations. The ECHR was drafted under the auspices of the Council of Europe, an international organization that currently has 47 European states as members.

Article 8: The ECHR explicitly guarantees a right to privacy in its Article 8, which states:

1. Everyone has the right to respect for his private and family life, his home, and his correspondence;

2. There shall be no interference by a public authority with the exercise of this right except such as is in accordance with the law and is necessary in a democratic society in the interests of national security, public safety, or the economic well-being of the country; for the prevention of disorder or crime; for the protection of health or morals; or for the protection of the rights and freedoms of others.

European Court of Human Rights: The Council's European Court of Human Rights has an important role in interpreting the key reference texts of the council. It bears the ultimate role of enforcing and interpreting the ECHR. This tribunal has decided a series of important cases concerning media invasions of privacy, the activities of the police and security agencies, the issuing of identity papers, monitoring of communications by employers, and other privacy topics.

Leading Cases

Von Hannover v. Germany, 59320/00 Eur. Ct. H.R. (2004)

Princess Caroline of Monaco sued German magazines for publishing photographs of her. The ECHR found that "the decisive factor in balancing the protection of private life against freedom of expression should lie in the contribution that the published photos and articles make to a debate of general interest." The photos in this case "made no such contribution" because the applicant exercised no official function and the photos and articles related exclusively to details of her private life.

Copland v. United Kingdom, 62617/00 Eur. Ct. H.R. (2007)

Collection and storage of personal information related to an individual's telephone, as well as her e-mail and Internet usage, without her knowledge, implicated Article 8 rights. Such an "interference" with Article 8 must be carried out "in accordance with the law" under Article 8(2), European Convention on Human Rights. There is a need, therefore, for a domestic law that regulates such activity, and such a law must also "be compatible with the rule of law" and its requirements.

Mosley v. United Kingdom, 48009/08 Eur. Ct. H.R. 774 (2011)

Holding that this case concerned "a flagrant and unjustified invasion of the applicant's private life" and that "there is a distinction to be drawn between reporting facts—even if controversial—capable of contributing to a debate of general public interest in a democratic society, and making tawdry allegations about an individual's private life." The ECHR found that Article 8 of the Convention on Human Rights did not require a prenotification requirement before news stories regarding a person's private life were published.

P.G. & J.H. v. United Kingdom, 44787/98 Eur. Ct. H.R. (2011)

Article 8's protection of private life can be affected by measures that occur "outside a person's home or private premises." One element, although not necessarily a conclusive factor, is "a person's reasonable expectations as to privacy." Yet, the ECHR also found that "files gathered by security services on a particular individual fall within the scope of Article 8 even where the information has not been gathered by any intrusive or covert method." Specifically, Article 8 was implicated "once any systematic or permanent record comes into existence" of monitoring a public scene through technological means, such as closed circuit television.

Von Hannover v. Germany (no. 2), 40660/08 & 6064/08 Eur. Ct. H.R. (2012)

Affirming decisions of the Federal Court of Justice and Federal Constitutional Courts regarding publication in Germany of photographs of Princess Caroline of Monaco. The ECHR held that the national courts "carefully balanced the right of the publishing companies to freedom of expression against the right of the applicants to respect for their private life." In the judgment of the ECHR, the key parts of the analysis of the national courts concerned whether the photos had "contributed to a debate of general interest" and "the circumstances in which the photos had been taken."

Axel Springer v. Germany, 39954/08 Eur. Ct. H.R. (2012)
Finding German courts were not justified in ordering an injunction blocking
publication of certain information "reporting on the arrest and conviction of
a well-known actor for a drug-related offence." The ECHR concluded that the
courts' interference with the "freedom of expression" protected by Article 10 of
the Convention lacked a "reasonable relationship of proportionality" between the
resulting restrictions and "the legitimate aim pursued."

Von Hannover v. Germany (no. 3), 8772/10 Eur. Ct. H.R. 835 (2013)
Holding that the German Federal Court of Justice's refusal to grant an injunction
prohibiting any further publication of von Hannover's photograph did not violate
Article 8 of the Convention. The ECHR found that the German court sufficiently
took the ECHR's rulings into consideration when balancing the right to respect for
private life against the right to freedom of expression. Given that it lies in the discretion of the Member States to ensure the rights given by Article 8, the ECHR declared that the German court's rulings did not constitute a breach of von Hannover's
privacy rights as enshrined in Article 8. The ECHR also accepted the German
court's findings that the photographs contributed to a debate of general interest.

Satakunnan Markkinapörssi Oy and Satamedia Oy v. Finland 931/13 Eur. Ct.
H.R. (2015)
Publisher Satakunnan Markkinapörssi Oy printed Finnish individuals' publicly-available tax-related data. The publisher collaborated with service provider
Satamedia Oy to send out tax information via text message upon an individual's
request. Extensive publication of personal, publicly-available tax information constituted a violation of Article 8, especially in light of Article 10's protection of a free
press. The ECJ also found that these text messages had low public interest value.

Council of Europe Convention on Privacy
ETS No. 108 (1981)

Background: Throughout the 1980s, the most important European-wide agreement regarding the processing of personal information was the Council of Europe's
Convention for the Protection of Individuals with Regard to Automatic Processing
of Personal Data (Convention). This document is a European treaty opened for signa-
ture in 1981 and one to which 46 nations have acceded. It was the first legally binding
international instrument in the field of data protection law. Among the countries
where the Convention has recently entered into force are Austria (2012), the Ukraine
(2011), Monaco (2009), and Armenia (2008).

Minimum Standards: The convention is a "non-self-executing treaty." Its standards
do not directly impose binding norms on signatory nations. Its requirement is for signatory nations to establish domestic data protection legislation that gives effect to the
convention's principles and provides a common core of safeguards for the processing
of personal information. Domestic statutory standards can, in turn, exceed those
basic safeguards. As Article 11 of the convention states, domestic law can "grant data
subjects a wider measure of protection than that stipulated in this convention."

Data Quality: The convention's common protective core contains a number of elements. Among the most important is the Article 5 requirement of "data quality." This term captures a number of concepts relating to FIPs. In its broadest sense, data quality requires that personal information be "stored for specified and legitimate purposes and not used in a way incompatible with those purposes." Moreover, the concept of data quality limits the processing of personal data to circumstances that are "adequate, relevant and not excessive in relation to the purposes for which they are stored."

Access and Correction: Beyond data quality, the convention calls for individual rights permitting a person access to and an ability to correct personal data. Domestic law also is to provide judicial remedies for violations of these rights.

EU Data Protection Directive
Council Directive 95/46 (1995)

The Directive has been replaced by the General Data Protection Regulation (GDPR), which does not take effect, however, until May 2018. As a result, the Directive is still important in understanding the harmonized law in EU Member States.

Primary Function: To facilitate the free flow of personal data within the EU by establishing an equally high privacy level in all EU member states. The directive establishes obligations for the processors of personal data and rights for the affected party. It also created the Article 29 Working Party.

Reasons for Its Creation: The directive was viewed as necessary because European integration both increased the sharing of data among member states and generated new demands for personal information within separate member states. The directive was also viewed as necessary because of divergences among the statutory protections among EU countries with national data protection legislation.

Harmonizing: The Data Protection Directive establishes common rules for data protection among EU member states. It is a "harmonizing" directive that requires member states to enact national legislation that reflects its principles. See Articles 5 and 24.

Key Terms: The directive relies on the following key terms:

1. *"Personal data"*—data about any "identified or identifiable natural person"

2. *"Data subject"*—the person to whom the data pertains

3. *"Processing of personal data"*—"any operation or set of operations … performed upon personal data" in a wide variety of means (collection, use, disclosure, storage, retrieval, erasure)

4. *"Controller"*—any person, business, organization, or government entity that "determines the purposes and means of the processing of personal data"

5. *"Processor"*—any person or entity that processes data for the controller

Article 3—Exception for Law Enforcement and National Defense: The directive contains a broad exemption for data processing relating to law enforcement and national defense. Its Article 3(2) states that the directive will not apply "in any case to processing operations concerning public security, defence, state security ... and the activities of the state in areas of criminal law."

Article 7—Criteria for Making Data Processing Legitimate: The directive permits the processing of personal data only under certain circumstances. These are when (1) a data subject has given his consent, (2) to fulfill a contract, (3) to meet a legal obligation of the controller of the data, (4) to protect a vital interest of the data subject, (5) to carry out a task in the public interest or (6) to fulfill a legitimate interest pursued by the controller or by a third party "except where such interests are overridden by the interests for fundamental rights and freedoms of the data subject which require protection under Article 1(1)."

Article 8—Special Protection for Sensitive Data: Article 8 provides for special treatment of data that is particularly sensitive for data subjects. Thus, it restricts the processing of certain categories of personal data, namely, information "revealing racial or ethnic origin, political opinions, religious or philosophical beliefs, trade-union membership and the processing of data concerning health or sex life." There are a number of explicit exceptions to this rule. Moreover, member states may, for reason of "substantial public interest," make further exceptions to the ones explicitly found in Article 8. The commission must be notified of all such further derogations.

Articles 10 & 11—Notice: These articles set out the kinds of notice to be provided to the data subject when information is collected directly from him and when it is not collected from a third party.

Article 12—Access and Correction: The data subject has a right of access to certain information from the data controller as well as an ability to correct, erase, or block information that does not comply with the directive.

Article 15—Restrictions on Automated Decisions: Subject to certain exceptions, the directive establishes a right for "every person not to be subject to a decision which produces legal effects concerning him or significantly affects him and which is based solely on automated processing of data intended to evaluate certain personal aspects relating to him, such as his performance at work, creditworthiness, reliability conduct, etc." Article 15(1). The exceptions provided are (1) when the decision "is taken in the course of entering into or performance of a contract" and there are "suitable measures to safeguard ... legitimate interests" of the data subject or (2) when the processing "is authorized by a law which also lays down measures to safeguard the data subject's legitimate interests." Article 15(2).

Article 17—Data Security: Member states must provide "appropriate technical and organizational measures" of data security.

Articles 22 & 23—Individual Remedies: Article 22 requires member states to provide for a "judicial remedy for any breach of the rights guaranteed him by the national law applicable to the processing in question." Article 23 further requires member states to provide that "the controller" of the data in question provide compensation to "any person who has suffered damage as a result of any act incompatible with the national provisions adopted pursuant to this directive."

Article 25—Adequacy Standard for International Data Transfers: A transfer of personal data is only permitted to a non-EU member state that has "an adequate level of protection." Article 25(1). The directive states: "The adequacy of the level of protection afforded by a third country shall be assessed in the light of all the circumstances surrounding a data transfer operation or set of data transfer operations." Article 25(2). There has been a formal finding at the EU level that the laws of the United States generally do not provide adequate protection. The Article 29 Working Group (for more on this entity, see below) has stated that the "current patchwork of narrowly focused sectoral laws and voluntary self-regulation in the U.S. is not adequate." Article 29 Working Group, Opinion 1/99.

Article 28—National Supervisory Authorities: Each member state must establish one or more public authorities to monitor the application of the laws and regulations adopted pursuant to the directive. The directive states: "These authorities shall act with complete independence in exercising the functions entrusted to them." Article 28(1). Member states are to consult with the supervisory authorities when creating the rules and regulations for the protection of individuals' rights with regard to data processing. Article 28(2).

Articles 29 & 30—Working Party: The directive created a new institution of data protection on the European level. It calls this entity the "Working Party on the Protection of Individuals with Regard to the Processing of Personal Data" (Working Party). Each member state is to designate a representative for the Working Party. This entity has "advisory status" and is to "act independently." Article 29(1). In Article 30, the directive sets out the numerous tasks of the Working Party.

Leading Case

Case C-101/01, *Criminal Proceedings Against Bodil Lindqvist*, 2003 E.C.R. I-12971 (Nov. 6, 2003)
The posting of information on a website constituted a "processing" of personal data within the sense of the Data Protection Directive. Without the data subject's permission, such personal information could not be posted, that is, made subject to "processing." The European Court of Justice also found that member states could enact data privacy protections beyond the areas that the directive had specified so long as no provision of European Community law precluded such action.

Case C-121/12, *Google Spain v. AEPD*, 2014 E.C.R. 317 (May 13, 2014)
The European Court of Justice (ECJ) required that Google remove from its search results links to a 1998 newspaper article about his foreclosed house. According to the ECJ, under what has become known as the "right to be forgotten," EU citizens have a right to the deletion of certain personal data under the EU Data Protection Directive. Operators of search engines must remove links to third party webpages when such links violate people's fundamental privacy rights.

Case C-362/14, *Maximillian Schrems v. Data Prot. Comm'r* 2015 E.C.R. (Sept. 23, 2015)
In this landmark case, the ECJ ruled, first, that national authorities must be able to independently investigate the Safe Harbor agreement and to decide on the adequacy of mechanisms in place before transfers of personal information to third countries. Second, the Court considered the adequacy of the Safe Harbor agreement itself. It held that it did not provide an adequate level of protection because EU citizens' data were exposed to the mass surveillance programs of U.S. intelligence agencies without limitations and redress.

Case C-230/14, *Weltimmo s. r. o. v. Nemzeti Adatvédelmi* és *Információszabadság Hatóság* Judgment (Oct. 1, 2015)
This case involved Weltimmo, a Slovakian company, that ran a Hungarian-language real estate website. The ECJ examined which national data protection law applied to a business operating in more than one EU state. According to the EU Directive, a key factor in determining the applicability of a member state's laws to an entity is whether the company operates a "relevant establishment" in said state. The ECJ held that Weltimmo had an establishment in Hungary for these reasons: (1) website language; (2) location of advertised property; (3) existence of a representative in Hungary in charge of collecting debts and judicial and administrative proceedings on behalf of Weltimmo; and (4) existence of business address and bank account in Hungary.

A Leading German Case on Search Engines

Google Autocomplete, **German Federal Court of Justice**
BGH VI ZR 269/12 (May 14, 2013)

In May 2013, Germany's Federal Court of Justice found that Google's Autocomplete function was capable of violating an individual's personality rights and that an autocomplete suggestion was Google's own content. The Federal Court of Justice held that although the operator of a search engine was not generally required to check Autocomplete suggestions in advance for privacy violations, it did have responsibility once it acquired knowledge of a legal violation of a right to personality. In such case, search engines were required to prevent their software from generating a result that would lead to the privacy violation.

The General Data Protection Regulation (GDPR)

European Commission, Regulation 2016/670 of the European Parliament and of the Council of 27 April 2016 on the protection of individuals with regard to the processing of personal data and on the free movement of such data, and repealing Directive 95/46/EC (General Data Protection Regulation) (May 4, 2016)

After years of discussion and negotiations, the EU adopted the General Data Protection Regulation (GDPR) in April 2016. This new regime will replace the EU Data Protection Directive 95/46 and take effect in May 2018. Unlike the Directive, which required the enactment of harmonizing legislation in Member States, the GDPR will be directly applicable in all Member States. It takes effect in May 2018.

The GDPR includes high penalties for violations, a new and narrower definition of "consent," a requirement for most businesses with more than 250 employees to have a privacy officer, data breach notification requirements, and a "right to erasure." The proposed regulation also contains protections against decisions based exclusively on "automated processing" and safeguards for sensitive data.

Directly Binding in Member States: Unlike the Directive, the GDPR does not require implementation in national law; it will be directly applicable to all member states of the EU. As the Recitals state: "Consistent and homogenous application of the rules for the protection of personal data should be ensured throughout the Union."

National Law-Making and Areas of Exclusion. Although generally directly binding, the GDPR does allow for certain kinds of national law-making. These include national laws that further specify obligations in areas covered the GDPR, such as "the processing of personal data for compliance with a legal obligation, for the performance of a task carried out in the public interest or in the exercise of official authority vested in a controller." There are also exceptions and national law-making power for freedom of expression and information, national identification numbers, and employee data. Moreover, the GDPR permits "a margin of manoeuvre" for Member States to specify certain kinds of rules, such as those for sensitive data and regarding the conditions under which data processing will be lawful. Finally, the Regulation does not apply to "activities which fall outside the scope of Union law, such as activities concerning national security." It also does not apply to activities by a natural person "in the course of a purely personal or household activity."

Important aspects of the GDPR include:

Article 3—Territorial Scope
The GDPR will apply to all organizations considered "EU establishments" that process personal data, regardless of where this processing physically occurs so long as the data are processed "in the context of the activities" of such an establishment. It also applies to non-EU established organizations "offering goods or services" or "monitoring" behavior within the EU.

Article 5—Principles Relating to Processing of Personal Data

The GDPR require that the processing of personal data be subject to these concepts: (1) lawfulness, fairness and transparency, (2) purpose limitation, (3) data minimization, (4) accuracy, (5) storage limitation, (6) integrity and confidentiality, and (7) accountability.

Article 7—Consent

Strict rules for consent give the data subject the right to withdraw his or her consent at any time. Moreover, when assessing whether consent is freely given, "utmost account shall be taken of whether … the performance of a contract, including the provision of a service, is conditional on consent to the processing of personal data that is not necessary for the performance of that contract."

Article 17—The Right to Erasure

Right to obtain erasure of personal data from the data controller under a number of specified circumstances, including when consent is withdrawn and where there is no other legal ground for processing. Erasure is also required when the data subject objects to the processing and "there are no overriding legitimate grounds for the processing." The data controller is responsible for taking reasonable steps to inform other controllers of his obligation of erasure.

Article 22—Limits on Automated Decision-making

Provides individuals with a right not to be subject to decisions with legal effect solely based upon automated processing and profiling, unless allowed by an exception such as consent or performance of a contract.

Article 24—Controllers

The GDPR heightens responsibility and obligations for controllers. It requires controllers to implement appropriate "security systems and to adopt robust privacy policies. The Regulation's accountability principle places the "burden of proof" on controllers to prove compliance with the provisions of the GDPR.

Articles 33 & 34—Data Breach Notification

Controllers must notify supervisory authorities and individuals without undue delay after becoming aware of a personal data breach. In the case of supervisory authorities, controllers must "where feasible" notify these entities not later than 72 hours after having become aware of a breach. Controllers do not have to report a breach in the event it is unlikely that the data breach would result in a risk to the rights and freedoms of the individual. The GDPR defines "personal data breach" as "a breach of security leading to the accidental or unlawful destruction, loss, alteration, unauthorized disclosure of, or access to, personal data transmitted, stored or otherwise processed."

Articles 37-39—Designated Data Protection Officer (DPO)

Public agencies and authorities and all "controllers or processors" whose core activity and purpose requires "regular and systematic monitoring of data subjects" or "processing on a large scale of special categories of data" must designate a DPO. Articles 38 and 39 then set out the provisions for the independence of the DPO as well as her tasks.

Articles 63-66—Consistency Mechanism

The European Data Protection Board (EDPB) has power in a number of instances to resolve disputes among Supervisory Authorities. These include situations where there is a dispute regarding which Supervisory Authority should be competent over an organization.

Article 68—European Data Protection Board (EDPD)

An institution that replaces the Article 29 Working Party. The EDPR consists of the European Data Protection Supervisor and the heads of the supervisory authority from each Member State. The Board's organization, tasks, and powers are set out in Articles 69-76. They include ensuring the consistent application of the GDPR by advising the Commission, issuing guidelines, and providing the Commission with opinions on a range of specified matters.

Article 83—Administrative Fines

Significant monetary penalties are possible under the GDPR. Depending on the category of violation, sanctions may result in monetary fines either (1) "up to EUR 10,000 000, or up to 2 % of the total worldwide annual turnover" or (2) EUR 20,000 000 or up to 4 % of the total worldwide annual turnover. The fines will be set depending on which provision of the GDPR is violated. Their amount also depends on "the nature, gravity and duration of the infringement" as well as other factors.

The EU-US Privacy Shield Framework (2016)

The U.S.–EU Safe Harbor Arrangement (2000-2015). The EU has never found the U.S. to provide an adequate level of protection, so the U.S. Department of Commerce and the EU Commission negotiated a Safe Harbor Arrangement in 2000. Organizations in the U.S. could voluntarily agree to adhere to the Safe Harbor principles for privacy and publicly attest to such adherence. These organizations were viewed as meeting the EU Directive's "adequacy" standard for information privacy. In 2015, the ECJ invalidated the Safe Harbor arrangement.

The Schrems decision. In Case C-362/14, *Maximillian Schrems v. Data Protection Commissioner* (Sept. 23, 2015), the ECJ invalided the 15-year-old, widely-used EU–U.S. Safe Harbor Framework, which provided a mechanism for data transfers between the EU and U.S. Austrian privacy-rights activist Max Schrems sued Facebook Ireland, arguing that his data protection rights were violated when Facebook transferred his personal information to US servers and thus exposing it to the NSA's mass surveillance program. The ECJ held that U.S. surveillance policies did not meet EU privacy rights standards. As a result, the EU invalidated the Safe Harbor for failing to guarantee an adequate level of protection for the personal data of EU citizens.

The Creation of the EU–U.S. Privacy Shield Framework. The U.S. government and European Commission were already negotiating a new framework for data transfers at the time of ECJ's *Schrems* decision, which invalidated the Safe Harbor agreement. On July 12, 2016 the Commission issued its implementing decision, which found the Privacy Shield to ensure an adequate level of protection for personal data transferred from the EU to self-certified organizations in the U.S. pursuant to it.

Principles of the Privacy Shield

The Privacy Shield seeks to impose strong obligations on U.S. companies to protect the personal data of EU citizens, and to establish robust monitoring and enforcement by the Department of Commerce and the FTC. Furthermore, it provides for stronger individual rights for EU citizens including:

1. **Notice**
   Participating companies must provide individuals with a variety of different information including: (1) type of data collected, (2) purpose of collection, (3) circumstances of onward transfer, (4) third-party identities, (5) rights of the individuals, (6) redress channels for the individuals.

2. **Choice**
   The Privacy Shield gives individuals a right to opt out of their information being disclosed to a third party, or used for a purpose that is materially different than the purpose for which it was originally collected or subsequently authorized by the individual. Opt-out mechanisms must be "clear, conspicuous, and readily available."

3. **Accountability for Onward Transfer**
   Organizations are liable for compliance with the Notice and Choice Principles when transferring information to a third party acting as a controller. To do so, organization must enter into a contract with the third party controller.

4. **Security**
   Companies must take reasonable and appropriate measures to protect personal information, taking into account the risks involved in the processing and the nature of the personal information.

5. **Data Integrity and Purpose Limitation**
   Companies possess a duty to ensure that personal data held and processed by the organization is "reliable for its intended use, accurate, complete, and current."

> ## Principles of the Privacy Shield
>
> 6. **Access**
>   Individuals are to have access to personal information about them and be able to correct, amend, or delete that information when it is inaccurate, or has been processed in violation of the Principles. Companies are to reply to individual complaints within 45 days.
>
> 7. **Recourse, Enforcement, and Liability**
>   The Privacy Shield provides the right to file privacy complaints directly with participating companies. The agreement requires independent recourse mechanisms that must be free of charge to individuals.

Transparency and Safeguards. The U.S. issued written confirmation to the EU Commission that access of public authorities for law enforcement and national security purposes to EU citizens' information will be subject to "clear limitations, safeguards, and oversight." There will be an annual joint review of the Privacy Shield, including the issue of national security access, which will be conducted by the European Commission and U.S. Department of Commerce. The U.S. has also created a new Ombudsperson, separate from U.S. intelligence services, who will handle individual complaints from EU citizens.

Compliance Review by Companies. Participation in the Privacy Shield framework requires an annual compliance review by companies. Companies exiting the Privacy Shield agreement must still comply with its requirements with respect to the data obtained and processed under Privacy Shield.

Enforcement. The Privacy Shield heightens enforcement mechanisms beyond those of the Safe Harbor agreement. The Department of Commerce and the FTC are given an oversight role under it. Individuals may also bring complaints under it to a national Data Protection Authority.

Other Safe Harbor Arrangements

U.S.–Swiss Safe Harbor Framework (2009)
Follows the same approach as the Safe Harbor with the EU. A U.S. organization that self-certifies under the U.S.–Switzerland Safe Harbor Framework is viewed as providing "adequate protection" under Swiss data protection law. As in the EU–U.S. Safe Harbor, these Safe Harbor principles require safeguards concerning: (1) notice, (2) choice, (3) onward transfers, (4) access, (5) security, (6) data integrity, and (7) enforcement. The Department of Commerce has issued a list of Frequently Asked Questions (FAQs) to supplement these Safe Harbor principles. It has also published a handbook, *U.S.–Swiss Safe Harbor Framework, Guide to Self-Certification* (March 2012).

The U.S.–Swiss Safe Harbor continues to exist after the invalidation of the U.S.–EU Swiss Harbor. The U.S. Department of Commerce continues to maintain its online U.S.–Swiss Safe Harbor List. The Swiss Data Protection Commission has criticized reliance, however, on the U.S.–Swiss Safe Harbor and called for use of contractual safeguards for Swiss–U.S. data transfers. The Swiss Data Protection Commission also advocated adoption of an analogous regulation as the EU–U.S. Privacy Shield between the U.S. and Switzerland.

Positive Adequacy Determinations by the EU Commission

Adequacy determinations of the EU (with the date of the finding):

- Andorra (October 2010)
- Argentina (June 2003)
- Canada (December 2001)
- Bailiwick of Guernsey (November 2003)
- Bailiwick of Jersey (May 2008)
- The Faeroe Islands (March 2010)
- Isle of Man (April 2004)
- Israel (January 2011)
- New Zealand (December 2012)
- Switzerland (July 2000)
- United States: Passenger Name Records Agreement (December 2000)
- United States: Safe Harbor Principles (December 2000)
- Uruguay (August 2012)

Adequacy due to EEA Membership:

- Norway
- Liechtenstein
- Iceland

Personal information may be transferred within the 28 EU member states and the three EEA members without any further requirements.

The Privacy Shield supplies an adequate level of data protection for U.S. companies that comply with its requirements

Positive Adequacy Determinations by the EU Commission

The United States has never formally sought an adequacy determination from the European Commission for its entire legal system, as opposed to the more limited EU recognition of the Safe Harbor Principles and Passenger Name Records Agreement. This reticence is likely due, according to Christopher Wolf, "because of the well-understood outcome: request denied." Christopher Wolf, *Delusions of Adequacy? Examining the Case for Finding the United States Adequate for Cross-Border EU–U.S. Data Transfers*, 43 Wash. U. J.L. & Pol'y 227 (2013).

Source: European Commission, Frequently Asked Questions Relating to Transfers of Personal Data from the EU/EEA to Third Countries, at http://ec.europa.eu/justice/policies/privacy/docs/international_transfers_faq/international_transfers_faq.pdf

Passenger Name Record (PNR) Agreements

- Australia
- Canada
- U.S.

The EU has signed bilateral agreements with these three countries to permit the transfer of passenger information provided during flight booking and check-in. The collected data may be used by law enforcement to combat terrorism and other serious crimes.

Model Contractual Clauses

The EU has approved two sets of model contractual clauses. If a company in a non-member state follows either of the model contractual clauses, it is deemed to have "adequate protection" under the EU Directive on Data Protection. The first set of model contractual clauses was approved by the EU in 2001. The second set of model contractual clauses was approved by it in 2004.

Binding Corporate Rules (BCRs)

BCRs can be used instead of model contract clauses as a means to meet the "adequacy" test. If a company chooses to use them, the BCRs must be uniform throughout the entire organization. The EU has set the following requirements for BCRs:

- BCRs must be enforceable by "data subject."

- BCRs must indicate a clear duty of cooperation with data protection authorities in the EU.

- In principle, the approval of a BCR must come from each data protection authority (DPA) in each of the countries from which data are to be transferred. The Working Party has developed a so-called standard application for approval of a BCR, and a procedure for filling out a single copy of a form, which can be submitted to the "lead DPA" for approval. The Article 29 Working Party has developed a multifactor test for determining the lead DPA.

Discovery from EU Member Nations in U.S. Litigation

Strict data protection laws in Europe may conflict with U.S. discovery rules. Civil discovery in the U.S. tends to be largely managed by the parties to litigation and proceeds under a broader test that permits more material to be discoverable than is usual in civil law jurisdictions. A European company's transfer of certain personal data to the U.S. might violate European privacy law.

The **Restatement (Third) of Foreign Relations Law § 442(1)(c) (1987)**, provides a set of factors for U.S. courts in deciding the permissibility of ordering information sought for production that is located in a foreign country:

> the importance to the investigation or litigation of the documents or other information requested; the degree of specificity of the request; whether the information originated in the United States; the availability of alternative means of securing the information; and the extent to which noncompliance with the request would undermine important interests of the United States, or compliance with the request would undermine important interests of the state [or country] where the information is located

In **Volkswagen, A.G. v. Valdez, 909 S.W.2d 900 (Tex. 1995)**, the Texas Supreme Court rejected a finding of the trial court ordering discovery of documents from Volkswagen that were located in Germany. It found that the trial court abused its discretion in failing to balance the competing interests of the parties and in disregarding German law in its entirety. The Texas Supreme Court applied the Restatement (Third) of Foreign Relations Law § 442 (1987). Among its findings was that production of the document would violate German privacy law and bear little importance to the litigation.

Directive on Privacy and Electronic Communications (E-Privacy Directive)
Directive 2002/58/EC (2002) (Amendments 2009)

Primary Function: To protect "the right to privacy in the electronic communication sector." Like the Data Protection Directive, it seeks to harmonize the regulations in the member states in order to ensure an equivalent level of protection in them.

Confidentiality and Security: Requires member states to ensure the confidentiality of communications through their national legislation. It requires providers of tele-communication services to protect the security of their systems and services.

Opt-Out: The directive permits the use of information in the terminal equipment of a user, as through cookies, only if the user is provided with clear and comprehensive information about the purpose of the processing and is given a chance to opt out.

Opt-In: The directive directs member states to permit unsolicited telephone calls, e-mails, and faxes only when the affected party has provided opt-in consent.

Exceptions: The directive does not apply to issues concerning "public security and defence, state security and criminal law." These issues are regulated through the EU Data Retention Directive (see below).

Cookies and the 2009 Amendments: The EU amended the E-Privacy Directive in 2009 to make cookies subject to prior user consent following the provision of "clear and comprehensive information" to the affected party. It forbids the placing of cookies without such consent with an exemption for cookies "strictly necessary in order for the provider of an information society service explicitly requested by the subscriber or user to provide the service."

EU Data Retention Directive
Directive 2006/24/EC (2006)

Primary Function: The Data Retention Directive requires member states to enact laws that mandate storage of telecommunications information "for the investigation, detection, and prosecution of crime." Under the Data Retention Directive, member nations of the European Union are to enact statutes that require providers to store certain telecommunications data. Article 1(1) of the directive provides: "This directive aims to harmonise Member States' provisions concerning ... the retention of certain data which are generated or processed by them, in order to ensure that the data are available for the purpose of the investigation, detection and prosecution of serious crime, as defined by each Member State in its national law."

Limits on Data Retention: The directive mandates retention of certain specified categories of information "for periods of not less than six months and not more than two years from the date of the communication." Article 6.

Leading Cases

Decision of Federal Constitutional Court, **1 BvR 256/08, 1 BvR 263/08, 1 BvR 586/08 (March 2, 2010)**
In Germany, the Federal Constitutional Court ruled that parts of the German statute enacted pursuant to the directive violated the German constitution, the Basic Law. The Constitutional Court found that the statute's technical conditions

for the data storage were not secure enough, that the statute did not clearly establish legal norms for the use of the stored data, and that the statute could "cause
a diffusely threatening feeling of being under observation that can diminish an
unprejudiced perception of one's basic rights in many areas." In the current form
of the law, "such retention represents an especially grave intrusion" into the constitutional rights of citizens. It required the immediate deletion of the personal telecommunications data already collected and for amendments to the law that would
provide stricter conditions for the use and storage of such information. In 2015,
the Bundestag enacted another data retention bill, which among other provisions,
requires telecommunications providers to store all data required by the law within
Germany.

**C-293/12 & C-594/12, *Digital Rights Ireland & Seitlinger v. Minister
for Comm'ns, Marine & Nat'l Res.* 2014 E.C.R. I-238 (April 8, 2014)
(joined cases)**
On 8 April 2014, the European Court of Justice declared the Data Retention
Directive 2006/24/EC (2006) invalid. It held that it did not meet the principle
of proportionality. The Data Retention Directive lacked sufficient safeguards to
protect the fundamental rights of respect for private life and of protection for personal data. The Court also found that data retention generally served a legitimate
and general interest by protecting public security and would be permissible if
subject to clear and precise conditions.

European Data Protection Supervisor (EDPS)

The EDPS is an independent supervisory authority that protects personal
data and privacy in EU institutions and entities. It does so through:

- Oversight of the EU administration's processing of personal data
- Advising the EU on policies and legislation that affect privacy
- Cooperating with other international authorities with the goal of
  ensuring "consistent data protection"
- Participating as a member of the European Data Protection Board,
  which the GDPR establishes in its Article 68.

NORTH AMERICA

Canada

Charter of Rights and Freedoms (1982)
The Canadian Charter of Rights and Freedoms does not contain an explicit right to
privacy, but Sections 7 and 8 serve to protect privacy.

Section 7: Everyone has the right to life, liberty, and security of the person and the right not to be deprived thereof except in accordance with the principles of fundamental justice.

Section 8: Everyone has the right to be secure against unreasonable search or seizure.

Leading Cases:

Hunter v. Southam, Inc., [1984] 2 S.C.R. 145
Section 8 of the charter protects only against violations of reasonable expectations of privacy.

Regina v. Plant, [1993] 3 S.C.R. 281
Factors for determining the existence of a reasonable expectation of privacy include "the nature of the information, the relationship between the appellant and the Commission, the place and manner of the search and the seriousness of the offence under investigation."

R. v. Chehil, [2013] 3 S.C.R. 220
Use of a properly deployed drug detection dog is a search that is reasonable based merely on "reasonable suspicion." Because dog sniffs are minimally intrusive, narrowly targeted, and can be highly accurate, these searches may be conducted without prior judicial authorization.

Even though indicia like a dog's past performance and the risk of cross-contamination can be relevant to determining a dog's reliability, no specific evidentiary requirements will apply mechanically to every case. The prosecution does not have to prove that the dog is infallible, just as it does not have to prove that an informer's tip is infallible.

R. v. Vu, [2013] 3 S.C.R. 657
The privacy interests at stake when computers are searched require that these devices be treated, to a certain extent, as a separate place. Therefore, police must obtain a specific search warrant to search a computer; police must satisfy the authorizing justice that reasonable grounds exist to believe that any computer they discover will contain the information things for which they are searching.

R. v. Telus Comm'ns Co., [2013] 2 S.C.R. 3
Canada's Supreme Court found police were required to comply with rules regarding interception set out in the Criminal Code if they want to secure the prospective and continuous production of text messages from a mobile carrier. It found that the police cannot merely obtain a general warrant but must obtain an intercept order and comply with the conditions needed to intercept voice communications if they want to copy text messages.

R. v. Spencer, [2014] 2 S.C.R. 212
Police obtained information about ISP subscribers without a warrant. The Canadian Supreme Court ruled that Canadians have a "reasonable expectation of privacy in their use of the Internet" and that a police investigation does not exempt warrant requirements. Finally, the Court ruled that asking ISP to voluntarily disclose subscriber information constituted a search under the Charter.

R. v. Fearon, [2014] S.C.R. 621
Holding that police may search cellphones without a warrant incident to an arrest. The Canadian Supreme Court discussed and rejected the result reached by the U.S. Supreme Court in *Riley v. California*, 134 S. Ct. 2473 (2014).

Privacy Act (1985)
Limits the collection, use, and disclosure of personal information by federal government institutions. Vests powers in the Privacy Commissioner to receive and investigate complaints, initiate an investigation, and make findings and recommendations. Grants a private right of action only in relation to a refusal by a government institution to provide individual access to his or her personal information held by the government.

Personal Information Protection and Electronic Documents Act (PIPEDA) (2000)
PIPEDA regulates all private-sector entities that collect personal information on Canadians and personal information used in connection with any commercial activity. PIPEDA is based on the OECD Privacy Guidelines and, more directly, the Canadian Standards Association (CSA) Model Code for the Protection of Personal Information, which articulates 10 privacy principles. PIPEDA's Schedule 1 reprints most of the CSA Model Code.

PIPEDA's 10 Privacy Principles
(from the CSA Model Code)

1. **Accountability**
    Responsibility for data transferred to others; must have point person for PIPEDA compliance.

2. **Identifying Purposes**
    Purposes for data use must be articulated when collected.

3. **Consent**
    Consent requirements and opt-out rights.

4. **Limiting Collection**
    Data collection limited to that necessary for purposes. No deceptive collection.

5. **Limiting Use, Disclosure and Retention**
    Data use limited to purposes of collection. Data no longer needed must be deleted.

6. **Accuracy**
    Data must be kept accurate.

7. **Safeguards**
   Must protect data security.

8. **Openness**
   Privacy policies must be transparent and understandable.

9. **Individual Access**
   People are entitled to know about the data gathered about
   them and can challenge accuracy of it.

10. **Challenging Compliance**
    People can complain to an organization about failures to
    comply with PIPEDA.

PIPEDA requires that the individual must consent prior to the collection, use, or disclosure of personal data. It also incorporates the OECD's purpose specification principle, security safeguard principles, openness principle, accountability principle, and data quality principle, among others. Under PIPEDA, the Privacy Commissioner of Canada has the power to investigate citizen complaints and to conduct audits.

PIPEDA has provisions that acknowledge the federalistic structure of Canada. It permits a province's privacy law to displace it only when the provincial privacy law is "substantially similar" to it. PIPEDA does not contain an explicit benchmark regarding the meaning of "substantial similarity," but assigns an important task to the national privacy commissioner in making this determination. In a report to parliament, the privacy commissioner stated that, in the view of his office, substantial similarity means "equal or superior" to PIPEDA "in the degree and quality of privacy protection provided." Privacy Comm'nr of Canada, *Report to Parliament Concerning Substantially Similar Provincial Legislation* (2001).

The EU Commission issued a decision in December 2001 that found PIPEDA to provide an adequate level of protection.

Digital Privacy Act, S.C. 2015, c. 32 (Can.)

Amending PIPEDA to established breach notification requirements and heightened requirements for valid consent. The amendments also increase penalties for violations of PIPEDA.

Canada's Anti-Spam Law (CASL) (2010)

Scope: Canada's Anti-Spam Law (CASL) prohibits electronic spam, alterations of transmission data and installation of certain computer programs on another person's computer.

It also prohibits the use of false or misleading representations in an email for the promotion of products or services (Section 52.01 of the Competition Act), collection of personal information by means of unauthorized access to computer systems, and the unauthorized compiling of lists of electronic addresses (Section 7.1 of PIPE-DA)

In addition to commercial e-mail, CASL also regulates spyware, malware, and botnets. As a result, it regulates more areas than the CAN-SPAM Act in the U.S.

Enforcement: CASL's regulatory scheme also includes strong administrative monetary penalties and a private right of action. According to CASL's clause 21(1), every person who contravenes this statute's clauses 7 to 10 is liable for an administrative monetary penalty. Clauses 7 to 10 refer to sending unsolicited commercial electronic messages; altering transmission data; installing computer programs; and aiding, inducing, procuring, or causing to be procured any of the former actions. The maximum penalty for such violation is $1 million in the case of an individual, and $10 million in the case of an organization.

CASL also provides for a private right of action that enables a person affected by an act or omission that constitutes a contravention of the statute's clauses 7 to 10 to obtain an amount equal to the actual amount of the loss or damage suffered, or expenses incurred, and statutory damages for the contravention.

Regulations and Guidelines for Canada's Anti-Spam Law (2012)

The Canadian Radio-television and Telecommunications Commission (CRTC) is the main regulatory agency responsible for pursuing administrative penalties for violation of CASL. The act also gives it authority to issue regulations and guidelines regarding compliance with the act.

In March 2012, the CRTC issued its final regulations for CASL. These regulations set out the information that an organization must include when it requests consent for receiving commercial e-mail. In October 2012, the CRTC released two sets of guidelines regarding CASL.

The first, CRTC 2012-548, specifies the kinds of identification that a message gives regarding the sender and gives examples of acceptable mechanisms for subscribers to unsubscribe from mailings as well as the kinds of consent requests that are acceptable.

The second guideline, CRTC 2012-548, is perhaps the most important of these documents. It expresses a negative opinion on "toggling," a set of practices involving pre-checked boxes. In toggling, the person whose consent is being sought must *uncheck* the box to indicate that she does not consent. Toggled boxes generally are considered to provide "opt-out consent." The second guideline states, "The Commission considers that in order to comply with the express consent provisions under the Act, a positive or explicit indication of consent is required. Accordingly, express consent cannot be obtained through opt-out consent mechanisms." As a result, express consent under CASL must be through opt-in. In this regard, CASL will set stricter requirements than CAN-SPAM does in the U.S.

Common Law Torts

Canada recognizes only one of the Warren and Brandeis privacy torts, that of intrusion upon seclusion (see below). Other Canadian torts have been applied to protect privacy, and Canada recognizes the breach of confidence tort in the UK and a few other commonwealth countries. *Lac Minerals v. Int'l Corona Res.* [1989], 2 S.C.R. 575.

Jones v. Tsige, **2012 ONCA 42 (Jan. 18, 2012)**
The Court of Appeal for Ontario recognized the U.S. privacy tort of intrusion upon seclusion—intentionally intruding upon a person's seclusion or solitude, or into his private affairs.

Provincial Privacy Laws

- Alberta Personal Information Protection Act, S.A. 2003, c. P-6.5 (2004)
- British Columbia Privacy Act, R.S.B.C. 1996, ch. 373 (1968)
    - Personal Information Protection Act, S.B.C. 2003, ch. 63 (2004)
- Manitoba Privacy Act, C.C.S.M. ch. P125 (1970)
- Newfoundland and Labrador Privacy Act, R.S.N.L. 1990, ch. P-22 (1990)
- Quebec Charter § 5
    - Quebec Civil Code §§ 35-40
    - Quebec Act, R.S.Q., ch P-39.1 (1993)
- Saskatchewan Privacy Act, R.S.S. 1978, c. P-24 (1978)

Mexico

Constitution
Article 16 provides privacy protection to one's person, family, home, documents, and possessions, as well as communications.

Federal Data Protection Act (FDPA) (2010)
The act is an omnibus law, following the EU model, that requires a lawful basis for collecting, processing, and disclosing personal information. Unlike the EU model, however, the statute embodies the "habeas data" concept embraced by several South and Latin American countries—the individual to whom the data refers is treated as a "data owner" with legal rights, such as those of access, that derive from this status. [**For more on habeas data, see the box at right.**] The Federal Data Protection Act of Mexico also creates a supervisory authority, the Federal Institute of Access to Information and Data Protection. The Federal Institute is granted strong powers to hear objections to data processing practices and issue decisions to protect the rights granted by the Federal Data Protection Act.

Other Statutes
Mexico has many federal laws related to privacy, addressing government records, marketing, credit reporting, and electronic surveillance.

SOUTH AMERICA

Argentina

Constitution of the Argentine Nation
Article 43 provides for a right to "habeas data." A person can "obtain information on the data about himself and their purpose, registered in public records … or in private ones."

Law for the Protection of Personal Data (2000)
Argentina was the first country in South America to adopt a comprehensive data protection law. The law is based on the EU Data Protection Directive, several provisions of the Argentina constitution, and earlier national laws. Among its measures are rules of procedure that permit "habeas data" as a judicial remedy. The Argentina data protection law also prohibits international transfers of personal information to countries without adequate protection. In June 2003, the Commission of the European Community decided that Argentina provides an adequate level of protection for personal data.

> ## Habeas Data
>
> The concept of "habeas data" is common among South and Latin American countries. Habeas data is a special judicial measure that permits any person to know the content and purpose of the data pertaining to her in public records or in certain private records. Habeas data is a novel concept from the late 1980s, first introduced in the Constitution of Brazil. It is a legal mechanism that permits an individual to find out what information is held about her and to gain certain traditional information privacy rights with respect to that data.

Brazil

Constitution
The constitution of Brazil explicitly protects privacy in its Article 5. It also contains a constitutional right to habeas data.

Privacy Statutes
Brazil lacks any omnibus information privacy law. It does contain some sectoral privacy laws. These include a consumer protection law (1990) that regulates personal data recordkeeping and a federal law (1996) that regulates wiretapping.

The proposed Data Protection Bill (2011) has yet to be enacted; the draft legislation follows the EU model. It requires consent prior to transfer as well as breach notification. It also contains a requirement of consent for the transfer of personal data outside Brazil. The draft legislation establishes a Data Protection Authority with the power to issue sanctions and requires opt-in consent for processing of sensitive personal data.

MIDDLE EAST

Dubai

Data Protection Law (2004)
One of the seven emirates of the United Arab Emirates, Dubai is an important business hub in the Middle East. In 2007, it amended its Data Protection Law (2004) and strengthened it in various ways, including the creation of an independent Office of Commissioner of Data Protection.

Israel

Protection of Privacy Act (PPA) (1981)
The PPA applies to both public and private entities. It requires certain databases to be registered with the government. The PPA also establishes an office, the Israeli Law, Information, and Technology Authority (ILITA), that plays the central role in overseeing the PPA's database registration provisions. In an opinion from December 1, 2009, the Article 29 Working Party found that Israeli data protection law provides an "adequate level" of data protection in the sense of the EU Data Protection Directive. The EU Commission will take this finding into regard as it makes its own decision on this issue.

Other Statutes
Israel's Basic Law on Human Dignity protects privacy of the home and one's papers and belongings. Israel also has a law that protects the privacy of digital information (Computer Law of 1995) and that regulates credit reporting (Credit Data Service Law of 2002).

ASIA

Japan

Constitution
Article 13 provides a "right to life, liberty, and the pursuit of happiness." In 1963, the Supreme Court held that this provision protects a right to privacy.

Act on Protection of Personal Information (PPI) (2005)
This omnibus privacy law requires businesses to provide information to an individual about how they use, store, and process her personal data. It also limits disclosures of data to third parties unless they meet a set of statutory conditions. Such disclosures can be made pursuant to a law or ordinance; when necessary for the protection of

human life, safety or property and it is difficult to obtain the consent of the individual; when necessary to improve public hygiene and promote the health of children and it is difficult to obtain the individual's consent; and when cooperation is necessary for certain government activities and consent of the individual would hinder achievement of that purpose.

In September 2015, an extensive amendment to the PPI was enacted. The amendment to PPI will enter into force on a date set by cabinet order and occurs before September 2017. This Amendment places new restrictions on data transfers to foreign countries. It permits transfers to third parties in foreign countries only when there is prior consent, a transfer to a country with protections equivalent to that of Japan, or the transfer is to a third party with an internal protection system that meets standards set by the Japanese Personal Information Protection Commission. The amended PPI contains additional details regarding the law's definition of personal information. Finally, it contains a new definition of sensitive personal information, which will require prior consent before organizations can collect it.

China
China does not have an omnibus privacy law. Its civil law does protect against harm to reputation, and its criminal law protects against those who violate "rights of communication freedom."

China's Several Provisions on Regulation of the Order of Internet Information Service Market (2011)
Regulates entities providing "Internet information services" by restricting them from providing personal information to third parties without consent or collecting data not necessary to provide services. Requires notice to users, security safeguards, and notices of harmful data disclosures to the telecommunications authority.

Hong Kong

Personal Data Ordinance (1997)
The ordinance regulates the public and private sectors. This law created an oversight authority, the Office of the Privacy Commissioner for Personal Data.

Hong Kong Personal Data (Privacy) Amendment Ordinance (2012)
Updates the 1996 ordinance to provide notification and consent for the use, transfer, or sale of data for direct marketing, requirements for contracts for outsourcing, and other provisions. The Ordinance provides for strong penalties. For the transfer of personal data to third parties, it permits a maximum penalty of HK$ 1,000,000 and imprisonment for five years. For other direct marketing contraventions, it allows a maximum fine of HK$ 500,000 and imprisonment for three years.

Other Statutes
Hong Kong has also enacted sectoral protections for employment data (2001) and consumer credit data (2003).

Singapore

Personal Data Protection Act ("Singapore PDPA") (2012)

The Act follows the general structure of the EU–Data–Protection Directive. The Singapore PDPA's rules regarding the transfer of data also follow the provisions set out in the EU–Directive, so that the standard of protection in the receiving country is of crucial importance. Unlike the EU model, however, it contains no extra definition for sensitive data and most provisions do not apply to business information. Regardless of its size, organizations subject to the Singapore PDPA must designate a data protection officer. Currently there is no requirement for an organization to register its use of personal information with the data protection authority. The PDPA also establishes a national Do Not Call (DNC) Registry to allow individuals to register their telephone numbers and to opt out of receiving marketing phone calls, mobile text messages, and faxes from organizations.

South Korea

Personal Information Protection Act (PIPA)(2011)

South Korea enacted an omnibus data protection law in 2011 as well as sectoral laws, such as the "IT Network Act" or "Act on Real Name Financial Transactions and Guarantee of Secrecy." Among Asian countries, South Korea is now considered to offer the strictest privacy laws. It is also an example of an Asian country following the EU model of data protection legislation. Key concepts under the PIPA include a requirement of prior consent and an obligation that data processors reveal the purpose of processing, using, and collecting of data.

All organizations must also register with the Minister of Public Administration and Security and appoint a data protection officer. If a data subject accuses a data processor of non-compliance, the burden of proof rests with the data processor. This requirement is intended to force companies to keep detailed records of their data processing to prove compliance. Penalties for noncompliance consist of imprisonment or fines of up to 100 million Won, which is approximately $92,000.

Under the IT Network Act, a service provider must notify the Korean Communications Commission (the "KCC") or the Korea Internet & Security Agency (the "KISA") if it discovers a breach or intrusion of data security. A service provider must analyze the cause of the intrusion and prevent it from being spread. Individuals can withdraw their consent to data processing and transfers at any time.

Amendment on PIPA (2015)

This Amendment, effective in July 2016, allows for punitive and statutory damages to be tripled from the actual harm suffered from a data breach. Consumers may claim statutory damages of up to 3 million Korean Won unless the allegedly responsible company can prove that it was not at fault for the data breach.

India

Constitution
Article 21 protects a right to privacy as a component of the right to "personal liberty."
In 1964, the Supreme Court held that this provision encompassed a right to privacy.
Kharak Singh v. State of UP, (1964) 1 SCR 332.

Statutory Protections
India also has sectoral privacy protections for financial transactions (Public Financial
Institutions Act of 1993), communications (Telegraph Act of 1885) and telecommunications (Common Charter of Telecom Services). In 2013, it devised rules that
create a data breach notification requirement following "cyber security incidents" for
service providers, intermediaries, data centers, and corporate entities.

India's Information Technology Rules (April 2011)
The full title of these regulations is "the Information Technology (Reasonable security practices and procedures and sensitive personal information) Rules, 2011." In
these regulations, India defines the information that constitutes "sensitive data" under
the act and spells out the circumstances under which these data may be collected. It
also requires organization and corporations to develop clear privacy policies concerning how they handle user information.

Philippines

Data Privacy Act (2012)
The Data Privacy Act is a consolidated data privacy legislation that follows both the
EU model and the APEC framework. The Act mandates that all personal information
controllers comply with a set of requirements before processing or other activities
may take place. It includes some of Asia's toughest sanctions for privacy violations.
Among its penalties, the statute permits fines and prison sentences for first time
breaches, ongoing liability of controllers for personal information sent offshore or
provided to third party processors, and the deportation of foreigners who breach the
Act.

EUROPE, NON-EU COUNTRIES

Russia

Constitution of the Russian Federation
Article 23 protects "the right to privacy, to personal and family secrets and to protection of one's honor and good name." It also protects privacy of communication. Article 24 forbids collecting, using, or disclosing personal information without consent.
Article 25 protects privacy of the home.

Law on Personal Data (2006)

Omnibus privacy law that restricts private-sector information gathering without consent and provides rights regarding government records.

Russia's Cross–Border Data Transfer Rules (2011)

Amendments to Russia's data protection law created new rules on the cross-border transfer of personal data. It permits this transfer to countries that are parties to Europe's Convention for the Protection of Individuals with regard to Automatic Processing of Personal Data (1981). It also authorizes the Russian Federal Service for Oversight of Communications, Information Technology and Mass Media (the Russian Data Protection Agency) to approve a "whitelist" of approved data transfer countries that are not parties to the convention. On this approved list are to be those countries that provide adequate protection of personal data. The amendments also permit a cross-border transfer if the data subject consents to the transmission.

Localization Law, Federal Law No. 242-FZ

A new law requires that the personal data of Russian citizens be stored within Russia. The deadline for compliance was September 1, 2015.

Other Statutes

Russia has a law protecting against the interception of electronic communications (Communications Law of 2003).

Turkey

Law on Personal Data Protection (2016)

In March 2016, Turkey adopted its first information privacy law. The statute establishes a new Personal Data Protection Authority with the ability to impose both EUR 300,000 fines and prison sentences of up to four years. The law also creates the Board of Personal Data Protection, which oversees breaches of personal data.

APEC Privacy Framework (2004)

Origin: Ministers of nations that form the Asia-Pacific Economic Cooperation (APEC) adopted the Privacy Framework in 2004. The APEC Privacy Framework seeks to enable multinational businesses to implement uniform approaches to the use of personal data. The resulting guidelines strongly reflect the OECD Privacy Guidelines.

Advisory Only: Unlike the EU Data Protection Directive, the APEC Framework does not mandate that member states enact its principles into law. The APEC Framework is advisory only.

APEC Privacy Framework's Nine Principles

The nine principles of the APEC Privacy Framework are:

1. Preventing Harm

2. Notice

3. Collection Limitation

4. Use of Personal Information

5. Choice

6. Integrity

7. Security Safeguards

8. Access and Correction

9. Accountability

Accountability: One of the most interesting of these principles is accountability. The APEC Framework states that organizations that process information should be "accountable for complying with measures that give effect" to its principles. In its commentary to this principle, the APEC Framework further observes:

> Efficient and cost effective business models often require information transfers between different types of organizations in different locations with varying relationships. When transferring information, personal information controllers should be accountable for ensuring that the recipient will protect the information consistently with these Principles when not obtaining consent. Thus, information controllers should take reasonable steps to ensure the information is protected, in accordance with these Principles, after it is transferred.

The idea of accountability has proven influential at the international level. The idea is that accountable privacy requires processes tailored to the specific risks of the data risk at hand. For an example of the influence of this concept, the Article 29 Working Group in 2010 called for a "statutory accountability principle" as a way to help move data protection from theory to practice. Article 29 Data Protection Working Party, Opinion 3/2010 on the Principle of Accountability, at 3. Accountability concepts involve data controllers implementing "appropriate and effective measures" that are "scalable"—that is, proportionate to the risks involved. As the Working Party discussed this concept, "the types of measures should be coherent with the risks represented by the data processing and the nature of data."

APEC MEMBER NATIONS		
Australia	Japan	Russia
Brunei Darussalam	Malaysia	Singapore
Canada	Mexico	South Korea
Chile	New Zealand	Taiwan
China	Papua New Guinea	Thailand
Hong Kong	Peru	United States
Indonesia	Philippines	Vietnam

APEC Cross Border Privacy Rules System

In 2011, APEC members introduced the Cross Border Privacy Rules (CBPR). This is a voluntary accountability-based approach to permit data flows among the APEC nations. It has four elements:

- Criteria for organizations that wish to become an APEC CBPR system-certified Accountability Agent;

- An intake questionnaire for organizations that seek to be certified as CBPR-compliance by an Accountability Agent;

- Assessment criteria for use by Accountability Agents in reviewing an organization's answer to the intake questionnaire; and

- A regulatory cooperative arrangement sets up a multilateral mechanism to permit cooperation by Privacy Enforcement Authorities in participating APEC economies. It also establishes an Electronic Commerce Steering Group with responsibility for the APEC Privacy Framework.

Source: Cross Broder Privacy Rules System, at http://www.cbprs.org/

FTC Enforcement of the APEC Cross–Border Privacy Rules System

In re Very Incognito Techs., Inc., FTC No. C-4580 (May 4, 2016)
On May 4, 2016, the FTC approved its first APEC order, settling a case with Very Incognito Technologies, Inc. ("Vipvape"), a vaporizers manufacturer. Vipvape falsely alleged on its website that it was a certified company under APEC's Cross Border Privacy Rules framework. The settlement prohibits Vipvape from misrepresenting its participation, membership or certification in any government or self-regulatory privacy or security program.

AUSTRALIA

Constitution
The constitution lacks an express provision protecting the right to privacy.

Australia's 13 Privacy Principles (2014)

The 13 principles of Australia are:

1. Open and transparent management of personal information

2. Anonymity and pseudonymity

3. Collection of solicited personal information

4. Dealing with unsolicited personal information

5. Notification of the collection of personal information

6. Use or disclosure of personal information

7. Direct Marketing

8. Cross-border disclosure of personal information

9. Adoption, use, or disclosure of government related identifiers

10. Quality of personal information

11. Security of personal information

12. Access to personal information

13. Correction of personal information

Privacy Act (1988)
As amended in 2014, the act establishes 13 privacy principles. These principles are known as the Australian Privacy Principles (APPs) and replace the previous eleven National Privacy Principles (NPPs). The Office of the Privacy Commissioner is responsible for the administration of the Privacy Act. The Privacy Act establishes limits on transfers to another country. A 2000 law amended the original Privacy Act to expand it from the public sector to the private sector. The act established a "co-regulatory" scheme. Companies can apply to the privacy commissioner to substitute their own privacy practices if they are "overall equivalent" to the NPPs. Further exemptions are possible for "small businesses" and employment records. Data can readily be transferred abroad because any restrictions that do apply are not strictly written.

FOR FURTHER REFERENCE

Treatises and Books

Colin J. Bennett, *Regulating Privacy: Data Protection and Public Policy in Europe and the United States* (1992)
Important early study about differences in policy approaches to privacy in Europe and the U.S. Argues that the American experience demonstrates "the enormous problems associated with enforcing data protection standards without a commission or some other agency whose sole responsibility is privacy."

Colin J. Bennett & Charles D. Raab, *The Governance of Privacy: Policy Instruments in Global Perspective* (2006)
Study of development of global privacy standards finds that while their overall level is being "traded up"—that is, improved—nonetheless, surveillance practices may not be reduced.

***Personality Rights in European Tort Law* (Gert Brüggemeier et. al eds., 2010)**
Mapping the landscape of tort privacy law in different European countries and drawing comparisons with the U.S.

***Data Protection Law in Singapore: Privacy and Sovereignty in an Interconnected World* (Simon Chesterman ed., 2014)**
A series of essays exploring Singapore's Personal Data Protection Act (2012) and other aspects of privacy law in Singapore. Essays also explore Malaysia's Data Protection Law and draw comparisons with other Asian jurisdictions.

Axel von dem Bussche & Markus Stamm, *Data Protection in Germany* (2013)
Concise treatise on the Federal Data Protection Act and its requirements. Coverage of issues such as customer and supplier data protection, employee data protection, and international transfer of personal data.

Lothar Determann, *Determann's Field Guide to Data Privacy Law: International Corporate Compliance* (2d ed. 2015)
A concise and practical guide to the many dimensions of international privacy law.

Gilles Dutertre, *Key Case-law Extracts: European Court of Human Rights* (2004)
Extensive selection of decisions of the European Court of Human Rights in its Article 8 cases.

David H. Flaherty, *Protecting Privacy in Surveillance Societies: The Federal Republic of Germany, France, Canada, and the United States* (2014)
Classic account of the role of data protection agencies in Europe and the development of information privacy there and in North America.

Law, Privacy and Surveillance in Canada in the Post-Snowden Era
(**Michael Geist ed., 2015**)
Focusing on the role of the Canadian counterpart to the NSA, the Communications Service Establishment, and other Canadian aspects of global surveillance

Françoise Gilbert, *The Global Privacy and Security Law Reference* (2016)
3,000-page treatise covering 66 countries; updated three times each year.

Reinventing Data Protection? (**Serge Gutwirth et al. eds., 2009**)
Strong and up-to-date collection of essays looking at a wide variety of different issues in EU data protection.

Eloïse Gratton & Lyndsay Wasser, *Privacy in the Workplace* (3d ed. 2014)
Detailed examination of Canadian workplace privacy law.

Graham Greenleaf, *Asian Data Privacy Laws: Trade & Human Rights Perspectives* (2014)
Magisterial treatise on the development of and current status of information privacy law in all Asian states.

Rosemary Jay, *Data Protection Law and Practice* (4th ed. 2012)
Leading guide to the UK's Data Protection Act and relevant case law.

Christopher Kuner, *European Data Protection Law: Corporate Compliance and Regulation* (2d ed. 2007)
Examines European data protection law as it relates to legal compliance issues for companies.

Christopher Kuner, *Transborder Data Flows and Data Privacy Law* (2013)
Examining the transfer of personal data across national borders under data protection law. Coverage includes the EU and other global regulatory regimes, such as the APEC Privacy Framework, Organization of American States, and World Trade Law.

Barbara McIsaac et al., *The Law of Privacy in Canada* (2016)
Multivolume treatise on all aspects of Canadian privacy law.

Cloud Computing Law (**Chris Millard ed., 2013**)
A wide-reaching examination of the European law of cloud computing, including the issues of public sector cloud procurement and the privacy of personal data in clouds.

Abraham L. Newman, *Protectors of Privacy: Regulating Personal Data in the Global Economy* (2008)
Political scientist explains why nations in the EU adopted comprehensive information privacy statutes and why the U.S. has taken a narrowly focused sectoral approach. Also explains why the EU approach, and not the U.S. approach, has been broadly adopted throughout the world.

Andrew B. Serwin, *Information Security and Privacy: A Guide to International Law and Compliance* (2016)
Up-to-date treatise examining EU privacy law and that of individual countries, worldwide.

***European Privacy: Law and Practice for Data Protection Professionals* (Eduardo Ustaran ed., 2012)**
Detailed guide to EU privacy law.

Articles and Other Sources

Francesca Bignami, *European Versus American Liberty: A Comparative Privacy Analysis of Antiterrorism Data Mining*, 48 B.C. L. Rev. 609 (2007)
Examination of comparative regulations for data mining in the EU and the U.S. arguing that the Bush administration's warrantless surveillance program at the NSA would be illegal in Europe and might be legal under the then-applicable U.S. law.

Dennis D. Hirsch, *Going Dutch? Collaborative Dutch Privacy Regulation and the Lessons It Holds for U.S. Privacy Law*, 2013 Mich. St. L. Rev. 83 (2013)
Argues that the Dutch model of collaboration between regulators and industry in rule drafting offers an effective solution to the challenges of crafting effective privacy law. US policymakers can learn from the 20-plus years of Dutch experience using this collaborative model.

Edward Lee, *Recognizing Rights in Real Time: The Role of Google in the EU*, 49 UC Davis L. Rev. 1017 (2016)
Discussion of significant role of Google in developing the "right to be forgotten" (RTBF) in the EU. Google plays this role by deciding individual RTBF requests made to it.

Miquel Peguera, *In the aftermath of* Google Spain: *How the "Right to be Forgotten" Is Being Shaped in Spain by Courts and the Data Protection Authority*, 23 Int'l J.L. & Info. Tech. 325 (2015).
Analysis of over two hundred "right to be forgotten" cases in Spain finds courts "wrestling in search of a proportionate and balanced outcome that fully takes into account all the rights and interests at stake."

Joel R. Reidenberg, *The Data Surveillance State in the United States and Europe*, 49 Wake Forest L. Rev. 583 (2014)
U.S. law has generally focused on access restraints for government to obtain privately held information, ignored the collection and storage of data. In contrast, the EU focuses more on restricting the collection and retention of data and less on government access. This article recommends stricter retention limits combined with stronger access controls, increased transparency of government access to personal information, and personal liability of government officials for overreaching.

Joel R. Reidenberg, *Resolving Conflicting International Data Privacy Rules in Cyberspace*, 52 Stan. L. Rev. 1315 (2000)
Development of models of different strategies for developing international cooperation and achieving a high level of privacy protection for personal information in international data transfers.

Ira S. Rubinstein, Gregory T. Nojeim & Ronald D. Lee, *Systematic Government Access to Personal Data: A Comparative Analysis*, 4 Int'l Data Privacy L. 96 (2014)
Drawing on the analysis of the law and practices in 13 countries in an earlier volume of this journal, this article develops both (1) a descriptive framework for comparing national laws on surveillance and government access to data held by the private sector, and (2) a normative framework based on factors derived from constitutional and human rights law. The article calls for a robust, global debate on the standards for government surveillance premised on greater transparency about current practices.

Paul M. Schwartz, *The EU–U.S. Privacy Collision: A Turn to Institutions and Procedures*, 126 Harv. L. Rev. 1966 (2013)
Exploring the path that the U.S. has taken in its information privacy law and the reasons for the relative lack of American influence on worldwide information privacy regulatory models. This article also analyzes the likely impact of the Proposed Data Protection Regulation and how it may destabilize the current privacy policy equilibrium.

Paul M. Schwartz, *Information Privacy in the Cloud*, 161 U. Pa. L. Rev. 1623 (2013)
Comparative analysis of U.S. and EU privacy regulations of cloud services and the current uncertainty around many established privacy doctrines, including the definition of personal information and jurisdiction issues. Identifying weaknesses in how both systems regulate cloud companies and developing proposals for both legal systems.

Paul M. Schwartz & Karl-Nikolaus Peifer, *Prosser's Privacy and the German Right of Personality: Are Four Privacy Torts Better than One Unitary Concept?*, 98 Cal. L. Rev. 1925 (2010)
Contrasts German and U.S. tort privacy law and finds considerable similarities as well as significant differences regarding a relatively higher protection of celebrity identity in Germany and lesser post-mortem protection for the tort of right of appropriation.

Paul M. Schwartz & Daniel J. Solove, *Reconciling Personal Information in the United States and European Union*, 102 Cal. L. Rev. 877 (2014)
The privacy law of the U.S. and EU greatly differ in their definitions of personal information. The U.S. approach is narrow and inconsistent, while the EU approach is overly broad. Schwartz and Solove propose a tiered risk-based approach to bridge the gaps between US and EU privacy law—"PII 2.0"—which focuses on whether

data identifies a person, whether the data is identifiable, or whether there is a minimal risk that the data is identifiable. The article suggests that more Fair Information Practice Principles (FIPPs) be applied as the risk of identification increases.

Peter P. Swire & Robert E. Litan, *None of Your Business: World Data Flows, Electronic Commerce, and the European Privacy Directive* (1998)
Path-breaking early study of the European Data Protection Directive and its possible impact on commerce.

James Q. Whitman, *The Two Western Cultures of Privacy: Dignity versus Liberty*, 113 Yale L.J. 1151 (2004)
Argues that deep-seated cultural and legal differences in Europe and the United States have led to an approach to privacy centered on personal dignity in the former and individual liberty in the latter.

NOTES:

NOTES: